COMPANION GUIDE TO
The Coast of
South-West England

Uniform with this volume

THE

Coast of North-East England

In preparation

The Coast of South-East England
The Coast of East Anglia and
the Thames Estuary

THE COMPANION GUIDE TO

The Coast of

South-West England

John Seymour

COLLINS
ST JAMES'S PLACE, LONDON

William Collins Sons & Co Ltd
London · Glasgow · Sydney · Auckland
Toronto · Johannesburg

First published in 1974
Reprinted 1975
© John Seymour 1974
ISBN 0 00 219048 6
Printed in Great Britain
Collins Clear-Type Press
London and Glasgow

Contents

❧

Illustrations

❧

CHAPTER I

Lyme Regis to Beer

❧

THE frontier between Dorset and Devon strikes the sea at some very indeterminate point along the shingle a few hundred yards west of **Lyme Regis**. The latter town therefore should not come into this book, but we have got to begin somewhere, and, whether travelling by sea or by land, we are unlikely to reach the eastern extremity of the Devon coast without going to Lyme Regis.

The little part-natural part-artificial harbour called the Cobb, which has, we are told, one of the oldest breakwaters in the world, generally manages to find the room to squeeze in one more yacht, but in the summer it is woefully overcrowded. It is a somewhat precarious little harbour, in that in a fresh south-easter you cannot enter or leave it, it nearly dries out at low water, and the small fleet of motor trawlers often has to steer for Brixham and take shelter there, being unable to get home. There is a very good little yacht chandlery hard by the Cobb run by Mr and Mrs Owles. The harbour is becoming silted up owing to the misguided policy of the council in blocking the natural channel to the west of the harbour to build a car park. Before this was done the natural scouring of the seas helped to keep the harbour clear.

A couple of hundred yards west is a big building, once a cement factory, then a military establishment, and now the Lyme Regis Adventure Centre run by the County of Dorset. Here young people can learn sailing and canoeing, do nature study on the famous Undercliff, and engage in other activities. And this is practically within spitting distance of the Devon border.

And, with Devon, we come to the **Undercliff**, which for geologists and naturalists and lovers of wild scenery is one of the very special places in England. Here, at various periods of history, the cliffs have slipped, fallen and foundered, to leave a never-never land of chasms, ridges and practically unattainable table lands, over which a predominantly ash forest has grown, sheltering a rich flora and fauna, and the whole scene is a paradise for people who love wild places. Fortunately for such as do most people don't, and so you can wander about in this wilderness, even in high summer, and meet nobody at

9

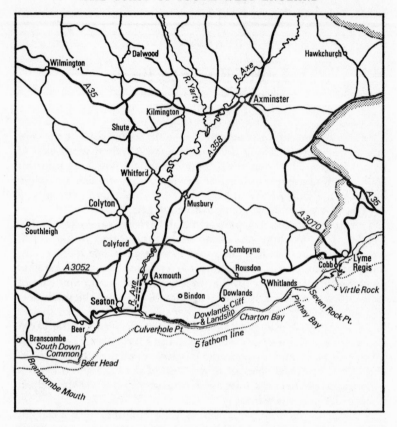

all if you don't want to. There are paths though – one through path in particular – on which you will probably meet other people. The whole area is in the care of the Nature Conservancy, and you are supposed to get their permission to leave the sign-posted path.

To begin at the beginning we must consider the geology of these cliffs, and to do this we cannot do better than to buy a copy of *Guide 23* of the Geologists' Association: *The Coast of South Devon and Dorset between Branscombe and Burton Bradstock* by Derek V. Ager and William E. Smith, which is generally on sale in Lyme Regis. For the less geologically minded it may be enough to know that the reason for the spectacular landslip is the fact that porous Cretaceous rocks (chalk and Upper Greensand) rest unconformably on impermeable Jurassic ones, such as the Lias, water percolates through the former during winters of heavy rain, lubricates the slippery impervious rocks below, and the top layers slip, spectacularly, towards the sea. In some places this may be a straight slipping, at others a theory has it that a rotary movement takes place. Cracks appear in the fields behind the cliff top and these cracks go, not straight down into the earth, but curving outwards towards the sea. When the cracks are sufficiently lubricated by water the section of cliff between the cracks and the sea rotates, so that its inland section goes down and its seaward section comes up. Thus, after the great Dowlands Cliff landslide of 1839–40 an island rose up one or two hundred yards out to sea which was three quarters of a mile long and forty feet high. This, being of soft rock, was soon washed away.

The more geologically minded will wish to walk from Lyme Regis to Axmouth along the beach, for thus, although they will miss the marvellous scenery of the Landslip country, they will have a better look at the rocks. Lyme Regis itself is built on the Black Ven Marls, which are rather undistinguished-looking shaley rocks. The Marls at Lyme are known picturesquely as 'Shales with Beef'; surely our geologists are poets to a man? The thin layers of secondary fibrous calcite which lie at right angles to the bedding of the shale are supposed to look like beef. Well, they have never made my mouth water. As we go west the great mass of the Blue Lias rises up – elevating the Black Ven Marls as it does so. The Blue Lias consists of alternating layers of calcareous shale and limestone, laid down under warm Jurassic seas somewhere round a hundred and fifty million years ago. When the Jurassic seas overran the salty marls at the end of Triassic times a great many animals died, both the reptiles of the land and the fish of the sea, and their fossils are still here in myriads for us to observe. Here have been discovered ichthyosaurs, ammonites by the ton, the oyster *Gryphaea arcuarta*, crinoids and brachiopods. Some of the ammonites are huge: a foot or two across and embedded in the hard blue rock. The limestone beds that have withstood the erosion of the sea at Seven Rocks Point (which you can only look at at low tide) are very fossiliferous. As we go west, owing to the dip towards us of the Blue Lias beds, we come to progressively older and older rocks, until we arrive at those reaches of geological time before ammonites were invented, and so these Lower Lias beds are called Pre-*planorbis*: *Psiloceras planorbis* being the first of the local ammonites. It didn't enter the stage until about twelve feet above the bottom of the Blue Lias deposition. Further west still we come to older rock yet: the Rhaetic. This we encounter at **Pinhay Bay**. This is a limestone, sometimes called 'White Lias'.

In it are the remains of both fish and shellfish which are very uncommon in Britain.

West of Pinhay Bay the walking is hard, for there are large blocks of stone lying about on the beach. These blocks have fossils of the Upper Cenomanian. Before **Charton Bay** the Rhaetic leaves the beach level and bends upwards revealing the older Keuper Marls beneath it. The top ten feet of the latter are called 'Tea-green Marls' – those poets again. The Keuper series is Triassic: thus over 180 million years old. And from here on west the cliff is all landslip, and thus very difficult to read geologically. After a fault in Charton Bay the Lower Lias comes down to the beach, with many an ammonite in it, then we meet our old friend the Rhaetic again, then the bottom stratum of the cliff is Keuper Marl until we come, thankfully, to the mouth of the River Axe.

The above complicated rock formations can be better understood when it is realized that the Jurassic and earlier rocks had already been subjected to forces which gave them an easterly tilt before the sea came along and covered them and laid down upon them, unconformably, the Cretaceous chalk and Greensand. There is a very good section of these cliffs in Lyme Regis's excellent little museum.

This cliff exposure, and its extensions west to Branscombe and east nearly into Hampshire, is one of the two most interesting exposures of Jurassic and Cretaceous rocks in Britain. The other, which has notable similarities, is in North Yorkshire along the Cleveland Coast (see *The Companion Guide to the Coast of North-East England*). Both these stretches of cliff have been described as 'cradles of the science of Geology' because so much of the work of the first geologists was done on them.

But I cannot recommend this beach saunter as a comfortable walk. Large stretches of it cannot be done at all at high tide, much of it is boulder-strewn and the rest is shingle. Walking along the shingle is very tiring.

But not only is this stretch of coast of interest to the geologist, but to zoologists, botanists, and lovers of nature generally; and these can pursue their interests best by going to Underhill Farm, near Lyme Regis, and committing themselves to the cliff path which runs the whole length of the cliffs, mostly about half way up them, to where it comes out on top of Culverhole Cliff and brings you out on Axmouth golf course. It is possible to reach the top in other places too (notably near Whitlands and at Allhallows School) but it is as well to remember that you won't catch a bus up there, and if you start this walk you must be prepared to finish it, and it will be at least six miles of hard going before you will get a cup of tea. But the effort is well worth it. I think this walk must be one of the most enchanting in England. For much of the time you cannot see the sea, being cut off from it by high masses of sundered cliffs, and often, too, you cannot see the tops of the cliffs. You seem to be lost in a fairyland of graceful ash trees, ivy and creeper-clad, Old Man's Beard, wild flowers of a hundred kinds, grey squirrels scamper up the trees, you may see roe deer (particularly at night), there are more rabbits than we expect to see these days, foxes and badgers, stoats and weasels, buzzards, kestrels, sparrow-hawks and three kinds of owls. Here the nightingale sings, and is said to nest: if it does, the most westerly nests of nightingales in England.

A literary key to this bit of the world is a most excellent little booklet, called the *Axmouth Lyme Regis Undercliff* and produced by the Natural History Society of Allhallows School, deserving a wider circulation. Suffice to say that of the commoner plants it lists: Hart's Tongue Fern, Dog's Mercury, Wood Sanicle, Enchanter's Nightshade, Wood Violet, Primrose, Bluebell, Viper's Bugloss, Salad Burnet, Marjoram, Yellow Rockrose, Hairy Violet, Cathartic Flax, Stemless Thistle, Yellow Wort, Ploughman's Spikenard. Of orchids occur: Early Purple, Green Veined, Spotted, Marsh, Bee, Pyramidal, Fragrant, Twayblade, Greater Butterfly, Marsh Helleborine, Bird's Nest (*Neottia*) and under the beech trees on Pinhay Cliffs are the only Devon examples of Yellow Bird's Nest (*Monotropa*).

Of pretty little birds are: Lesser Whitethroat, Tree Creeper, Stonechat, Blackcap, Chiffchaff, Willow Warbler, Gold Crest, Rock Pipit, Long Tailed Tit and the three woodpeckers. All of these nest. And a total of a hundred and twenty species of migrant birds have been recorded. According to the *Transactions* of the British Mycological Society (Volume 43 [1970]) five species of fungus hitherto new to science have been discovered here. Among the more mundane (and smellier) are both the Common and the Dog Stinkhorn, and the rare, vermilion, and evil smelling *Clathrus ruber*. The latter attracts bluebottles as plants with more comely habits attract butterflies.

Not far west from Lyme Regis we come to the waterworks which pumps ten thousand gallons of water an hour to the top of the cliff for the South Devon Water Board. The pipes were fractured in 1960, in a minor landslide. The year after this happened a mass of clay was squeezed up out of the beach below to a height of fifteen feet.

But the greatest landslip of all was that at Dowlands Cliff in

1839–40. On Christmas Eve of 1839 a farmer who lived near the top of the cliffs here was informed by a coastguard that some of his fields and an orchard had disappeared over the cliff. On Christmas Day he felt his cottage shaking, and so he prudently got out of it. On 3rd of February 1840 much more of his land went. Altogether eight million tons of rock and earth foundered, including the afore-mentioned orchard, two cottages and fifteen acres of wheat. The resulting chasm, which separated the foundered mass from the mainland, was half a mile long and from two to four hundred yards wide and, as we have seen, an island three-quarters of a mile long and forty feet high was up-thrust out of the sea.

The resulting cliffscape was fantastic. High, vertically-sided table-lands (reminiscent, although on a tiny scale, of the complex escarpments near Addi Arcai in Ethiopia) soared above deep valley bottoms, the latter bare of vegetation and the former still clad with their crops and trees and the two cottages still standing. The following August the fifteen acres of wheat were harvested by boys and girls dressed in white with blue ribands (the girls styling themselves 'the Nymphs of Ceres') to the accompaniment of music from bands, a big crowd which included 'people of the best quality', the ministrations of food vendors, and the attentions of a number of landscape painters. The productions of some of these latter can be seen in the little museum at Lyme Regis. It is interesting to compare the landscapes depicted in them with the cliff scenery of the present day. In the year of the landslide the chasms were as raw and lifeless as the craters of the Moon. Now the whole area, chasms as well as table-lands, is covered with a fine climax forest of ash: a forest which has established itself with neither help nor hindrance from Man in a hundred and thirty years. Eight hundred acres here were declared a nature reserve in 1955, and is in the care of the Nature Conservancy.

At the top of the cliffs, midway between Lyme Regis and Seaton, is Allhallows School: a typical public school where boys in sombre clothing stand on the touchline and cheer their muddied heroes on the rugby field. It occupies a splendid position, with this marvellous nature reserve of landslips just beneath it. The mansion on which the school is centred was built by Sir Henry Peek between 1871 and 1883. This gentleman, who was a practitioner of the wholesale grocery trade, enclosed 250 acres for a park, rebuilt the ruined church of St Pancras, and refounded a parish, the parishioners of which were all his own family or employees. He was lucky enough to have a ship wrecked at the foot of the cliffs by his new house loaded with Sicilian marble, and this he had incorporated into his mansion.

At **Rousdon Mill**, near by, lived – in fiction at least – Joshua Meech – a character in Sir Walter Besant's *'Twas in Trafalgar's Bay*.

And so we come, by whatever means we do come, to the mouth of the **River Axe**. If we come in a boat we had better come at high tide, or very near to it, on a calm day. The river mouth is a mere gap through the shingle. To find it, sail hard up against the end of the cliff, for like all the rivers along this coast, owing to the easterly set of the tide the river mouth has been forced up against the high ground to the east of it by a shingle spit which has crept out from the west. But you *can* get in, if you have power or a commanding wind and the sea is dead calm. Unfortunately the last two conditions are unlikely to be fulfilled together. In days when sailors could really sail, however, many ships did get in, and the place was a flourishing port. In 1346 'Seton and Axmouth' sent two ships and twenty-five sailors to the Siege of Calais, and right up until the time the railway came and killed it all, ships of 150 tons were sailing into Axmouth, bringing coal and timber and other goods.

Axmouth is certainly an ancient harbour, although whether it was indeed the harbour at the end of the Fosse Way is open to conjecture. It is hard to imagine a harbour of such importance being built at a point with so little natural advantage on a coast with such magnificent havens as Southampton Water, Poole Harbour, Exmouth and all the rest of them. On the other hand, it is believed that the shoreline here has been retreating at the rate of about three feet a year, and this would put it, in Roman times, at some five miles further out than it is now, and who knows what sort of a natural harbour there was there then? Certainly Seaton is quite sure that it was the Roman Moridunum: so much so that it has the name emblazoned on its foreshore. Nobody can really say now whether it was, or whether it wasn't. By the Middle Ages the harbour was 'a mene thing where smaul fissher boats alone put in for soccur'. Bishop Lacy granted a forty-day indulgence to people who helped to build a new harbour (it is supposed that a landslide had closed the old one). Leland wrote in 1537 that the harbour and town had been much larger once but 'there lyith between the two points of the old haven a mighty rigge and barre of pibble stones, and the river Axe is dryven to the est point of the haven and ther, at a very smaul gut, goith into the sea.' Like then like now. Leland adds that men had tried to dredge and train the channel, but with no success.

Certainly anchors, trenails and keel timbers of pre-Norman ships (one of seventy tons) were discovered as far upstream as Musbury, so the Axe is a harbour of some antiquity.

Soon after Leland's time the Erle family of Bindon (the latter a beautiful Tudor mansion still existing a mile to the east) spent a fortune on trying to improve the harbour, but when Sir Thomas died his neighbours 'stole away most of his work'. According to Stukely writing in 1724 a sailor named Courd found gold on Hawkesdon Hill and built a pier in the Axe. The *Book of the Axe* (1875) relates that Squire Hallett, of Stedcombe Manor, spent large sums on the harbour, built a large pier, and owned two schooners regularly trading to London. Many vessels at this time came in with coal for the local lime kilns, and sailed forth with hides, flints and pebbles. An engraving of 1850 shows five ships lying in the harbour.

In 1867 the railway came and put an abrupt end to the harbour, and, except for harbouring a few yachts, it has never been a harbour since. In 1877 a toll bridge was built, which still cuts off what had been the haven from the sea, and is to the Age of Concrete what Ironbridge, in Shropshire, was to the Age of Iron. For it is one of the first concrete bridges in the world and is, like so many concrete structures, hideously ugly. The Harbourmaster's new cottage was also built of this material: roof, door lintels, window frames – the lot. It still stands, west of the bridge, and is inhabited, and is very interesting to concrete-lovers. The toll bridge was freed of toll in 1907, when Sanders Stephans, the lord of the manor, paid £2000 to free it.

The mouth of the Axe is now a pleasant place. The river washes the foot of the vertical cliff to the east of it, and we can walk from Seaton to the river mouth along the 'mighty rigge and barre of pibble stones' that Leland knew, and watch the strange sight of the swift current of the river, at low tide, crumbling down the steep banks of shingle, which will be built up again by the waves and tidal currents when the sea comes in again. Except at times of spate it is possible to wade across the river mouth (although an official notice warns us against doing so). Back at the bridge we can look upstream to where the river has been artificially inned to make room for a railway (ships used to tie up to Seaton church: as witness mooring rings near the walls of that building) and we can look over a stretch of mud and saltings where wading birds resort, and teal and wigeon feed in the winter. Less than a mile upstream is **Axmouth**, a pleasant village, with the thatched Harbour Inn, which is a very good inn indeed, the Hills family, the members of which run the only licensed salmon net on the river, and an interesting church.

The Axe is the only river in England in which every salmon, large or small, that tries to go up or down it, gets trapped, inspected, recorded, tagged, and put back into the water again. Every adult salmon that swims into the river from the sea to spawn, or to make love to a lady salmon, and who escapes the net of Mr Hills, or the gaffs of such gentlemen adventurers as practise their trade when others are sound asleep, gets caught in a trap of Heath Robinson complexity but great effectiveness (situated just below the A 35 bridge). It is then anaesthetized, lifted out in a strange sort of a lift, weighed, tagged if not already tagged, allowed to recover gently from the anaesthetic, and released upstream. Every smolt, milt, or spent fish coming down stream slides over a grid and into a trough where the same thing happens to him. The weir is cunningly designed to work at any state of the tide or spate of the stream, is manned day and night, and is owned by the Ministry of Agriculture, Fisheries and Food. Some three hundred adult salmon are taken thus every year. About one out of every two hundred salmon tagged in Britain is caught by Danish salmon fishermen off the coast of Greenland: a sobering thought for salmon lovers.

The Axe came very near to being an important harbour indeed. The great engineer Telford made a survey in 1825 for a proposed ship canal from the Axe to the Bristol Channel. The summit of this canal would have been near Chard and 280 feet above sea level, but a lot could have been lopped off this altitude by a cutting. In the wall of Axmouth church is a copper bolt placed there in 1837 as part of a survey to determine the difference between the levels of the English and the Bristol Channels. The ship canal idea is not so outlandish as it may seem: even today the Dutch or Belgians would do it as a matter of course, and take some of the enormous weight of traffic off the roads.

As for the little town of **Seaton**: it is now a small holiday resort, very quiet, very pleasant, with a steep shingle beach which is not very popular with small children. The sea, which grades beach material from fine sand to boulders, grades people too. Young children don't like shingle beaches. Rich old people don't mind shingle, having long ago given up the bucket and spade, and don't like young children. Therefore parents of the former tend to go to sandy beaches, and the latter to retire to places with shingly beaches, and Seaton has plenty of retired people of the middle classes. On the beach, besides old ladies and dogs, are to be found beryls, garnets, jaspers and agates. There is a fine church at Seaton of the Decorated period, with a fulsome but amusing epitaph to one John Starre, there is a very good boatyard down by the Axe turning out boats of the local traditional design, there is a handful of fishermen who launch open boats from the beach but mostly just in the summer when they can take holidaymakers out for hire, there is a factory making model railways (Peco) which has just opened a big branch at Beer, and there is a firm which, until recently, bought pebbles collected off the beach, though this activity has now been stopped. These pebbles were sent away to be ground up for pottery bodies and glazes, shellac, and other industrial uses.

It is written that there is a mahogany counter in an ironmongers in Fere Street from the Finnish barque *Berar* which was wrecked in 1896, and in Tolman's Yard is her figurehead, but I have never seen these. Roman villas were unearthed at Seaton: the mosaic from one is in Exeter Museum.

Hard by Seaton is **Beer**, and you can get to it by a very pleasant walk over a high cliff. You can also get to it in a boat if you are prepared to beach on a forty-five degree shingle slope, but it is unfair to beach regardless and throw yourself on the mercy of the fishermen to haul you up to safety with their windlasses. After all they have a living to earn, they are very short of space on their little beach, and if they didn't look out they could spend all day hauling people up and down for fun. If a mariner is in genuine difficulties it need not be said that they will help him. Otherwise, if you are self-contained in the matter of hauling up the beach you should beach to the westward of the fishing boats, where you will not be in their way.

The fishing boats in use along this coast are very distinctive, and about as different from the beaching boats of the East Coast as they could possibly be. To an East Coast man they look like washing tubs. They have enormous beam for their length, terrific freeboard, they are clinker built, have long keels and bilge keels and when they beach they lie right over on to one or other of their bilge keels. They come to the beach head on and are launched stern on. They are hauled up the terribly steep shingle beaches by motor winches (until recently picturesque hand capstans were used). Holly sticks are laid underneath them to keep them from sinking into the shingle. When they are launched they have to be man-handled over the ridge in the shingle, the engine is started and put running astern, they are given a yo-heave-ho and down they trundle into the breakers with the propeller already turning to pull them off. They have a very effective and simple arrangement for hooking on when they come to the beach again – and if there is a sea running there is no time to be lost. The high freeboard and tubby shape are dictated by the steepness of the beaches these little boats have to land on: the long, low, narrow cobles of the North-East Coast would be swamped on these beaches.

Beer men have a reputation along this coast for being willing to put to sea when other, perhaps sager, men prefer to stay at home. There are about eleven full-time or nearly full-time boats at Beer now, four of them fitted with otter trawls and the rest engaged in lobstering or crabbing, and taking holidaymakers out in the summer. Besides these though Beer men own two large decked trawlers which they operate from Lyme Regis, as they are too big to haul up on Beer beach. The Beer beach boats tend to be from about twenty-two to twenty-eight feet long, and from eight to eleven foot beam. Old men can remember when there were seventeen boats working from Beer beach, some of them twice the size of the present ones.

Beer regatta, an event moveable to suit the tides, is a great event, when the Beer trawlers and crabbers are raced *under sail*. The older of these boats were of course built for sail, once setting the traditional South Coast dipping lug sails on main and mizzen – the mizzen sail being clewed out on the end of a long bumkin. The sails used for racing now are gaff rigged. Beer, and its hinterland, have become something of a rich Londoner's resort now, but the little fishing community still hangs on and keeps its independence and self-respect.

Beer Quarry is famous among geologists. It is not only a quarry but an underground mine too, although the mine part of it is no longer used. The chalk overlying the famous Beer freestone is quarried for agricultural purposes (by Soil Fertility Limited) and such freestone as is needed for building purposes comes from the limestone thus revealed. The stone is a carbonate of lime, is a freestone (that is it cleaves easily into rectangular blocks), gritty, soft enough to cut with a saw when first quarried but hardened by exposure to air. The quarries are said to have been worked by the Romans, and the roofs and some of the arches of Exeter Cathedral were built of it. In the waste tips are to be found plenty of fossils: sharks' teeth, *Terebratulina lata*, *Inoceramus labiatus*, and *Conulus castanea* being common.

Beer was once famous for lace making, before such arts were considered beneath the dignity of village girls; and the lace for Queen Victoria's wedding dress was made at Beer, also similar accoutrements for Queen Alexandra and Princess Alice. Beer was also famous for smuggling, and one Beer man, Jack Rattenbury – the

'Rob Roy of the West' – left his memoirs: *Memoirs of a Smuggler*, 1837. Rattenbury was born at Beer in 1778 and, according to his memoirs at least, led a life of constant adventure, being captured by Spanish privateers, travelling from Vigo to Vienna, back to Oporto, home again, captured by French and taken to Bordeaux from where he escaped, caught and tried at Dartmouth for smuggling and forced to enlist in the Navy but he escaped from this institution, and ultimately settled down to a peaceful existence catching fish.

Now we may as well deal with the 'Beer Spaniards'. Some of the Beer fishermen have black hair. A Spanish galleon was wrecked near Beer in 1588 and some of the crew came ashore. There are names like Meco and Margal in the parish registers. In 1871 a Spanish anchor was found in Beer Cove.

Leland: 'There was begon a fair pere for socour of shippelettes three years sins at this Bereword; but ther cam such a tempest as never in mynd of man had before bene seene and tare the pere in peaces.'

Beer Head, which is of chalk, has many caves. One of them is supposed to connect with Beer Quarry. I don't believe it.

CHAPTER 2

Branscombe to Exmouth

❧

Bovey House, now an hotel, is a splendid Tudor mansion. A secret chamber was found in a chimney, and another thirty feet down a 130 foot well. Between Beer and Branscombe you can walk along the cliff top, and look down at some sundered cliff into a sort of 'lost world' like that of the Lyme Regis Undercliff country, and there are splendid chalk pinnacles.

At **Branscombe** there is the usual steep shingle beach and some capstans, used in summer only by boatmen who take holidaymakers out. There is a refreshment room at this beach, open only during the summer. Branscombe is almost too pretty for words: it was much commended by that marvellous English writer H. J. Massingham in *In Praise of England* and before that by W. H. Hudson in *Afoot in England*. The church at Branscombe is quite special, and should be visited even by people who are not normally interested in churches. It is beautiful in so many different ways. There is an excellent guide on sale within, which is also a guide to the surrounding district and the big houses. There is too much in the church to see to describe here, but do not miss the monument to Joan Wadham which depicts her twice with her two husbands and her no less than twenty children. There is a good pub in Branscombe, the Mason's Arms, which the rich frequent and where you can get good ploughmen's lunches even if you are not actually a ploughman, and beyond the church (west) is the Fountain Head, one of the pleasantest and homeliest village pubs imaginable. The blacksmith's forge (built 1580) in the village is famous, but not working which is sad. It is thatched, like most of the village, and here might be the place to discuss the Devon thatcher's art, for there is much of it along this coast.

Devon thatching is mostly of 'wheat reed', which is not reed at all but straw. The difference between 'wheat reed' and 'wheat straw' is that the latter has been through the drum of a threshing machine, while the former has had the grain threshed out of it without actually passing through the drum and is thus unbroken. In East Anglia most thatch is of 'Norfolk reed', which may well have been grown

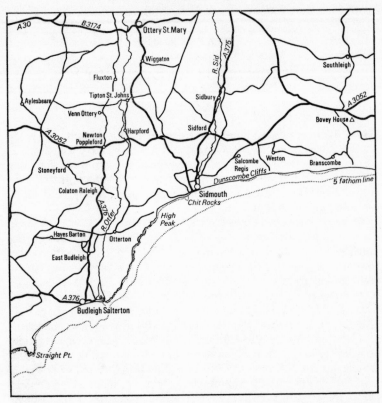

not in Norfolk but in Suffolk, or even have come over from Holland. 'Norfolk reed' will last for seventy years, but in Devon would be prohibitively expensive. 'Wheat reed' (unthreshed wheat straw) lasts perhaps half as long as 'Norfolk reed'. 'Wheat straw' (threshed wheat straw) only lasts about twelve years at the most and is a deplorable roof covering. There is a special machine which fits on the top of a threshing drum for threshing the corn out of 'wheat reed', and an example of an older machine which did the whole process can be seen in the Farm Museum at Mawla in Cornwall. Devon thatch, like all English thatch, is 'thick' thatch: that is the individual straws are laid almost horizontally, and thus the roof is nearly as thick as the individual straws are long. Thatch in many other countries, such as Africa and the West of Ireland, is 'thin' thatch: that is the individual straws are much more nearly parallel to the slope of the roof: the technique is quite different. This only lasts two or three years in a wet climate. The Devon thatchers are highly professional men – quite as much so as their East Anglian counterparts. They have their own terms for the tools they use: the *wink* is the wire tool for twisting up straw cord for tying down the thatch, the *stripper* is a sort of horse, or rack, for combing out and preparing the 'reed' on, the *biddle* is a curiously shaped plank with spikes on the bottom of it. The spikes are thrust into the thatch already done and the thatcher kneels on the plank to work higher up, for it is of course in the nature of all thatch that the lowest courses must be laid on first. The *drift* is a wooden plank with horizontal scores cut in it and a handle. This is used to smooth the surface of the new thatch by knocking the ends of the 'reed' in.

The name Branscome probably comes from St Brendon the Voyager, who had a chapel in nearby Seaton; but the church is dedicated to Saints Winfred and Branwallader. St Winfred was a Devon man, born at Crediton about A.D. 680, consecrated Bishop of Germany by Pope Gregory II and made an archbishop by Gregory III. He was martyred with fifty followers in Friesland in 755 and buried at Fulda.

Just below the church a footpath takes off across a green valley and disappears into the woodland over the other side and out on to the bleak cliff top, which is pocked with tumuli and an Iron Age camp, and we look down over the cliff at a beautiful foundered cliff among the crevices and recesses of which sensible people have built holiday bungalows and established pretty gardens in which rabbits graze for nine months of the year. These little holdings do not, in my opinion, spoil the cliff scenery but embellish it, for they speak of human happiness and contentment.

You can then walk along the cliff top – not necessarily going too near it, though, because the Upper Greensand under the chalk is apt to crumble. **Weston Combe** is beautiful. Weston is a collection of large old farmhouses. **Dunscombe Cliffs** are also dangerous, but beautiful, and some of the many springs that come from their lower slopes have petrifying qualities.

Salcombe Regis is approachable up a pleasant path along the lovely combe. The farmer there keeps the most amiable sows out of doors and lambs his sheep in *November*. Salcombe Regis is tiny, beautiful, and with a lovely and very interesting little church: pillars and font transitional-Norman, chancel door Norman, window in south wall some kind of Early English, Early English trefoil piscina. There is a panel in the chancel, of 1695 with an inscription in Hebrew, Latin, Greek and English: a wide enough spectrum for the most linguistic of passers-by. Over the village school are the words: 'Suffer little children'.

You can walk along the cliff top to Sidmouth, but better perhaps to plod laboriously along the shingle beach, because from here you get a view of the fine and weird *arêtes* of the cliffs. The cliff here is crowned with Upper Greensand (we have left the white cliffs of Old England behind us for good now: no more chalk from here on westwards. There was chalk once but it has all been eroded away). This soft greensand has been cut into strange peaks and pinnacles (compare the cliffs north of Filey, in Yorkshire). It is inadvisable to sit close to the bottom of these cliffs – lumps fall off. Below the Greensand here is Keuper Marl and below that, just before you get to the Sid, you will see Triassic sandstone appearing at the foot of the cliffs.

Not far from the top of the cliff is the Sir Norman Lockyer Observatory. It was founded by Sir Norman in 1912, and is now run by the University of Exeter.

You can usually get across the mouth of the **River Sid** dryshod, for the water percolates subterraneously through the shingle bank that generally blocks its mouth. When, however, there is a heavy spate in the Sid the observer may have the fun of standing on this shingle bank and watching it slowly disintegrate, until the fresh water impounded by it breaks through and rapidly carves a big channel, and the water inside is lowered many feet in a few minutes. There is a place upstream on the Sid called Ronscombe Girt. When there is a flood at Sidmouth the local people say: 'Lord Ronscombe has been busy again!'

Just to the west of the river is the **Sidmouth** fishing fleet: some four or five good vessels of the local beach type, hauled up the shingle by motor windlasses, but there are several of the beautiful and interesting hand capstans there too. The Sidmouth fishermen have had the sense to organize themselves into a body called 'Sidmouth Trawlers'. They run a good shop, open all day and round the year, just behind their landing place. They sell a good variety of fresh fish here: much of it caught themselves, but of course no fleet of this size could supply every kind of fish in all weathers and some of it comes from Brixham.

Sidmouth is an ancient port, for it sent three ships and sixty-two men to the Siege of Calais. Risdon, writing in Charles II's time, said: 'Sidmouth is one of the chiefest fisher towns of this shire and serveth much provision unto the eastern parts, wherein her principal maintenance consists. But in times past, it was a port of some account, now choked with chisel and sands by the vicissitudes of the tides.' Certainly Sidmouth sent ships to the Newfoundland trade.

But Sidmouth got in very early on the 'watering place' vogue. This was boosted by the fact that on Christmas Eve 1819 the Duke and Duchess of Kent arrived, very broke and beset by creditors, with their baby daughter Princess Victoria, and stayed at Woolbrook Cottage in what is now called Royal Glen. These royal personages have since been followed to Sidmouth by the Gaekwar of Baroda, the Grand Duke of Hesse, Earl Jellicoe and Mr and Mrs George Bernard Shaw. The Duke of Connaught wintered here in 1931, thus graciously setting an example to the English upper classes not to take their money abroad to Monte Carlo in the depression. A man named Peter Orlando Hutchinson used to ride round Sidmouth on a cannon pulled by a donkey, wearing a para-military uniform of his own devising, and he wrote the *Sidmouth Guide*, taking thirty years to do so.

Sidmouth beach is just steep shingle, and thus generally pretty bereft of children. Instead of these you can find, however, agates, carnelians, chalcedony and jasper, and also aged men scratching about in the shingle after gales looking for coins and other articles let fall by holidaymakers. Iron pyrites used to be mined from the cliffs and sent to Plymouth for the manufacture of sulphuric acid. On the 8th of June 1893 a huge bit of cliff fell off High Peak, near by, with a terrible noise which lasted ten minutes, and for miles the sea was covered with red dust.

Sidmouth was being much attacked by the sea until the sea wall was built in 1835 at the cost of £2000. This wall was repaired in 1924 at a cost of £106,000. Before the wall was built houses used to get taken by the sea from time to time, and one householder, Dame Partington, gave rise to a legend. Sidney Smith used her case as an example of the futility of opposing reform. She used to sweep the sea out of her house at Chit Rocks after gales with her mop, but the time came when the sea washed away her house, and her mop, and the whole headland on which she had lived.

Now Sidmouth is just a small, highly respectable, seaside resort, much resorted to by the staid and elderly. There are some notable rows and crescents of early 19th century houses in it, good and very high-class shops, a good library, a café (the 'Winter Garden' which has an interesting collection of early gramophones in it), a brewery which is now merely a depot for Devenish of Weymouth and a frontful of very good and expensive hotels. The medieval glass in the church showing the Five Wounds of Christ is interesting.

Sidbury, just inland, has an intriguing church with a Saxon crypt under the chancel and a room for storing gunpowder over the porch.

Ottery Saint Mary has a most splendid church, largely Early English, with some notable bench ends. In 1335 Grandisson founded a college here, in 1520 Cicely, Countess of Dorset, built the North Aisle, Cromwell personally ordered all the church ornamentation to be destroyed because he met with no success in recruiting soldiers for the siege of Exeter, and there are thirteen panels outside the church and eight inside marking the places touched by the bishop with holy oil at the consecration.

Coleridge was born at Ottery Saint Mary in 1772, son of the parson. He celebrated the place in *Sonnet to the River Otter*. Thackeray used to spend his school holidays at Larkbeare, near by, with his stepfather, Major Carmichael Smyth. In his *Pendennis* his 'Clavering St Mary' was based on Ottery St Mary, 'Chatteris' on Exeter, and 'Baymouth' on Sidmouth.

Sidmouth is unlikely to be visited by the sailor. It is in a deep bay, there is no harbour and the shingle is very steep. The pedestrian however will enjoy walking westward along the top of the cliffs, with the footpath winding up to the summit of **High Peak** through a larch plantation, from where there is a great view both inland and along the shore. Here is what is left of an Iron Age camp (most of it fell into the sea) which was excavated in 1961, when a Neolithic occupation was found to underlie the 5th to 6th century foundations.

Down below the cliff, just to the east of High Peak, is something we have not seen at all along this coast: a sandy beach. It is approachable from Sidmouth at all except high spring tides. Down the steep grassy bank from High Peak is a splendid little bay with three rocks in it: the biggest called Hern Point Rock, and this makes a lovely anchorage when the wind is off-shore. There is a pub ashore: the Three Rocks, but closed in the winter. **Ladram Bay** has a huge caravan site. An Italian barque came ashore here once in a terrible gale.

Footpaths lead to **Otterton**, most pleasant and well worth visiting. It was part of a manor given to the monastery of St Michel in Normandy by William the Conqueror, and the Benedictine priory here was a cell of that. It is now a large straggling village, with a stream running down the street and no less than nine farmsteads in the village itself. There is a delightful walk from it (take a footpath just south of the church) along the bank of the River Otter to Budleigh Salterton. Very beautiful with beech trees along the banks.

You are allowed to catch trout in the Otter if you are residing at the time in either Budleigh Salterton or East Budleigh.

East Budleigh is interesting for its Raleigh associations. Sir Walter is generally agreed to have been born in Hayes Barton farmhouse, either in 1552 or 1554 (at least he was according to John Shirley's *Life* of 1677) and this farmhouse can be visited in the summer time and the room can be seen where Raleigh was supposed to have been born. Apart from the Raleigh story the house itself is well worth viewing for it is very fine indeed. There is one beam in it eighty feet long, which goes the length of five rooms, like the keelson of a barge.

The church in East Budleigh has a slab tomb to the first wife of Raleigh (Joan Drake) and sixty carved bench ends believed to have been carved by returned sailors – some very fine – particularly the one of a ship. One of them, the foremost on the left of the centre aisle, has the Raleigh family arms. The second, dated 1537, has been defaced: it is conjectured that this was done at his execution. There is a fine 15th-century door. The vicarage, on the way to Hayes Barton, had secret hiding places and was once the home of 'smuggling parsons'.

Now the mouth of the **River Otter** is fordable by the agile although a notice solemnly warns us not to try. The river is not navigable, but it was not always so. In 1347 three ships belonging to this port, with 141 men aboard, were captured by the French, which goes to show that the Otter was once open. Leland says, mid-16th century: 'lesse than a Hunderith Yeres sins shippes usid this Haven, but now is clene barrid.' All the rivers along this coast, the Axe, the Sid and the Otter, were once ports. Now they are all, except the Axe, 'clene barrid'. Why? Has more shingle been created and washed along the shore?

The beach of **Budleigh Salterton** shelves so steeply that pleasure steamers used to ram it in fine weather and let down a ramp for the disembarkation of their passengers. Sometimes a south-easter flings up a continuous high bank of shingle which cuts off the small beach boats which are all that are left of the Budleigh fishing fleet and makes it awkward to launch them. The large round pebbles on this beach are said by people who know more about pebbles than I do to be partly Devonian and partly Silurian, from 'a pre-Triassic extension of the rocks of Calvador and La Manche'.

Budleigh Salterton rivals Seaton in its claims to have been the Moridunum of the Romans, and one A. F. Drake wrote a book in 1924 pooh-poohing Seaton's claims and *proving* that it was Budleigh

Salterton. We must leave it to the experts. Meanwhile Budleigh is just another small and rather attractive seaside resort, not entirely bereft of retired lieutenant-colonels. Sir John Millais painted 'The Boyhood of Raleigh' here, using his own sons for models. The cliffs, where there are cliffs (there are some fine wind-eroded ones towards Ottermouth, though very small), are of New Red Sandstone. Near the path from the beach, walking west, is the only typical South African *rondavel* I have seen in England. We soon come to a delightful cliff-top pine wood, with areas of gorse. The beach below is quite straight and quite regular, and it is interesting to follow it with the eye from where we are to where it stops – quite suddenly – against the sandstone cliff of Straight Point.

Straight Point has on it what must be the worst-sited rifle range in the world. The beautiful promontory, which could be a delight to anyone who visits it, is fenced round like a concentration camp and recruits to the Royal Marines fire out to sea – right across the only practicable approach from the east to the River Exe. Every time a boat sails along this particular part of England a rocket goes up, all training of the Royal Marines has to stop, and very often a launch is tent out to apprehend and tow away the offending vessel. I doubt if is would be possible, in England at least, to find a more unsuitable place for a weapons range. You are not allowed to walk round the promontory outside the concentration camp fence, but fortunately you can, and the view from the end of the promontory is lovely: particularly on a clear day when you can see the whole great sweep of Lyme Bay – right as far as Portland Bill. At low spring tides it is possible too to walk round the promontory on the beach, but it is something of a scramble.

Thus we come to **Sandy Bay**, where are many caravans and a great big sandy beach. The nearly vertical sandstone cliffs are fine, and it is strange to notice that patches of 'Norfolk reed' grow on even very steep parts of these cliffs where water happens to be springing from the rock. The sandy beach below gives way to parallel ridges of rock with an eastwards strike, which stretch out to sea in a manner unwelcoming to stricken ships. The **Orcombe Rocks** are fascinating, with fine wind-eroded sandstone on which somebody has kindly placed ladders so that people can clamber about. This is National Trust land, very beautiful, but in the summer highly populated. Soon we strike the motor road which follows (and completely spoils) the shore to Exmouth. It is very much used as a speed track by the local hot-rodders. A road here is quite unnecessary.

As for the navigator – if he approaches the Exe from the west he has nothing to fear at all so long as he manages to pick up the red and white bell buoy at the entrance of the channel (and so long as he doesn't stop one of the Royal Marines' bullets). From the buoy on, if it be flood tide, he will be whipped up the channel whether he likes it or not – for the tide runs like a mill-stream. The channel is buoyed on both sides and is quite straightforward. If he is trying to beat up-wind on a falling tide, though, he will not get very far, and should beware of being carried by the fierce sideways-going ebb over the sands of Pole or he may end in disaster. Until these sands dry out the tide whips over them in a spectacular manner. Beating against the wind down on the ebb is fraught with the same peril: on the port tack you are apt to keep on going and end up on the hard sand in a nasty wind-against-tide swell.

Exmouth (map, p. 33) is officially merely a part of the Port of Exeter, but in fact is very much a little port of its own. In its little artificial harbour are several small trawlers and the place is a resort of coasters up to 800 tons. A somewhat bizarre traffic nowadays is the import of thousands of tons of apple juice from France in tanker ships from which it is pumped into big tanker lorries. The government heavily subsidized Devon farmers to grub up their cider apple trees, so now England's traditional cider country has to pay out foreign exchange for foreign apple juice.

We meet here, for the first time in our progress west, a kind of fishing boat very well designed for two purposes. This is the powerful half-decked trawler: decked in forward but with a big sheltering canopy, and abaft of this canopy a completely open boat. The trawl winch is set down in the bottom of the boat, in the open after part, and here also there are two gallows' for the trawl warps. The lay-out of the boat reminds one of the *botters* of the old Zuider Zee and the dimensions are about the same too: from thirty to forty-five foot long and very beamy for the length. This particular design – of a semi-open boat of a size and power that would normally indicate a fully decked vessel – is dictated by the vessel's second use: that of taking amateurs out fishing. There is plenty of room in the open part of the boat for a large party of amateurs and they are unlikely to fall overboard owing to the high gunwales. When not taking anglers these vessels make very good trawlers.

If you wish to enter the Dock at Exmouth in a sailing boat I would advise you to choose slack water – unless you have a strong commanding wind and very much know what you are doing. The tide runs past the narrow entrance at a great speed, whether on the ebb or the flood, and you could easily get swept against one of the piers.

Inside is a swing bridge, but there is room to tie up while it is being swung.

Exmouth is a port of great antiquity and once of great importance. It is known that the Romans had a harbour here, and – that useful index of the size of a port in medieval times – the Siege of Calais was attended by no less than ten ships from the Exe and 193 men. Exmouth sent at least one ship (the *Felix*) against the Armada. Holinshead wrote, in 1577: 'here was sometime a castle, but now the place hath no other defence than a barred haven and the inhabitants' valour.' By the 17th and 18th centuries the Exe was prominent in the Newfoundland cod trade. From 1714 to 1717 for which there are records, we know that the Exe sent 22 ships to Newfoundland, 28 to Oporto, 23 to Lisbon, 26 to New England and 45 to Rotterdam. In 1700 Topsham alone sent 34 ships to Newfoundland.

The export to Rotterdam and Portugal was wool. The Newfoundland trade, in which practically every port in the West Country was engaged, was an interesting three-cornered one. It started with the simple traffic of fishermen sailing to Newfoundland loaded with salt, catching and salting cod and bringing them back to England. Specialization then took place, some men living ashore in Newfoundland and catching the cod from dories, and others sailing across in large trading ships and transporting the fish only. It was then found that the Portuguese, Spaniards and Italians would pay a higher price for salt cod ('stock fish') than the English, and so a triangular trade started up: salt and manufactured goods from England to Newfoundland, salt cod to the Mediterranean countries, and wine and fruit back to England. This was contemporary with that other most profitable three-cornered trade: trade goods to West Africa, slaves to West Indies, sugar and rum back to England. The sailors of the West Country early made the Atlantic Ocean their playground.

In the 19th century Exmouth had a big sailing fishing fleet. In 1869 she had 58 fishing vessels including four trawlers. It was inevitable, however, that this should be knocked out by Brixham: the latter port being so much nearer to the fishing grounds. Exmouth was a big ship-building place: one yard alone, Redways, employing three hundred men in 1843 and building ships up to the size of the *Amazon*: 1,100 tons. But in 1880 the yard caught fire, and the business was transferred to Dartmouth. Rope and sail making were important too.

Exmouth was another early entrant into the pleasure resort

business: by 1750 even 'people of quality' were resorting there. The result of this is an elegant 18th and early 19th century look about much of the town. Exmouth is now a very underrated place. It has developed of late years as a 'popular resort' – i.e. a place where people without much money but with large families of small children go. The reasons for this are not far to seek. *Sand* (we have already examined the *grading* effect of the sea currents on the average age of holiday and retired populations), the pleasures of a big open sea shore combined with those of a big estuary, a ferry service over to the beautiful Dawlish Warren, a motor boat service up to Exeter, the interest of a commercial and fishing port, good sea angling and withal a beautiful and interesting old town. Exmouth has a great deal to offer the visitor: and what if there are plenty of young people there?

The area north of the Dock, called The Point, is a strange little township of its own: a 'shanty town', and in calling it this I do not mean any disrespect. The land, owned by the Dock, is let to people who have built small bungalows on it, some of which are permanently occupied, others used as holiday chalets. The place has a very pleasant atmosphere. Alas, the pressures of high finance look as if they are going to sweep it all away. There is now a scheme to build what has come to be known as a 'marina' – in other words a yacht harbour – here. It is a very unsuitable place. The sand (called the 'Shelly') dries out very far, enormous dredgings would have to take place, and the tide is very strong.

CHAPTER 3

The Exe to the Teign

꙲

IF you are in a boat you will have to steer south-west to get north to Exeter, for you will have to round that high sandbank known as the Great Bull Hill. The channel is very well marked now all the way to Topsham, but you must keep to it, for the sand dries out very high. It is a beautiful estuary (a post-glacial submergence of a river valley) although with the disadvantage of having a railway running along both banks. In the winter some 5000 wigeon resort here and a large company of Brent geese. The west side of the channel is all bird reserve, but the ancient craft of *punting* is still practised, by two people at least, on the wide sand flats to the east of the channel.

The punt is a grey painted vessel, pointed at both ends, with a small fore deck and a small after deck, so low in the water that it looks like a floating plank. A very big gun is mounted on the fore deck, the recoil of which is taken by the breeching ('britchin'') rope which passes round the stem of the punt from the breech of the gun. Nelson's cannon had the same arrangement. The punter sits in the cockpit and rows until he either sees or hears the birds – generally the latter, for punting is best at night or in a fog – and then he 'lies down to them' – lying on his belly behind the big gun. He propels the punt forward with two 'setting sticks' or hand paddles – when he gets within range aims the gun by aiming the punt – then pulls a lanyard (small cord) which fires the gun. There is a devastating roar – and the punt shoots backwards in the water owing to the recoil. The punter sits up and seizes his oars and rows the punt towards the stricken birds as fast as he can. He may have got twenty or thirty ducks or geese at the shot. This form of hunting sounds ruthless, but in fact it does far less harm to the birds than the indiscriminate shore-popping that goes on night and day all around our estuaries, and which wounds and frightens birds far more often than it kills them. Punting was the main occupation of many commercial fishermen in the winter when fishing was slack, and kept many a fisherman's family from starvation. It is hard, cold, and hazardous, and the punter is lucky to get one shot in a week.

If the traveller is on foot a path leads north from Exmouth, be-

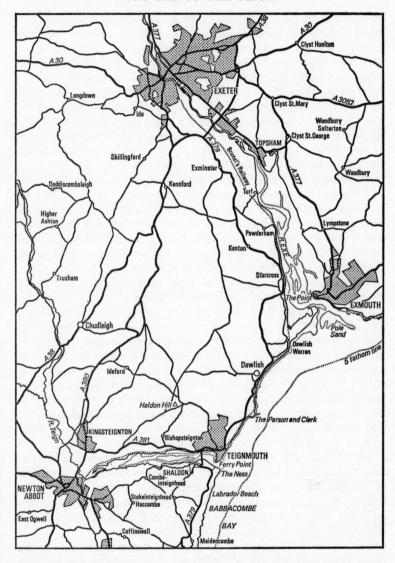

tween the estuary and the railway, to **Lympstone**. This is a beautiful little place with a very Dutch-looking tower, a wharf, old lime kilns, many boats and five salmon licences. A licence allows the holder to use a net 140 fathoms long and with a 4½-inch mesh or larger from the 14th of February to the 16th of August. Lympstone was once a great fishing village, with big ships in the Newfoundland fishery and oyster beds nearer at home. At one time there were 63 fishing vessels there. The place, as a port, died out about 1800, and seeing that there is only five feet of water at its quays at high spring tides this is not surprising. The little cliffs to the north are Permian sandstone, and the huge group of buildings on the most conspicuous site just upstream from the village which disfigures the whole estuary is the training centre of the Royal Marines. If any private person had wanted to put up such a monstrosity on such a site he would, quite rightly, have been stopped.

Topsham is a little town of great antiquity and beauty, made hideous and uncomfortable nowadays by motor cars, for which its network of extremely narrow streets were never designed. The citizens should take the bull by the horns – now before it is too late – and ban motor vehicles completely from most of it. It would then become a delight. After all – Norwich has a traffic-free area larger than the whole of Topsham and it works very well there.

Topsham is thought to have been the port of Roman Exeter, for – even before the infamous weir was built by the Countess of Devon – it was hard to get ships much higher up the Exe. It is still a port, for about four ships a year come in and discharge Tuborg lager from Denmark, also some timber comes in and potatoes go out. Ships of up to 800 tons can dock. There is a large and growing industry here now, in this unlikely place: the marinating of sprats, mostly for export to other countries where they are canned. Sprats are also salted and smoked, and very good smoked sprats may be bought in the fishmongers. The firm that handles the sprats is called Marinpro, and absorbs most of the sprats caught by pair fishing and midwater trawling from the South-West fishing ports.

But Topsham is said to have come to importance when the Countess of Devon built her weir (at Countess Wear, now a suburb of Exeter) and thus prevented ships from getting upstream to Exeter. We know that in 1290 there was an inquisition to enquire into the allegation that the Countess had thus obstructed the navigation, and in 1422, 1461 and 1462 there were more such enquiries. But inquisitions or no the weir stayed there until 1539, when there was an Act of Parliament empowering the City to 'plucke down' the offending obstruction. But meanwhile Topsham had flourished, for Exeter's loss was Topsham's gain, and for centuries all trade to and from Exeter had had to go through Topsham, and be carried between the two places in carts.

In 1316 the Earl of Devon built a quay at Topsham, and this was in use until 1861. By the 19th century there were four ship-building yards in the little town, building up to 500 tons. By 1874 ship-building was dead. Old men in Topsham today though can tell you of when four 140-ton ketches were owned in Topsham: the *Topsham*, the *Buttercup*, the *Young Fox* and the *Effort*, and besides these a big iron 'engine-ketch' (i.e. an auxiliary) called the *Crown of Denmark* which was only sold away after the Second World War. In latter days these ships carried cement, stone and brick.

And now Topsham acts as one of the wealthier suburbs of Exeter. There is still an active little fishing industry in the shape of ten salmon licences (see Lympstone). There is a total of eighteen licences in the whole estuary. Catches have fallen sadly in recent years: in 1942 Jim Voysey caught 120 fish in four days (selling at 8/6d a pound) and his cousin, also named Jim Voysey, once caught a salmon weighing 61¾ pounds! Topsham has not been physically spoiled and is a beautiful place. Many of the houses are of Dutch brick, for they were built of brick carried back from Holland as ballast in days when wool exporting from Topsham was an important trade. In the church are two Chantry monuments: one to Admiral Sir John Duckworth, who forced the Dardanelles, and the other to his son who was a colonel and who led a charge at Albuera. Topsham has great atmosphere and several good pubs.

Exeter as a cathedral and university city is outside the scope of this book, but as a port it must be mentioned. In the 12th century it was the fourth city of England. In the 14th century it was exporting much wool, raw at first but more and more of it manufactured as time went on, chiefly into serge.

The cost of carting everything down to Topsham for shipment became unendurable, and it was decided that something must be done to get ships up to Exeter. In 1563 a man from Glamorgan named John Trew was commissioned to make a canal, and by 1566 the canal was opened, having cost £5000. Trew had a single sluice gate into the estuary (which could only be opened of course when there was 'a level' of tide outside) but inside three pairs of 'pound sluices' or true locks. These were the first true pound locks ever to be built in England, and were anywhere a very new invention. The pound lock is a device for lifting or lowering vessels from one level to another, and was imagined by Leonardo da Vinci although he never saw one. John Trew has been called 'the Father of the English locked canal'.

In 1676 a Dutch engineer was called in (as Dutch engineers

generally have to be called in where there is anything to do with tidal water) and work was done under him which allowed ships of 10 tons to get to the middle of Exeter. But ships were getting bigger all the time, and by 1698 Exeter was being starved as a port because so few ships could get there and in that year a character named William Bayley was employed to improve the canal. He decamped with the funds. And so the Chamber, desperate, employed 'a heroic company of women – all in white, with clean straw hats, armed with mattocks and shovels, with drums beating and the city musick playing before them . . .' to dig a bigger canal. In 1701 ships of 300 tons could get to Exeter. By 1831 the canal was extended downstream – to its present entrance at Turf, and the canal was now 5½ miles long. A side lock (still in use) was left opposite Topsham. But it all came to nothing, or nearly nothing, in the end. By 1850 the railway had come and that was that. Now the canal is used by yachts and a few pleasure boats, and a little ship which carries the produce of Exeter sewage works down to the sea, to be dumped on top of what once were escallop beds. An occasional small coaster carrying timber and an occasional small oil tanker comes in. It is sad and (silly) that the big gas works built right by the canal gets its coal by rail, when it could get it so much more cheaply and conveniently by sea, and it is sad that Exeter seems to have given up all desire to be a port again. And this the city that once owned 230 ships in the serge trade to the Continent, imported linen direct from Antwerp, wine from Spain and Portugal, tobacco from the West Indies and salt cod from Newfoundland. Defoe said of Exeter: "Tis full of Gentry and Good Company, and yet full of Trade and Manufactures also.'

The most interesting thing about Exeter now is the new Maritime museum run by I.S.C.A.: the International Sailing Craft Association. This occupies a large and beautiful warehouse between the canal and the old river port of Exeter, and has floating accommodation outside for an almost unlimited number of small ships and vessels besides a great deal of indoor accommodation. At the moment of writing the exhibits include four Arab dhows – one quite large one, several traditional craft of the British Isles including coracles, curraghs and a coble, and traditional 'native' craft from places as far away as the Gilbert Isles, Sierra Leone and Lake Titicaca. In this superb site, and with a little official encouragement, this museum might make Exeter a world centre of interest in sailing vessel matters. An excellent aspect of the museum is that such of the craft as can be sailed are taken out and sailed, so that their habits and qualities may be studied and observed, and a Bahraini pearling dhow being flogged up and down the Exe estuary is a sight worth seeing. The marvellous Exeter waterfront is terribly under-used: there seems to be the all-too-common official disapproval of anything that floats.

Meanwhile, it is interesting either to walk down the towpath or take a boat down to **Double Locks**. Here there is an hotel, and the lock itself is of interest being of a very ancient design: a turf lock instead of a masonry one. It replaced the three pound locks built by John Trew: the first in England. The balance beams of the great gates, incidentally, are made from the main mast of H.M.S. *Exeter*, which was removed after the battle of the River Plate.

Further down we come to the end of the canal where it debouches into the estuary at **Turf**, where is another large pub which stands on an island between canal and estuary and is one of those lucky places which cannot be reached by motor car. When approached from the other way – by boat up the estuary – it looks like an oasis or desert island, with big ilex trees growing on its island lawn and surrounded by a bird-haunted wilderness.

Powderham has the Starcross Yacht Club, which claims to be the oldest yacht club in England and thus in the world. It also has Powderham Castle, the seat of the Earls of Devon, and open to the public from 30th May to 3rd September. It was built about 1400 but has been much restored, not to say rebuilt. It has fine furniture.

Starcross is interesting, although unfortunately cut off from the water by Brunel's railway. The most interesting building in it is the great engine house that once provided the air pressure for Brunel's 'Atmospheric railway'. This was a device which caused trains to go along by the atmospheric pressure provided by frequent air pumps. The pressure came along a channel closed by leather flaps, and the flaps had to be greased to make them anything like air tight and the rats ate the flaps. The whole thing was an expensive failure (it cost £426,000) and was replaced by a conventional locomotive-powered railway, which was converted to standard gauge in 1892. The pumping house at Starcross was later a Wesleyan chapel. Now it should be preserved, being a fine and interesting building.

Meanwhile Starcross dreams, if the traffic of the A 379 allows it to dream of anything, of having been an important trans-shipment port for Exeter, and of having had, before the days of universal pollution, a big oyster industry. It also owned a big fleet of smacks which used to sail out to sea to dredge escallops in the bay, and there was until recently an important mussel industry. The oysters became inedible owing to pollution inside the estuary, the escallops because of the dumping of sewage outside it, and the mussels were destroyed by flocks of oystercatchers that occasionally black out the sky. When oystercatchers could be shot and sold for more than the price of a charge of shot they were kept in reasonable control. Now they are protected, and nobody thinks of protecting the poor mussels, nor the fishermen who used to gain a living from the latter.

Dawlish Warren. Leland: 'a great vaste plaine and barren field at the west side and very point of Exeter Haven.' Still like this, but also a 'great vaste' caravan camp, golf course, chalet complex and 'amusement' centre. In the summer swarming with thousands of parents with their happy children. The Warren is supposed to be getting smaller from erosion – all such places are. I imagine it has been getting smaller – and bigger – and smaller – ever since the Ice Age and perhaps before. All such places have. In the 1920s it had a whole village of bungalows built on it. These are locally supposed to have been 'swept away by storms' – in fact they were swept away by the storm of the Second World War, when holiday bungalows were not needed but military installations were. There used to be a lake between what is now the golf course and the southern part of the Warren and it was called Greenland Lake. Now it is dry mud and reminds me of the Etosha Pan, in Damaraland. In winter the whole place has a lonely atmosphere, with large flocks of waders. In summer it is too crowded with *Homo sapiens* to admit of many birds, though it supports some rare wild flowers. The Warren bears the same relation to the Exe as the Spurn does to the Humber, except that it sprouts from the opposite bank. Deep water comes up to a few feet of the sand in the estuary right at the end. There is a channel called the Western Way through the Pole Sands to the east of it, marked in summer by one lonely badly sited beacon – in winter often not at all. This channel can be used at high tide to avoid the long slog right round the end of the sand spit. In the old days schooners and even brigantines used to use it. It would be nice if it could be more adequately marked.

From here on the pedestrian can follow Brunel's railway along a footpath between it and the sea, that is so long as it is not high tide with a south-easter blowing. If it is, even the trains sometimes have sheets of salt water blown over them, and a walker would be washed away.

Dawlish is a pleasant little seaside resort, especially pleasant for train spotters. There are two Flaxman monuments in the church. The Daw has been tamed by waterfalls and is peopled by black swans and ornamental ducks. Once, in 1810, it came down in such a spate as to sweep part of the town away.

The cliff path here rather peters out, and the railway takes to tunnels. Without some rather difficult trespassing – physically difficult as well as politically – it is hard to follow the cliff edge and the law-abiding might like to take to the road. From seaward the rocks called the Parson and Clerk look wonderfully named: the Parson seems to be thundering a hell-fire sermon over the humble head of his less learned brother. The Clerk is a challenge to rock climbers, and would make a superb perch for a latter-day Simon Stylites.

The coast footpath can be resumed again after the rocky headland, but again, in a south-easter, beware being washed away. Here we see the full splendour of Brunel's railway. The mighty masonry embankment that he built has to stand up to the full force of the waves. Four times the latter have prevailed, though, and the embankment has been temporarily broken.

Teignmouth has been much burnt down by pirates. Danish ones did the job in 790 and again in 1001, and Stow in his *Annals* for 1340 tells us that 'certaine French pyrates sailed towards the coasts of Devonshire and coming up to Teignmouth they set fire to the Towne and brent it up.' In 1690 Admiral Tourville attacked it and managed to set fire to 116 (some authorities say 160) houses of the 300 then in the town and destroy eleven ships. Two of his galley slaves escaped on this occasion and were given a great welcome by the town people, and £11,000 was raised throughout the land to help Teignmouth rebuild. A plaque in French Street commemorates this battle, and two cannon balls, chained together to make them nastier, were dug up in Britton Street.

But despite all these tribulations Teignmouth has been important. Domesday mentions twenty-four salt works in the river, and Teignmouth sent seven ships and 120 men to the Siege of Calais. In 1770 the port had 43 ships in the Newfoundland trade: a big fleet. One of the Newfoundland fishermen was a Mr Bawdon, who lived to 106, never in his life having taken physic, lost a tooth, or known pain. So it must have been a healthy life if a rugged one.

Ball clay now competes with holidaymakers in providing the town's livelihood, with fishing coming a good third. Teignmouth was early a 'resort'. John Keats came here with his dying brother, and finished writing *Endymion* here (the preface is dated Teignmouth April 18th 1818). There is a plaque on the house wherein he lodged.

The town is a very pleasant resort, with plenty of sand, a pier, a big open space called the Den (from Dene – meaning sandy place), and the never-ending interest of a working commercial port. Also it has what every good seaside resort should have: an estuary. There is a small fleet of fishing boats, several of them of the half-decked open-well trawler kind, there are big mussel layings up the river and the mussels are placed in cleaning tanks on a quay to be purified before sale. This is organized by the Teignmouth Fishermens' and Watermens' Association. If you want a boiling of winkles there is an old gentleman who frequents the Lifeboat Inn who will always get you one, and on the Shaldon side of the river there is another old gentleman who goes out and ring-nets prawns and you can often buy a mess of these. The ring-net – perhaps one of the oldest fishing engines ever used – is an iron ring (once wood weighted with stones) with a net tied to it. It is baited, lowered to the sea bottom with a rope, and hauled up again as the prey are busy eating the bait.

As for the ball clay industry: the clay is quarried up river near Kingsteignton. It is called ball clay because it used to be cut into blocks (seventy of which went into an Old Ton of 22½ hundredweight) which were called balls. The stuff itself is derived from decomposed granite (as is the quite different china clay), it fires out white, makes good earthenware, electric porcelain, wall tiles and similar things. It is also used as a filler for rubber and an extender for paint. The quarries were opened in 1743, when John Astbury started sending the clay by sea to Staffordshire for his own potteries there. It was brought down-Teign in barges, loaded by hand into old Newfoundland ships put to this new traffic, sailed round to the Mersey, loaded into narrow boats at Runcorn and hauled by horses up the narrow canal to Stoke on Trent. Now it comes from the open casts by lorry (causing awful congestion on the road) and is loaded by conveyors into ships alongside the quays. These take most of it to the Continent. There is heavy traffic: generally three or four ships loading and more at anchor out in the bay waiting to come in. The New Quay was built in the 1820s to be used for loading Haytor granite into ships to be sailed to London for the building of London Bridge. In 1825 work was started on the great Shaldon Bridge, which was 1672 feet long and had thirty-four wooden arches and a drawbridge. The present bridge is new but of the same pattern, and still has a drawbridge in the same position as the old one but it is seldom used. In 1932 the Teignmouth Quay Company was founded, the berthage improved, and now ships of 200 foot long and 14 foot draught can be loaded.

The granite that was shipped from Teignmouth, incidentally,

was brought down from Dartmoor along a unique tramway with granite rails. This was ten miles long and had a drop of 1300 feet in it. Uphill the wagons were hauled by horses – eighteen horses pulling a train of twelve empties. Downhill most of the motive power was gravity. In places the tracks can still be seen.

Sailing into Teignmouth has its perils, for the sands of Ferry Point alter with every gale, and south of the channel, near the Ness, are pretty horrid sandstone rocks. There is one small buoy in the entrance, sited according to no comprehensible logic, and the attitude seems to be that if you don't know the way in you had better stay out. The tide runs very strongly both in and out. Once you do get inside you turn sharp right, and there is plenty of room to anchor, further up, and a very steep clean beach just inside the point although much occupied by tripper-carriers. There is a brisk trade in taking out sea anglers.

Up the estuary you get avocets, spoonbills and red breasted mergansers amongst other birds. Brunel's railway spoils the north bank: the south is better for walking along. Teignmouth is a very nice harbour to visit. There are many good sailors' pubs. The Kangaroo has the oddest name: the Old Quay, down by the docks, is the friendliest. Morgan Giles, the famous yacht builders, had their yards near the Ferry Landing. They have now gone out of business and Honour Marine build in glass fibre in their old premises.

On **Haldon Hill**, inland, are beautiful plants such as Bog Asphodel, and fossils of the Greensand. South of the Teign, reached either by the nice little ferry which runs every ten minutes (foot only), or by the big bridge, lies **Shaldon**. Once you get back from the sea front here you enter a charming village of narrow streets and old houses, something like Topsham. At **Stokeinteignhead** is a church with a fine screen of Richard II's time and a clerical brass of 1375. At **Haccombe**, further inland, there are two horseshoes nailed to the church door. These are to commemorate a wager between two gentlemen named Carew and Champernowne as to whether the former would be able to swim his horse over the estuary. He could. **Forde House**, in Newton Abbot, is Jacobean, and Charles I slept here and dubbed Richard Reynells a knight. William of Orange slept here and Sir William Courtenay, who owned the house at the time, slept elsewhere that night as he didn't want to compromise himself in case the prince's cause came unstuck. It is a very fine house, with good Jacobean carving, fine plaster ceilings, very early wall paper and the ghost of an immured nun.

CHAPTER 4

The Teign to Brixham

◆

JUST south of Shaldon Ness is a fascinating tunnel which leads to an isolated beach, and if it is not used by smugglers it ought to be. **Labrador Beach** (map, p. 33) is so called because a Captain Trapp, a Labrador trader, built a house above it in the 18th century. It is a delightful beach, and you can get tea there in the summer. Captain Trapp's house is now gone: it harboured smugglers at various times and on one occasion a French spy.

The cliffs along here, and south, are of a crumbling Permian sandstone, high and steep and indented with many combes. Walking along them is a healthful exercise because there is much up and down to it. The combes, being sheltered so perfectly from north and west, have the vegetable lushness of places much further south and are interesting to botanists. They are hard of access, being steep-sided and thorny.

Maidencombe has a beautiful thatched farmhouse, now a guest-house. At **Watcombe** Brunel built the mansion he intended to live in, but died before it was completed. There are delightful sylvan walks around here, but it must be realized that from here on south the country becomes urban or suburban.

Oddicombe Beach has a cliff railway down to it, with all that that implies. South is a large open space, with an ancient field system visible on it, which terminates in Long Quarry Point: a most theatrical place where a green field lies down near the sea at the base of steep cliffs of Devonian limestone which have resisted the sea better than the surrounding Permian sandstone. If you climb down to this lost field (which you can do if you are agile) you will find it hard to believe that you are not half a mile from **Babbacombe** and the whole straggling conurbation of Torbay. Keats loved Babbacombe: what would he think of it now?

Anstey's Cove is splendid, and accessible by the beautiful Bishop's Walk.

And here we might as well consider **Kent's Cavern**, for this lies a little inland from Anstey's Cove. This large and labyrinthine cave in the limestone played a very important rôle in the develop-

ment of man's understanding – or misunderstanding – of his world
and universe. From 1825 to 1829 the Rev. J. MacEnery, a Roman
Catholic priest, began to excavate in its sooty and dusty deposits.
He ruined his health by his labours, but he dared not publish his
findings, for what he discovered upset the whole cosmology of his
Church, and of natural science as it existed at that time. For he
convinced himself beyond any doubt that Man had existed in the
world for hundreds of thousands of years longer than anyone up to
then had supposed.

Kent's Hole, as it was first called, had for long been an object of
local interest. One W. Maton, about 1745, wrote how 'two ancient
females, and not the most comely of their years, conducted us to the
spot, provided with candles, tinder boxes, and other necessaries for
the expedition . . .' and, sticking the candles in slotted sticks, led
Maton and his friends into the labyrinth. But in 1865 a remarkable
man named William Pengelly, a scientific investigator of the first
order, arrived from his home at Looe in Cornwall and – having
excavated Windmill Hill Cavern near Brixham – undertook the
complete and systematic excavation of what was to prove beyond
any possible doubt that *Homo sapiens* had co-existed with many
animals that were known to have been extinct for several hundred
thousand years. Between 1865 and 1880 he had discovered no less
than 1378 man-worked flints, together with many other implements,
intermingled with the bones of Cave Bear, Sabre Toothed Tiger,
Woolly Rhinoceros, Mammoth and many other extinct creatures.
A whole pack of Cave Bear must have been drowned, once, by an
inrush of water into these caves. Pengelly laboured below ground in
the dusty darkness five hours a day for sixteen years, and his health
was ruined as had been MacEnery's, but the exact and systematic
record that he kept was – and still is – of the first scientific importance.

The cave is now opened by a private company, and people are
conducted round it, winter and summer, by pleasant and well-
informed guides. The cave is electrically lit, and it is fascinating that
under each ordinary electric light bulb grows a hart's tongue fern,
for ever unstirred by the winds of Heaven, for ever at exactly the
same temperature and humidity (for these never change winter or
summer), their day and night regulated by whether anybody
switches on or off the electric light. A foretaste of the controlled
environment of the future? These ferns have not been planted by
man: their minute spores are believed to have been washed through
the porous limestone from above by water. The great cave is fun to

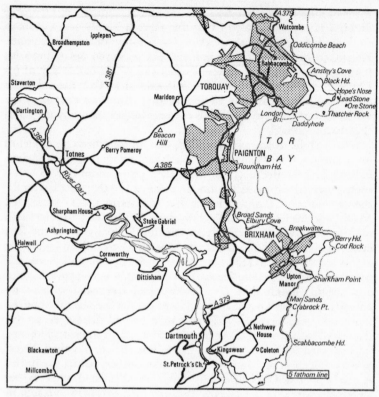

visit, the stalactites and stalagmites superb, and the fossils in the little museum outside imagination-stirring. The gentlemen's and ladies' lavatories are labelled, respectively: CAVE MEN, and CAVE WOMEN.

South of Anstey's Cove we come to **Black Head**, which is solid dolerite. **Hope's Nose** exists as a remnant of Devonian limestone. It is a good place for bird watching. There is a good little booklet called *Hope's Nose and its Birds* by Lt.-Col. Kennedy, published by that unique organization the Torquay Natural History Society; it can be bought at the society's museum.

Beyond the **Lead Stone** (or Flat Rock as the unimaginative call it) is the **Ore Stone**, a challenge, often taken up, to rock climbers. South-west is **Thatcher Rock**, and climbers sometimes connect this up to the mainland with a ropeway. **Daddyhole Plain** is a pretty weird place, with a great cleft in the cliff known as the Daddyhole.

At **Rock End** there is a fine cliff garden, and then comes **London Bridge** a natural arch of rock. And so we come to Torquay Harbour, which is fairly and squarely in the heart of **Torquay**, which town is a combination of Los Angeles, Monte Carlo and the New Jerusalem.

The actual inlet of the sea called Torbay did not exist in Pliocene and early Pleistocene times, for the sea level then was a hundred feet lower than it is now. Forests grew in what is now Torbay, and their remains can still sometimes be seen at exceptionally low tides. Subsidence of the land, or elevation of the sea, or both, started at the end of the Pliocene, the rising sea cut into the soft Permo-Triassic deposits to form Torbay, leaving the harder Devonian rocks of Berry Head and Hope's Nose outstanding.

In 1196 William Brewer, Lord of the Manor of Torre, founded a Premonstratensian abbey on the shores of Torbay. In 1200 King John gave the monks the right of fishing between the Ore Stone and Berry Head. Leland, 16th century, wrote of: 'a peere and socour for boates in the bottom of Torre Prior.' In 1570 a smuggler was found to have 'thirty hoggesheddes of wine in a sellar in Torbay and Sugers in quantities not known.' About this time some of the sailors of Sidmouth came and built a quay at Torbay, their own harbour proving more and more inadequate. In 1750 Torquay Harbour was improved. In 1800 the village was 'nothing more than a few cottages, with their little herb gardens, while beneath cluster the cottages of fishermen, whose boats lie within the shelter of a rude pier, which gives this hamlet its name of Torquay.' But in this year, or soon after, Sir Laurence Palk started building South Pier, 220 feet long, and by 1806 the Inner Harbour was completed.

In 1864 Torquay was chosen as the venue of a grand regatta by the Royal Victoria Yacht Club, but during the event a south-easter sprang up and the assembled yachts had to claw out of it and run dangerously for Dartmouth. It was seen that the place was dangerous (now *yachtsmen* were involved – not just common fishermen) and so the Haldon Pier, an outer sea defence, was started in 1867: the top of Beacon Hill being blasted off to provide stone for it. Most of this pier is in fact made of huge concrete blocks. James Mountstephen was the engineer for this work. By 1870 the Outer Harbour was completed, and another, less hazardous, regatta was held, which was a great success. In 1886 the Torquay Corporation bought the harbour from Lord Haldon. It has been called the finest artifici al harbour in South-West England, and who shall say that it is not?

Torquay was well on the way to becoming an important fishing and commercial and even ship-building harbour. Sailing trawlers began to use it early in the 19th century, but eventually left it in favour of Brixham. Schooners of up to 200 tons were built here – the last ship, the 50-ton cutter *Charlotte*, was launched in 1855. Ships of up to 1000 tons used to bring timber from Canada, anchor out in Torbay and chuck the timber into the water, where it was lashed into rafts and towed into the harbour. But this commercial traffic, too, died a natural death.

Other developments were on the way. During the Napoleonic wars Torbay was a favourite anchorage for the British fleet, which would lie sheltering from the predominant westerlies here waiting to sail out and annoy the French. It was once predicted that Torbay would be the graveyard of the Royal Navy, for a switch in the wind to south-east, gale force, would have proved disastrous. This did not happen (then at least – it happened later as we shall see when discussing Brixham), and while the fleet lay in Torbay so often the officers would send for their wives, who would lodge in Torquay, where they found the climate mild and delightful. The little village of Torquay was in a perfect position: sheltered by high hills from the west, north and east, exposed to the southern sun, far to the west of England where the Gulf Stream operates, its climate more Mediterranean than English. Napoleon, while a prisoner on board the *Bellerephon* anchored out in the bay, was loud in his praises of the place and compared it with Porto Ferrajo in Elba. Soon 'people of quality' began to arrive, and Torquay became a fashionable resort. The Duchess of Sutherland lived, not in Sutherland, but at Sutherland Towers in Torquay and there she entertained Princess Alexandra of Wales. The Marquis of Bute built Bute Court. Disraeli used to frequent Braddon Hall. German princes and Russian archdukes became ten a penny. Of writers, Lord Lytton died here, Philip Gosse wrote his *Manual of Marine Zoology*, Elizabeth Barrett Browning lived in what has become the Regina Hotel, Charles Kingsley spent some time here and William Scoresby Junior, that grossly underestimated writer and sailor (see WHITBY in *The Companion Guide to the Coast of North-East England*), died at Upton, where he was vicar, in 1857.

As for Torquay today, it is part of the super-city of 'Torbay', which has swallowed up Torquay, Paignton and Brixham, on the well-known principle that bigger means better. That Brixham, an ancient place with a strong tradition and flavour of its own, should have been absorbed by this conurbation is most sad. Torquay is a fine resort for those who like large seaside towns. It has 'every amenity'. It has a superb harbour, a superb bay, a superb position. It has a most excellent library, the Natural History Museum is very good (with a great collection from Kent's Cavern amongst other things), in Torre Abbey there is a permanent art gallery and many exhibitions are held. There is a great 12th-century tithe barn there called the Spanish Barn, because 397 prisoners of war from the flagship of the Armada – the *Nuestra Senora del Rosario* – were kept here, when their ship was brought into the bay as a prize.

The numerous other amusements and delights of this large and growing town are listed in the official guide book, which can be had almost anywhere free, so I will not describe them here. The place has the charm of a city built on steep hills. From a vessel out in the bay it all looks enchanting – particularly at night when the whole great semi-circle of the bay is brilliant and twinkling with lights. Torquay is a very civilized place.

Paignton, where are more sandy beaches to be found than exist at rocky Torquay (Permian Sandstone to the north of Roundham Head, Lower Devonian to the south of it), is another ding-a-ding holiday resort. It has its roots. A Saxon named Paega built a church here – but even he was anticipated, for he built it on a Bronze Age site. The bishops of Exeter built a seaside palace here (now called Coverdale Tower, because it is thought that Miles Coverdale translated the Bible in it). Paignton church is 15th century and interesting; the west door and east pillars of the nave are in fact Norman. Kirkham chapel has a really great 15th-century stone screen (Devon being a county of good screens).

In the Middle Ages there were two Paigntons: Paignton Well up by the church and Paignton Quay down by the water. The latter was of old a fishing place: Paignton fishermen even now have the right to dry their nets on the south end of the Green (but who wants to dry nylon and corlene anyway?). In the 17th century most Paignton men were away at the Newfoundland fishery. Paignton ships imported culm (anthracite dust) and coal into the place, and cider and the famous Paignton cabbages were shipped out. The very first Act of Parliament in Queen Victoria's reign was the Paignton Harbour Act of 1838, and it caused the North Pier to be built. In 1880 a perceptive Birmingham speculator bought much of the land about and developed it, turning the Harbour Master's house into a café and the coastguard station into a public lavatory. Paignton, which lacks the hilly charm of Torquay, has great beaches, a splendid collection of shrubs and plants just south of Roundham Head (many of them sub-tropical), a good Zoo, a good Aquarium and many other delights. The harbour is used by tripper-carrying boats and by four full-time crabbers; it is an important depot for the crab and lobster fisheries. Whether this last activity will be badly compromised by the decision of the Brixham Fishermen's Co-operative to start handling shell-fish themselves, remains to be seen.

The steep shingle beach at Beer.

Above, Branscombe village; *below*, Torquay harbour.

CHAPTER 5

Brixham

✣

AND so we come, via Broad Sands and Ebury Cove to the splendid and ancient town of **Brixham** (map, p. 44). Brixham is haunted and dominated, and let us hope it always will be, by the memory of the most splendid fleet of little ships that ever sailed the seas: the Brixham Sailing Trawlers. Brixham claims, quite rightfully, to be the Mother of the Trawl Fisheries, and we shall consider this aspect of the town first: William of Orange and all that can come later.

Brixham was of old a fishing port, besides being a commercial port of some significance too. In the early 19th century Brixham developed the first great trawling fleet in the world.

The trawl, a bag net dragged along the bottom of the sea by a boat, is known to have been used as early as the 14th century, but for long was frowned on by the authorities. It was held that it damaged the fishing grounds, which it does. In any case, until the introduction of the fore-and-aft rig, which is said to have been brought from the Continent by sailors returning from the Seven Years' War (that is in about 1763), fishing vessels were not powerful or manoeuvrable enough to work the trawl effectively. But, about the turn of the century, the adoption of the big and powerful main-sail set on a boom and gaff made trawling practicable, and indeed inevitable.

The clean ground and good shelter of Lyme Bay encouraged the fishermen of Brixham to develop this form of fishing, as did the opening of the turnpike to Bath and Bristol, where there was a large population of wealthy and discriminating people willing to buy such luxury trawl fish as soles and turbot. The trawl is about the only practicable method of taking sole: that fish that clings so lovingly to the sandy bottom of the sea and is so reluctant to take any bait. As decade followed decade the Brixham trawlers grew not only in numbers but in size and power until was evolved the finest working sailing vessel ever built: the Brixham trawler. The typical ship of the heyday of the industry, when three hundred of them fished from Brixham, was from sixty to seventy feet in length, ketch rigged (a big mast forward and a little one aft), setting jib, foresail, mainsail, main-topsail, mizzen and mizzen topsail, and towed a beam trawl. The beam trawl is a bag net the mouth of which is held apart laterally by a wooden beam, the head rope of which is lifted above the ground by the fact that the beam is supported by iron heads which are like sledge runners. The modern otter trawl cannot reliably be worked by a sailing vessel as it depends on a constant speed to keep the mouth open by the kite-like action of the 'doors' or otters in the water, and so the otter trawl was not possible until the development of power.

The largest of the Brixham smacks were called Dandies, the medium class Bumble-bees and the smallest Hookers. A Dandie might cost, to build, £1000. The general custom was to divide the catch into shares, the ship getting one, the gear another, the Captain and each man one and there were generally two men beside the skipper. The skipper, who was generally the owner too, might hope to make about a pound a day, the fishermen four shillings, but of course this varied enormously according to the catch. There was many a week in which the ships couldn't put to sea at all because of the weather, and then captain, owner and crew got nothing. There was no 'national insurance'. On the other hand, sometimes they struck it rich.

As time went on the Brixham smacks outgrew the port in which they had developed. The bottom of Lyme Bay got scraped so thoroughly that hardly a fish was to be found there, the ships explored further and further out into the Channel, rounded Land's End into the Irish Sea, and finally – the greatest break-through of all – sailed into the North Sea itself. The East Coast fishermen had been too obsessed with the Icelandic cod grounds, which they exploited with hand lines and long lines, to worry about the new game of trawling. In 1840 a Brixham Trawler, which had ranged as far as the Dogger Bank, shot her net and hauled it in absolutely full of soles. She had discovered, quite by accident, the Silver Pits, perhaps then the richest trawling ground in the world. When news of this discovery got out the Brixham smacks flocked round to the North Sea, and they established the present East Coast fishing ports by a process that has been aptly called colonization. Loading their wives and children and their furniture aboard their ships they sailed east and north, and went ashore at Lowestoft, Great Yarmouth, Boston, Grimsby, Hull and Scarborough (although Barking men claim some of the credit for the colonization of Great Yarmouth). Boston was early of the greatest importance but when the railway got through to Great Grimsby it fell right out, for the Boston fleet moved to Grimsby. Even now one of the biggest trawler owners in Grimsby is called the Boston Fishing Company.

And so much of the fishing blood was drained out of Brixham, the mother of the trawl fisheries, that Brixham itself declined. In 1822 6000 tons of fish were landed in the harbour and under 500 tons at Hull. In 1928 2160 tons were landed at Brixham and 94,000 tons at Hull. The First World War, with its plethora of wrecks in the English Channel, struck another great blow. Not only were Brixham smacks sunk by the enemy by the dozen but the trawling grounds were littered with wreckage which, in the absence of electronic navigational aids, worked havoc with the nets. A few of the great smacks sailed on into the 1930s and then, alas, the diesel engine was perfected enough to knock them out altogether. The sailors could compete against steam (in fact they used steam to drive their trawl winches) but not against the diesel. The last sailing trawler, the *Ruby Eileen*, was built in 1927 (although some people say the *Servabo* was the last), and by 1939 only six were still trawling. The Second World War killed these, as it killed so many other good things, and now only a handful of the great smacks still live, converted as yachts or as training ships for boys, and they are still the grandest ships of their size that have ever sailed the seas: when it is realized that a great fleet of them used to circle these islands in any weather that God could send, winter and summer, often keeping the sea for months together (the North Sea fleets used to transfer their catches at sea into *trunkers* – special fast cutters built for the purpose) and that hardly a smack was lost to bad weather, and that they would hang on fishing in weather that would send a modern diesel trawler scuttling for port, some idea of their marvellous efficiency can be obtained. The arms of Brixham are a lion rampant. They should be a Brixham Trawler passant on a field of azure: lions have been extinct here since they lived in Windmill Cavern during the Pleistocene.

The only Brixham Sailing Trawler left in Brixham now is the poor degraded hull of one, which supports a ludicrous matchboard mock-up alleged to look like the *Golden Hind*. It is pathetic that the town cannot find it in its heart to keep one as a boys' training ship, or just as a floating museum piece.

But Brixham is growing very fast as a fishing port nevertheless. Steam never really took hold in Brixham – coal was too dear there and Brixham's children on the East Coast too vigorous for their old mother to compete against; but with the diesel came hope. During the Second World War a company named Torbay Trawlers was formed, which began to operate some eighty-foot motor trawlers. During the war there was an influx of Belgian fishermen into the port: some of these managed to flee from the invading Nazis in their trawlers and they were welcomed and took up residence at Brixham. It is interesting to compare this influx of foreigners, fertile with new ideas, with the Huguenot influx into Brixham in the 16th century. Nevertheless the Brixham fleet grew slowly after the war, fell on hard times, and by 1964 the only fish merchant in Brixham decided to close down. It looked like the end.

But the fishermen – led by one of the Belgians – themselves took charge. They put everything they had got into it and formed the Brixham Fishermen's Co-operative. They undertook all their own buying and selling, and since then the industry has grown by leaps and bounds. Six years ago there were but eight trawlers fishing out of Brixham – at the time of writing there are 56, many of them big ones, some powered with engines of over 500 horsepower. The Belgians went back to Belgium and bought up old Belgian trawlers, other people went to France and looked for ships. The present fleet is owned by 45 individuals or syndicates, and employs 150 men afloat plus many more, of course, ashore. All the men fish on shares (i.e. so many shares of the catch for the boat and gear and a share each for the men) and most of the owners go to sea. It is a democratic industry.

And now a great development is taking place in the harbour. A large and bang up-to-date fish dock is being built at a cost of £330,000. This will have nine deep-water berths (a limitation of the Inner Harbour is that it dries out at low water), ice-making plant, auction floor, lorry landing stages, merchants' office accommodation, slip for hauling out vessels and even a viewing stage up aloft upon which the public can stand and watch other people work without getting in their way.

But trawling is an extractive industry, and it is only a matter of time before the trawling grounds of the Western Channel get fished out. Trawlers can only operate here now because of the Decca navigator system, which enables a skipper, with the marvellous fishing charts now available, to fish within a few yards of any of the 380 wrecks that litter the sea bottom between Start Point and Portland, waiting to rip the belly out of a trawl. With the entry of Britain into the Common Market the fish-hungry French will be over this side in droves, having already exterminated the fish on their side of the Channel, and the trawling grounds of the Western Channel will have a very short life indeed.

But other developments may happen to save Brixham as a fishing port. One possibility is sprats, which seem to have taken the place of pilchards along this stretch of coast. Already they are being caught in vast numbers by Brixham pair fishers (two mid-water trawlers towing a net between them) and sent to Topsham to be marinated, or to other centres to be canned as 'bristling', or direct to English, French or even Italian cities for the 'fresh' trade (you can't for the life of you buy fresh sprats in Brixham – even when they are being unloaded by the ton on the quays. The West Country people still haven't learnt that you can eat sprats). There should obviously be a cannery in Brixham itself.

Another possibility is the old fishery of pilchards. The pilchards no longer come as far east as they once did, but there is nothing to stop fishermen from hunting them out in the Atlantic where they are still to be found. Then there is tuna, which have recently been found to exist in large numbers in the eastern Atlantic. The Portuguese and Bretons have known about them all the time.

One development of great interest is the introduction into Brixham of 'twin-boom fishing', bringing with it the return of the beam trawl. The orthodox modern trawler hauls an otter trawl along the bed of the sea: a bag the mouth of which is held open by two 'otters', or boards, set kite-fashion so as to drag the net open by pressure of the water. But for several decades now the trawlermen of Holland and Germany have been hauling, not one otter trawl, but two beam trawls, slung from the ends of two booms which are lowered over each side of the vessel, and steeved up when the trawls are hauled, simultaneously, to bring the 'cod ends' level with the deck for emptying. The convenience and efficiency of this method of fishing is obvious to the observer, but there is one great danger attached to it. If one of the two trawls snags on a rock or wreck the trawler will possibly be immediately overturned. On the German coast, particularly, there has been considerable loss of life owing to this cause, and unrelaxing vigilance is required of the crew. But there are now two vessels fishing this method from Brixham – the *Scaldis* and the *Sara Lena* and there will no doubt soon be more. The advantage in thus going back to the more ancient beam trawl is that very heavy ground chains can be used, which literally plough the sea-bottom, and stir out the soles which have taken more and more to burying themselves to escape the ground ropes of the more orthodox trawlers. Orthodox trawlermen decry the new method of fishing, saying (probably rightly) that it destroys the grounds.

So much for Brixham as a fishing port. As a trading port it also has a history, and in years gone by its trading fleet was probably more important than its fishing fleet. Brixham was one of the leaders in the three-cornered Newfoundland cod trade: trade goods (including Paignton cabbages) to Newfoundland, salt cod to the Mediterranean, wine and fruit to England. As the Portuguese took over the Newfoundland trade the fruit trade flourished alone, and many fast schooners were built for this trade in which speed was essential. The names of Brixham schooners in old shipping lists give an idea of their profession: *Choice Fruit, Tangerine, Orange Girl, Golden Grove, Fruit Girl, Levant, Teneriffe, Lisbon Packet.* By the late 1860s Brixham was one of the most prosperous little towns on the English South Coast and nearly 200 schooners were owned in the port – a fantastic fleet for such a small place, and they sailed to very many parts of the world. Then the steamers came, and gradually the sailors were knocked right out. An attempt was made to start steamers in Brixham, but failed completely, and now Brixham has no merchant fleet whatever. Commercial activity, apart from fishing and taking out holidaymakers, is limited to bunkering ships at the oil jetty on the Breakwater, and putting Trinity House pilots on, and taking them off, ships bound up and down Channel in pilot cutters based at Brixham for the purpose. Big ships often lie for shelter under Berry Head, and big tankers anchor there to pump their cargo, or part of it, into small tankers to lighten themselves.

Brixham has a large and beautiful harbour, and very welcome it is if you have been running down Channel before a south-easter. It is easy to get into and completely safe. It wasn't always like that. The old natural harbour of Brixham was just a tidal creek (some of it dammed to drive two tidal mills) and ships could neither get in nor get out except at high tide. Two small half-tide breakwaters were built (the New Pier was completed in 1804) but it was not until 1843 that the work was commenced to turn Brixham into a deepwater port with the construction of the present great breakwater. Work went slowly on this until it was given great urgency by the terrible gale of January 1866.

A large concourse of shipping had taken refuge from a southwester in Torbay – when the wind suddenly swung round to the east and blew at hurricane force. Such an event had long been feared. Now it must be explained to the non-seafaring that a sailing vessel can sail to windward – or *against* the wind – in normal weather by tacking, or zig-zagging backwards and forwards at an angle to the wind – working up to windward a little with each zig or zag. But if the wind is over a certain velocity she cannot do this: no sailing ship in the world can sail to windward, in say, a Force 12. Thus this great fleet of merchant shipping suddenly found itself 'embayed' – that is trapped in a bay with the wind blowing straight into it. No ground tackle (anchors) can possibly hold against the kinds of winds and seas that were experienced that night and one after another cables parted, or anchors 'came home', and ship after ship was driven on to the rocks to be pounded to pieces by the ferocious waves. The fury of the gale made the use of the eyes impossible – no man could possibly look into it, and no man could stand, unsupported, against it. There was absolutely nothing the sailors of the stricken ships could do but let go all their anchors, veer out all the anchor cable they had got, and then hang on and wait for the inevitable. There was no lifeboat at Brixham then, and so the Teignmouth boat was dragged by a team of eight horses over the steep hills and combes to Torquay, where she was launched, but she was of no service in spite of the desperate and heroic efforts that were certainly made by her crew. Out of ninety-four ships anchored in the bay, sixty were totally lost. A hundred men were known to have been drowned, but many an entire ship's crew was lost about whom nothing was known at all: mangled corpses were being washed up around Torbay for days afterwards. The temporary lighthouse that had been built on the end of the partially built breakwater at Brixham was quickly washed away, and the women of Brixham turned out in that fantastic gale and managed to build a huge fire on the end of the Breakwater which was responsible for saving many ships, for at least sailors knew where to aim for to try to round up behind the only shelter that could possibly save them.

> They took the grandam's blanket,
> Who shivered and bade them go,
> They took the baby's pillow,
> Who could not say them 'No,'
> And they heaped a great fire on the Pier
> And knew not all the while
> If they were heaping a beacon
> Or only a funeral pile.[1]

Miraculously 34 ships survived, and many of them by getting behind the breakwater. On the morning after the gale wreckage was piled high against the eastern side of the breakwater and ships lay stranded all around the shores of Torbay. The existing Commercial

1. From 'The Wives of Brixham' by Miss B. Smedley.

Hotel of Brixham was turned into a hospital, but nearly every house in the little town sheltered exhausted survivors. In the Museum at Brixham one can see contemporary photographs of the wreckage.

This disaster spurred the citizens of Brixham into getting on with their breakwater, but it was not until 1916 that this great work was eventually completed. The finished wall is 3000 feet long. After the gale a lifeboat was established at Brixham, and there is still one there.

A remarkable man named Richard Wolston discovered iron ore near Brixham in 1842, and started manufacturing it into paint. Nine iron mines were eventually started in the country round about, and a paint factory established at Freshwater Quarry which could load direct into ships. Wolston made an attempt to bring a railway down into the town, but it was never completed. There is a kind of medieval folly building at Parkham, which Wolston built as a railway station, but it was never used for that purpose. The iron enterprise was successful, but eventually came to an end. Slate was quarried at Upton and Nethway, and limestone was, until quite recently, quarried on a large scale at Berry Head and shot straight down into ships in fine weather. If the wind came round to the east they had to get the hell out of it.

Brixham is now (despite being absolutely choked with holiday-makers in July and August) a place of great charm and character. The houses climb steeply up the hillsides on each side of the harbour, the harbour itself is all bustle and activity. The quay-side pubs are crowded and lively – particularly on days when the fishing fleet can't put to sea. If I have a criticism it is that it is difficult to buy good, cheap, fresh, unfrozen, locally caught fish in the many cafés and restaurants. I have sat in a café eating frozen plaice which has come from Iceland via Grimsby while looking out of the window at live plaice being unloaded from a trawler. And what about local sprats? And escallops? And lobsters and crabs *not* out of the deep freeze? Few things lose their flavour more than crabs on being deep frozen.

The statue of William of Orange beside the Inner Harbour looks its best when it has a Greater Black Backed Gull sitting on top of the royal wig. William arrived in the good ship *Brill*, on the 5th of November 1688, accompanied by fifty men of war and five hundred transports (actually one estimate is that he had a fleet of 670 sail). He had 1400 men with him, and five hundred horses had died during a gale which had beset them on the voyage. The *Brill*, incidentally, subsequently had a long history: she was re-christened

the *Princess Mary* and used as a royal yacht, the Hanovers sold her to
a London merchant who renamed her the *Betsy Cairns* and sent her
trading to the West Indies, she then fell to being a collier, and was
wrecked on the Black Middens in the 19th century. Thus we know
that she reigned for well over a hundred years!

It being low tide when William landed, he is said to have been
horsed ashore on the back of a fisherman by the name of Varwell.
Varwell, the story goes on, was given for this service a warrant, by
the prince, to visit him in London, after he had been proclaimed
king, and claim a reward. Varwell went to London, fell into bad
company, was robbed of his money and also his warrant, and when
he got to the palace found that the thief had already claimed the
reward and he himself was turned away with harsh language.

The people of Brixham are supposed to have welcomed William
with the following splendid piece of verse:

> And please King William your Majesty,
> You be welcome to Brixham Quay,
> To eat Buckhorn and drink Bohea
> Along with we,
> And please your Majesty.

Buckhorn was dried whiting, bohea was tea.

The prince replied, again according to popular report: 'Mine
goot people! Mine goot people! I mean your goot! I am come here
for your goot – for all your goots!'

After great feasting and jollification (William had come with a
fleet of 670 sail so he was not unaccompanied) the Dutch prince and
his army marched on London where he was acclaimed king. It is a
pleasing thought that one of the first things that the Prince of Orange
did when he arrived in England was to cross the River Lemon.

Of things to see in Brixham now the church near the harbour (All
Saints) was completed in 1824. It is large and impressive, and had
Rev. H. F. Lyte, the great hymn writer, as parson. Its carillon plays
'Abide with me' every evening at eight o'clock, 'When at thy Foot-
stool Lord I bend' at eight in the morning and 'Praise my soul the
King of Heaven' at noon. The old church, much higher up the hill
at Higher Brixham, has a fine roof to its south porch, and a
monument with an anchor to the men who died in the Great Gale.
Down at the Quay, where the fishermen run their own, very good,
fresh fish shop, is an aquarium and – a little way up the hill – a
museum which should not be missed. It has a particularly good
section on the Brixham Trawlers, and another on smuggling –

particularly smuggling of the 'scientific period' when all sorts of sophisticated techniques came in in response to increased pressure from the revenue men.

Philp's Cavern, south of the Harbour, is worth visiting. It was discovered in 1858, and was interesting in the same sort of way as Kent's Cavern was.

CHAPTER 6

Berry Head to Kingsbridge

❧

AT **Berry Head** (map, p. 44) heroic efforts are being made to preserve the pristine purity of the place against the assaults of multitudes
of holidaymakers – to the lengths of sinking a car park in dead ground
so that it can't be seen and hiding a café inside anti-Napoleonic
fortifications. Berry Head has an Iron Age fort (its name probably
came from *byrig* – Anglo-Saxon for fort), was much fortified in the
16th and 17th centuries, and came to a grand climax in the Napoleonic
wars when very strong fortifications indeed were built on it.

Torbay was a most important anchorage for the Channel fleet
during sailing days. Any sailor will see that, before the age of tugs
and engines, ships required for frequent action do not like entering
a river mouth or an enclosed harbour if they can help it. If the wind
blows straight into such places it is difficult – if not impossible – for a
sailing ship to get out of them. An open roadstead such as Torbay
is therefore favoured. Brixham was a fine watering place and
victualling place – very early too. A wharf on the inner side of the
Inner Harbour is still called the Queen's Watering Wharf, and was
connected by pipes to a reservoir under the Town Hall. So during
the Napoleonic wars the Channel fleet lay sheltered from the south-
westers in Torbay, taking on water and food and ammunition from
Brixham, ready at any hour to weigh anchors and make sail and go
out and attack the French. And so strong fortifications were built on
Berry Head to protect this useful anchorage. It's a grand and windy
place to visit now, and kittiwakes, fulmars, guillemots, razorbills,
cormorants and herring gulls are to be seen in profusion from its
high cliffs. There is deep water within a few yards of the head.

Brixham is built on a lump of limestone, but as we round Berry
Head we leave the limestone and enter a world of metamorphic
rock: gneisses and schists. The reason for this is that the great
upheaval caused by the igneous intrusions from deep down in the
earth that made Dartmoor altered the sedimentary rocks by pressure
and heat out of recognition. From here on westward we shall get
used to this changed rock, and fossils will no longer be apparent.

The heat and pressure that altered the original sedimentary rocks also destroyed the fossils.

Behind **Sharkham Point** is perhaps the nastiest rubbish dump in England: certainly if a prize were to be awarded for the worst-sited and most offensive garbage dump in the world this would win first prize. When is old England going to learn *not* to dump its sewage in the sea, and *not* to deface its green and pleasant land with rubbish dumps? Municipal composting is the complete answer to both these problems, and wherever it has been tried it has been successful.

Leaving this evil thing behind we quickly come to noble cliffs. At **Man Sands** is a lime kiln, proving that ships once beached here to unload the coal to burn the limestone. The pretty valley behind the beach has a fresh-water lagoon, and it is fascinating to watch the water bubbling out of the beach at low tide like a sort of geyser. Beyond **Crabrock Point** is a super beach, and seventeen pairs of fulmars were nesting, in 1971, behind **Scabbacombe Head**. Here are large, terribly steep ploughed hillsides – it seems hard to believe that a tractor can live on them. But live one does, a tracked tractor of course, and it only ploughs one way – downhill. Kale, early potatoes, short grass-and-clover leys, and sheep are farmed.

At **Coleton Fishacre** is an absolutely superb farmhouse, or small mansion, of stone. The owner seems to have abandoned it for a hideous modern house with blue shutters which defaces the view; but perhaps it is better to live in an ugly house and look out at a beautiful one, than the other way round.

The coastal path, if indeed there is one, rather peters out about here, and it takes determination, agility, and a certain ambiguousness about one's attitude to the law of trespass to get any further without leaving the sea. But it is physically (if not politically) possible to force one's way through very steep wooded cliffs to **Kingswear Castle**, which is private, and occupied by a member of Parliament, and was built about 1491 when Dartmouth Castle was built, and we shall discuss the latter when we come to it.

Kingswear is much occupied, one would hazard a guess, by retired Admirals. It is a good place to lie with a small boat, because one can tie up to the Railway Wharf and get ashore. Shopping facilities though are very limited, but the ferries that cross the river to Dartmouth are frequent and cheap. The motor ferry is far the cheaper, for pedestrians that is. The foot ferry has shelter but you pay for it. The local crabbers use the Railway Wharf to unload their catches, and you must not tie up to their stretch of wharf. The

Dartmouth fleet of crabbers is active and increasing, and there is talk of over-fishing. Even now the boats are having to range as far as Portland to shoot their pots, for the nearer grounds are becoming worked out.

There is a splendid little ship from Guernsey, the *Tol*, which comes into Kingswear to load live crabs and lobsters in her perforated hold (i.e. a hold into which the fresh water of the sea is allowed to enter to keep the fish alive) to take across the Channel to France. She makes the voyage across the Channel in all weathers: her crew claim that they have never yet been stopped by the weather. She has powerful motors now but was a Breton sailing crabber to start off with. In the winter, when crabs are scarce, she often loads winkles which have been brought all the way from Scotland by lorry, for the French, as her skipper will tell you, will 'eat anything

61

that moves'. Big rough-looking Breton crabbers and trawlers come in and tie up against the Railway Wharf too, to get away from bad weather.

Dartmouth is a fine and romantic place. It has a superb deep water anchorage, with no bar (unlike Salcombe), is accessible at all states of the tide, and thus has always played a great part in the maritime history of the English in what they have the cheek to call their Channel. Richard the Lion Heart assembled a fleet of over a hundred sail for his crusade here. Each ship, we are told, carried a crew of fourteen and four cavalrymen, and their mounts and arms, and enough food for them for a year. This fleet sailed on 18th March 1190 towards Messina. Edward III drew 31 ships and 757 men from the port for the Siege of Calais: the third biggest entry in the realm. The port sent the rather more modest fleet of two sail, the *Crescent* and the *Harte*, against the Armada, and they victualled with 349 pounds of butter, 1888 pounds of gunpowder, 125 hogsheads of beer, 28 water butts, a kettle, a peck of mustard seed and a mill wherewith to grind it. They were armed, we are told, with 64 pikes and 9 swords: although this seems a very incomplete inventory indeed.

As the Middle Ages drew on Dartmouth became a shipping town of the first importance. Chaucer's Shipman came from Dertemouth and a doughty man he was too: 'Of nyse conscience took he no keepe' – in other words he was probably something of a pirate. An archetypal Dartmouth ship-owner was Sir John Hawley, quite probably the very Shipman Chaucer based his character on. He died in 1408 and there is his memorial brass in St Saviour's church. He was a privateer – not to say a pirate when it suited him. And it was said:

> Blow the wind high, blow the wind low,
> It bloweth good to Hauley's Hoe.

His Hoe being the wharf whereon he unloaded his goods. He was seven times Mayor of Dartmouth and carried out great improvements, particularly to Dartmouth and Kingswear Castles. Few individuals have stamped their characters on a town more than Hawley did.

As privateering and outright piracy (of which there was a great deal – there are very many records of accusations against Dartmouth ship-owners for piracy even by fellow countrymen) became less profitable the Newfoundland cod fishery developed until Raleigh was able to call it: 'the mainstay and support of the West'. Until

1580 England's chief off-shore fishery had been off Iceland, and therefore chiefly conducted by East Coast men. But about this time the great cod grounds off the Newfoundland coast were being developed and Dartmouth men played their full part. At its peak the fishery employed 400 big ships, and Dartmouth had the biggest fleet of all. The government gave financial support to the industry, as it did also to the whale fishery, for it looked upon these two fisheries as the best cradle for the Royal Navy. A man who had been on the Newfoundland voyage a few times, or to the Arctic whaling, was sure to be a sailor.

A Newfoundlander was generally a brig, from eighty to a hundred tons, and she carried a crew of about forty. A form of organization was soon introduced: the ships sailed in one great convoy under the command of 'Admirals' and no ship was allowed to leave English waters until March 1st. The reason for this was that there was competition to get there first, in order to secure the best shore berths, and if competition had been uncontrolled it would have led to ships sailing earlier and earlier in the year when the weather was dangerous. On arrival in Newfoundland the crews went ashore and built landing and drying stages. About two dozen men would then start fishing from dories (small rowing boats) and the rest of the ship's company worked ashore. Of this shore party seven men were loaders and splitters, there were boys to help them, and three women to salt the fish and also act as 'housekeepers'. One can imagine that these women were pretty formidable characters. A crew would, in a good season, press out six tons of oil from the fish and this would be taken back to Devon and would pay for the salt. The salt cod themselves would, at the end of the season, be sailed to Spain or the Mediterranean and sold to salt-cod-hungry people. As time went on though ships and men began to specialize: some ships fished only while others were carriers only, and developed the three-cornered trade that we have noticed before. The last Dartmouth ship which made the cod voyage, incidentally, did so in 1907, so the industry had a long history. And who knows – it is not impossible that such a fishery might start up again? The cod are still there.

Dartmouth played a disproportionate part in the exploration of the New World. Sir Walter Raleigh, Humphrey and Adrian Gilbert, John Davis, all were based at one time or another at Dartmouth. John Davis was born at Sandridge House just below Stoke Gabriel (recently pulled down by vandals). In 1585, helped financially by the brothers Gilbert, he set sail in two thirty-ton ships to look for a North-West Passage. In 1586 he returned, having penetrated a great inlet and encountered Eskimos. The next year he sailed again and discovered Davis Strait – deep and free from ice. He pitched his camp at Cape Desolation and would have wintered there but his men were mutinous. He traded with the Eskimos for reindeer skins, codfish and copper, and he noted geese, ducks, partridges, pheasants and jays – to say nothing of unicorns! But every self-respecting explorer in those days saw unicorns. He also saw cranberries and bears. In Gilbert's Sound he thought he found gold, but, alas, it was copper pyrites. He discovered a Christian grave in Gilbert's Sound. He sailed into Hudson Bay a hundred years before Hudson was born.

His three northern voyages were interesting but not profitable, but he was one of the great navigators of the world, wrote *The Seaman's Secret* and *The World's Hydrographical Description*, and ultimately shipped with a Dutch expedition as navigator to the East Indies. He was killed by pirates aboard the *Tyger*, off Malaya, in 1605.

Sir Humphrey Gilbert, born at Greenway House on the Dart (now lived in by Miss Agatha Christie) was a step-brother to Sir Walter Raleigh (for his mother married the latter's father). He discovered Gilbert Strait, in 1583 sailed for Newfoundland and claimed it for the Queen. He found there a strange international collection of fishermen from Portugal, Spain, France and England, all living in a sort of stateless anarchy and getting on very well together. His end came on another occasion when he was trying to plant an English colony on Newfoundland. He sailed with the *Golden Hind* (40 tons), the *Squirrel* (10 tons), the *Swallow* and the *Delight*. Having reached the other side he sent the *Swallow* home with his sick, the *Delight* got wrecked, and the *Golden Hind* and *Squirrel* set off home. Sir Humphrey himself was on board the latter ludicrously small vessel when a great gale blew up and he was urged to transfer himself on to the *Golden Hind*. He refused, preferring to share the danger of his crew aboard the smaller vessel. The *Squirrel* foundered, but just before she did so he shouted across to the men in the other ship: 'Be of good cheer – we are as near to Heaven on sea as by land!'

As for Dartmouth today, the river is packed with yachts, there is a big place called a 'Boatel', also a 'marina', the Royal Dart Yacht Club at Kingswear, the Dartmouth Sailing Club and the Dartmouth Boating Association. There is a Royal Regatta each year towards the end of August. Having no bar and being so near the sea Dartmouth is an easy place to get in and out of (if you have a motor at least)

Above, Brixham harbour; *below*, Kingswear, from across the River Dart.

DARTMOUTH: *Above*, The Butterwalk; *below*, Bayard's Cove.

and upstream are twelve miles of what hardly anybody would dispute
to be the most beautiful estuarial river in England. Very difficult
sailing though, owing to the high and very steep banks the wind
comes at you from all over the place.

Starting downstream at **Dartmouth Castle** we will work our
way up to Totnes.

The Castle was substantially rebuilt in 1481, after many earlier
attempts at fortification, and is remarkable in being the earliest
surviving fortress specifically built for guns. The gun ports which
exist in it today are the original ones. The guns the place was built
for were not mounted on carriages, but lashed down to heavy planks.
They were not cast in one piece, but built up like barrels, with iron
hoops round them to try to stop them from exploding. Some of these
cannon had the optimistic name of *murderers*. They were supposed to
murder, of course, the enemy. Others were called *serpentynes*, and
these were of $7\frac{1}{2}$ inch calibre and were breech loaders. By the time
of Henry VIII (that great builder of coastal forts) guns were much
more efficient and were mounted on wheeled carriages with breeching ropes to absorb the recoil. The central government often took a
direct interest in Dartmouth's defences: Edward IV granted an
annuity of £30 a year for the Castle's upkeep.

Kingswear Castle, over the river, was abandoned when guns
became strong enough to command the river entrance from one side
only. There was a further battery of cannon up the river at **Bayard's
Cove**, a smaller port across the river, a chain across the river from
Dartmouth Castle (you can still see where it was anchored on the
other side), and the port must have been pretty impregnable. The
French did try to attack it: about 6000 Frenchmen and Bretons
landed on Slapton Sands from 300 ships under a leader named du
Chatel. They were attacked by local country people and du Chatel
was killed and three lords and twenty-two knights taken prisoner
and held to ransom. During the Civil War the castle was heavily
garrisoned. Dartmouth declared for Parliament but fell to Prince
Rupert after a month's siege. On 17th January 1646 troops under
Fairfax stormed it and took it in a few hours, in spite of the fact that
the garrison had a hundred cannon and the attacking Roundheads
no cannon at all. They seized all the cannon, and two Royalist men-
of-war, with the loss of one man killed and a few wounded. In both
the First and Second World Wars the Castle, and nearby batteries,
were in full use and guns mounted in them. Now the Castle is under
the Ministry of Works and is open to the public. It has a collection
of small arms from the Civil War. It helps to understand the peculiar

shape of the building to realize that it was first started as a round tower but then, for some reason, it was decided to build a square one. This latter was built up against the half-completed round one and then the two buildings knocked together. The reason why the earlier cannon ports are so low down is, of course, the fact that the cannon they were designed for were plank-mounted.

Gallant's Bower, above, was a Civil War defence and shows a more sophisticated ground plan, with bastions covering the curtain walls with fire.

St Petroc's Church, hard by the castle, may stand on the site of a cell occupied by St Petroc himself. The saint died in 594. Later it is thought that holy men lived here and maintained a lighthouse. By 1346 the Mayor of Dartmouth was at least considering 'endowing a chapel at St Petrox'. In 1438 an indulgence was granted for building and repairing. Mid-17th century the church was much rebuilt and added to, in the Gothic style even though this was not the Gothic period. There is a fine massive old font (far older than the rest of the church) and two fine brasses. The Norman-looking arches are in fact 14th century.

Back in town **St Saviour's Church** is fine indeed. The south door is the finest church door in England. The fine brass of that rip-roaring fellow John Hawley, between his brace of wives, lies under a carpet in the chancel. The screen is beautiful and supposed to be about 1480. The church was very much renewed and embellished in the 17th century. There is a marvellous carved and painted stone pulpit of late 15th century. It is altogether an unusual and interesting church, and its interior makes a great impact on the beholder.

The **Butterwalk**, restored after German bombing, houses among other things a very good museum. This has a really fine collection of ship models. Just round the corner is the **Newcomen Memorial Engine**. Thomas Newcomen was born at Dartmouth in 1663. In 1712 his first engine – and the first practicable steam engine ever (purists say, wrongly, that it was not a steam engine, but it was) started pumping water at a coal mine at Dudley, in the Black Country. It was 57 years after this that James Watt made the first major improvement to it, and by then there were 200 Newcomen engines at work, mostly pumping water out of mines. The engine on view here was built in 1725, while Newcomen was still alive. It is now made to work by electricity, but could still work perfectly well on coal and water. It was still in use right up to 1913, pumping water up to a higher pound on a canal.

The three ferries at Dartmouth are interesting. The lowest one, a car ferry, is of strange design, and it carries a Horse, Cow, Ass, Bullock or other Large Animal for 2 New Pence. The top car ferry is driven by paddles, but steers herself by a chain.

The **Britannia Naval College** was designed by Sir Aston Webb forty years after H.M.S. *Britannia* sailed into the river in 1863 to be a training ship for officers for the Royal Navy. Since then many kings and princes have studied the arts of seamanship and war here.

It is impossible to see much of the Lower Dart from the road (thank God) and walking is pretty difficult. A boat is really the only way. The sides are steep and heavily wooded and the river is breathtakingly beautiful. **Dittisham** has a car ferry, which contributes to ruining the peace of the place. There is nowhere for cars to park, and they just roar straight through the steep, narrow street causing noise and danger and stink. There is a fine friendly pub down by the ferry, a pottery over the road from it (and good pots too, surprisingly), and Dittisham's 'ploughmen' plums are famous. They are named thus as a corruption of *plumen* which they were called when the trees were first brought over from Germany. The Dittisham men once had the brilliant idea of carrying all their women out and marooning them on a rock called Haytor Rock, which I cannot identify (can it be the Anchor Stone?) until the ladies became less quarrelsome and more co-operative.

A local man, Captain Gervase Markham, wrote a treatise on cider making in 1631 which makes interesting reading. We are in the heart of cider country here, so we might as well here discuss the stuff. Cider was formerly made on every farm, and given free as a 'perk' to all labourers. The belief, fostered by the more sensational Sunday papers, that it affects the brain of the habitual drinker does not seem to apply to the Devon countryman, because there are many about, very bright and intelligent and in the finest of health, who have put down their dozen pints or so every day of their lives. Cider is made, quite simply, by crushing the juice out of apples, putting the juice away in wooden vats, and waiting. Nothing more is done, and nothing is either added or taken away. This process produces the *rough cider*, which is the wine of the country. For citified tastes some sugar is added. A good orchard will yield eight tons or upwards of fruit per acre, and a ton of apples should yield 165 gallons of cider.

While we are on the subject of local produce let us consider Devonshire cream. This used to be made, and still is by good farmers' wives, by setting milk in a shallow pan for twelve hours, then taking the matured cream and gently heating it but keeping it below boiling. When you can see the shape of the bottom of the pan as a circle on top of the cream the job is done. You let it stand for another twelve hours and 'fleet' (skim) off the clotted cream.

Stoke Gabriel, over the river and up it a few miles, is a beautiful village, only recently being spoiled by a rash of modern 'villas' and bungalows. It has a pub, the Church House, which claims to have been a pub in A.D. 1111, and another splendid pub, just down the hill, called the Victoria and Albert, in which there is much singing on Saturdays.

There is a big lagoon down near the shore at Stoke Gabriel which was once the pound of a tidal mill. There is a strong fleet of salmon netting boats here, with about two full-time fishermen and the rest part-timers, but all men with licences. This village has a lovely church, with a huge and famous yew tree near it, some amusing faces carved as finials on the window dripstones (one face whistling), a fine screen, and it is all beautiful and peaceful.

Further upstream, on the west bank, **Sharpham House** stands, clean lined, austere and dignified, on its high steep spur of land in a beautiful park. Now the home of Maurice Ash and his family it was built in 1770 by a sailor named Philemon Pownel with the money that he got for a Spanish ship that he took as a prize. The architect was Sir Robert Taylor. It is a most gracious and beautiful building, with a great surprise in the form of a glass-roofed cupola within, an elegant spiral staircase of most singular design (nobody can see how it stays up) and a large collection of the works of the very underrated Polish artist Ruszkowski, who lives at Lyme Regis. There are some Barbara Hepworths and a large – *revolving* – Henry Moore in the garden. The house is not really open to the public, but the Ashes are pleased to show it to the truly interested.

Totnes is getting far from the coast, but it was once a big port and still *is* a port, for timber ships still go up there. In Fore Street is the Brutus Stone, still used for mayoral proclamations, upon which, according to Geoffrey de Monmouth, Brutus the Trojan himself stepped ashore to be the founder of the British race, which was named after him. As he stepped ashore he uttered the following memorable piece of verse:

> Here I stand and here I rest
> And this place shall be called Totnes.

And Totnes it has been ever since. The parish church is a great one, but there is an absolute masterpiece of a guide on sale within.

Totnes is one of the few country towns left with a real book shop, and not just a place where they sell 'get better' cards for Auntie. This is rendered possible by the proximity of **Dartington**, which intellectually and artistically fertilizes the whole country round about. Totnes, which *could* fertilize the country in a more practical way, doesn't, but discharges untreated sewage straight into the most lovely river in England, turning the upper reaches of it into a stinking sewer.

And thus the Dart. It still plays its part in the history of England. On D Day 485 American ships sailed out of the Dart, carrying 33,000 men to land on the Normandy coast.

Back on the shore, the cliffs around **Blackstone Point** become difficult of access, but the National Trust has just bought some of them and a path will be made. Along the shore by the Dancing Beggars Rocks it is said that a submerged forest can be seen.

Stoke Fleming rejoices in the memory of George Barker Bidder, the 'Human Calculator'. He was, from an early age, a mathematical genius. He could do in his head what a computer would be used to do today. He was an assistant to George Stephenson, built several railways and London's Victoria Dock and the first-ever swing bridge (on the Norwich to Lowestoft railway). There is a brass in the church to Thomas Newcomen's father, who was rector here.

Blackpool, now a crowded place where picture postcards and ice cream get sold, would otherwise be a pretty beach at the foot of great sloping cliffs on which mighty Scots pines grow. It is here that Warwick the Kingmaker is supposed to have landed to oppose Edward IV. **Strete** is a pretty village, with a lovely cast-iron balcony on the King's Head. **Upton** is a very special place. A remarkably pretty village, with hilly narrow streets along which no motor carriage should be allowed to go, it has the ruins of a college, or chantry, founded by Sir Guy de Brian, standard bearer to Edward III, about 1350. Sir Guy was one of the very first knights of the garter. Sir John Hawkins's daughter-in-law is (probably) buried here – Lady Judith Hawkins. It is said that she was so grand that page boys used to have to unroll a red carpet all the way from Poole Farmhouse, where she lived, to Upton church, where she prayed. Slapton has Slapton Field Centre, run by the Field Study Centre. This is a large residential study and research centre which has parties of adults and children studying various aspects of natural history: most of them related to Slapton Ley and the shingle bank, which are part of the 300-acre reserve which is leased from the Herbert Whitley Trust. This also includes two splendid woods, much inhabited by foxes and badgers, difficult of access because of their steepness but well worth exploring by the adventurous.

Slapton Ley is a stretch of fresh water of 400 acres, cut off from the sea by a storm beach of very fine shingle. The lake contains pike, perch, rudd, roach and eels, and boats for fishing for these may be chartered from the Field Centre for a pound a day. Besides all the usual wintering and nesting birds that one could hope to find, crane, Scop's owl, Squacco heron, marsh harrier, spotted crake and great reed warbler have been reported. In 1874 S. P. Fox saw osprey, spoonbill, glossy ibis, little bittern, bustard and Pallas's sandgrouse. Colonel George Montagu did much of the research for his *Ornithological Dictionary* here. There is a monument on the beach set up by the Americans to the forbearance of the inhabitants in vacating this countryside and many villages, to make room for the Americans to train before D Day.

Stokenham has a record, in its church archives, of the hanging of a pirate in 1581 (see Start Point). In the south transept of the church is a window in memory of 28 people who went down in the *Spirit of the Ocean* in 1866. **Torcross** has an hotel. It was once the most easterly of pilchard stations, and men kept Newfoundland dogs which would swim out into the breakers, when the boats were returning from sea, to take the ropes in their mouths and carry them in to the waiting men and women on shore to be put on the capstans so that the boats could be hauled immediately out of the surf. After the big slate quarry near the **Limpet Rocks** we come to a long beach of shingle, with **Beesands**, which is a splendid little fishing place spoiled by some of the worst-sited caravans in Britain, with a handful of the tubby beamy beach boats of Devon hauled up by motor capstans (see Beer). Only three of these boats at the time of writing are full-timers. They shoot about eighty pots each, predominantly for crabs. The tendency is for Beesands men to go and live in Dartmouth and fish from there, with bigger boats which need a deep-water harbour. There is a rattling good pub called the Cricketers.

Beyond this cliffs of slate with a vertical strike come right down to the beach. These leave most pleasant little coves or cubby holes, with sandy floors, marvellously sheltered from the west wind, and warm when the sun is still in the east.

Hallsands is a very weird place indeed. There was a small fishing village here, perched up on flat rocks at the foot of vertical cliffs. The Admiralty allowed dredging of the sand in the bay for works at Plymouth and this so let in the fury of the sea that, in 1917, a great gale blew straight in and the waves destroyed the village. We can now see these weird remains of dwellings perched precariously on the rocks that remain. There are two ladies living in Dartington today who can remember when this disaster occurred.

Start Point (from Anglo-Saxon *steort* – a tail) has a lighthouse, a B.B.C. transmitting station, and its deadly **Blackstone Rock**. In the great gale of March 1891 the *Marana*, of Colombo, hit the Blackstone and was sunk with twenty-five of her crew of twenty-eight. She was loaded with sleepers, and these were littered along the coasts for miles. On the same night the *Dryad*, bound for Valparaiso, went down hard by losing all twenty-two members of her crew, and two schooners, the *Lizzie Ellen* and the *Lunesdale*, both suffered the same fate.

There is a marvellous walk along the shore from the Start to East Portlemouth. This coast is famous for early migrant birds from the Continent, and many colonies of seabirds breed here. It was at Start Point that, on 28th September 1581, Henri Muge, a 'pirate of the sea', was hanged in chains, to encourage fellow seafarers who happened to sail by to be more restrained. This fact is recorded in the parish records of Stokenham.

At **Lannacombe Beach** a very fortunate man lives right by the sea in a marvellously-sited cottage, and at **Woodcombe** the East Prawle men once kept their fishing boats, but now they use Salcombe. Just north of Prawle Point are some heavenly fields, cut off from the rest of England to the north by rocky outcrops, green and fertile and running right down to the sea. Slabs of greenish rock here are inhabited by redshanks and oystercatchers – and what a magnificent place for winkles! The coast here seems fresh, clean, beautiful and utterly unspoiled.

East Prawle is a rather isolated village in the middle of big farms. It is very much a farmer's village. There is a pub called the Pig's Nose (named after a nearby promontory) and another, in the next street, the name of which I forget but to which most of the local people go. There is one farm of eighty acres near Prawle – all the rest are huge. It is sad that the farms in the South Hams country seem to get bigger and bigger, swallowing each other up, depopulating the countryside of real countrymen, and turning honest farmers into 'agri-businessmen'.

Prawle Point (from Old English for a look-out) is the most southerly point of England if England is not held to include Cornwall, which it really should be. So here is Lloyd's Signal Station, although what it does now when every ship is in constant radio communication with her head office is anybody's guess. In March 1873 the *Lalla Rhookh* went ashore at Prawle with 1300 tons of tea. There were ridges of tea ten foot high on the beach. A ship loaded with lemons went ashore here once and the sea was turned a golden colour: lemons were selling round about afterwards for fifty for sixpence. Another tea clipper, the *Gossamer* of 735 tons, also came ashore here in 1868, and in 1793 His Majesty's Ship *Nymph*, 36 guns, came up with the slightly larger French frigate *Cléopâtre* and after a short sharp action captured her. Edward Pellew, the young and brilliant captain of the *Nymph*, wrote to his brother after the action with more exuberance perhaps than modesty:

'. . . We dished her up in fifty minutes, boarded and struck her colours.'

Pellew had manned his own ship with eighty Cornish miners, with but a small bunch of sailors to knock them into shape, and these landlubbers proved much better fighting stuff than the riff-raff picked up by the press gangs. The miners were tough and practical, and could easily understand and learn the other dangerous discipline of the sea.

East Portlemouth was once a more important place than it is now: bigger than Salcombe over the water. It supplied at least one ship against the Armada, and five ships and nineteen sailors for the Siege of Calais in 1346. Now it is a small village, straggling steeply down the hillside. The church of St Winwalloe is interesting, and Winwalloe was an interesting saint. He was driven out of Wales by the English, fled to Brittany and built a monastery at Landevennec which went on existing until the Revolution, and this had a daughter house at Landewennack in Cornwall. The saint died in A.D. 530. How East Portlemouth comes into it is not now known. It is a fine church though, although much restored, and in the churchyard are buried many sailors, including the captain and crew of the French brigantine *Pauline*, wrecked on Gaytor Rock on the 19th November 1877. The crew included little Salvat Doramy, the 'mouse' as French sailors (and Dutch ones) call their cabin boys. The church has a fine 16th-century screen with many saints.

Salcombe Harbour has much of the charm that the Dart has. Although not so long it is wider, has more interesting arms, dries out more at low water, and is beautiful. But it does not have the spectacular wooded-gorge beauty of the Dart. It is a fine wild-fowling estuary, with thousands of wigeon in winter, and a rich variety of other birds.

The harbour is encumbered with a bar, which makes entry difficult and dangerous at low tide, or at any tide when a southerly or south-easterly is blowing. This is the bar which inspired Tennyson to write 'Crossing the Bar', which he did after a bumpy passage in the yacht *Sunbeam* when he was staying with James Anthony Froude, the historian.

In spite of its difficult entrance Salcombe was at one time a big shipping port. It is interesting to read the list of imports from various ports brought home by Salcombe ships in the 19th century:

Barbados	sugar and ginger
Puerto Rico	coffee, cocoa and tobacco
Antigua	molasses and rum
Eleuthera	arrowroot
Dominica	lime juice, spices
U.S.A.	timber, fruit and cotton
South America	meat, grain, coffee and hides
Mediterranean	velvet, oil, wine, marble

(This list is reproduced in that excellent little book *Devon Harbours* by Vernon Boyle and Donald Payne [Christopher Johnson 1952].)

In the 19th century there were four big shipyards in Salcombe, and in five years 300 ships were launched. Steam killed the whole thing dead. Yachts are still built though, particularly in the old-established yard of Edgar Cove Limited (which also runs a big hire fleet) but there is no more commercial shipping. An open day boat called the 'Salcombe Yawl' has been developed, good for cruising or racing, but these are built on both sides of the river (some at **Goodshelter**). They are handy little boats indeed and sell for about £600. Some 500 yachts and cruisers berth permanently in the estuary, from fifteen to twenty visiting yachts come in every day in the summer and about 300 foreign yachts use the harbour every year. It is *par excellence* a yachting river. Salcombe is a growing crabbing port though, there are currently eleven full-time boats, each shooting about seven shanks with about forty-four pots on a shank (they call shanks 'strings' here). The new plastic pots manufactured at Weymouth are coming quickly into vogue. In the summer many boats take parties of amateurs out sharking: £14 a day for a boat, or £3.50 a man. About a hundred sharks a year are caught, going up to seventy pounders.

The fishing community still mans a lifeboat. In 1916 their lifeboat, the *William and Emma*, capsized off the harbour mouth and all but two of the crew were drowned. The two survivors were Eddie

Distin and Bill Johnson: and the latter died soon afterwards – he never recovered from his ordeal.

An interesting development at Salcombe is the Island Cruising Club. Founded in 1951 this owns a growing number of yachts, large and small, from 'bum-hangers' to the superb Brixham Trawler *Provident*, recently taken over by the Maritime Trust to be preserved but still operated by the Club. Beginners, old and young, are taught to sail by experienced members, and when they have learnt can go on long cruises, as far afield as Spain or Norway. Members sleep on dormitory boats moored out in the estuary, they help to maintain craft, and there is a good feeling of enthusiasm and *esprit de corps*.

Salcombe Castle, or **Fort Charles**, little of which remains, held out against the Roundheads in the Civil War very much better than Dartmouth did. Under Sir Edmund Fortescue, in 1646, it withstood a siege for four months against the investing troops of Colonel Weldon. When the defenders did surrender they obtained honourable terms, and marched out – 66 men and two laundry women – colours flying and drums beating and were allowed to go to their homes.

Kingsbridge, at the top of the estuary, is a fine old town, with many old traditions, including one whereby a glove is hung up at the market arcade with flowers hanging from the fingers. This signifies that there will be good fellowship and no arrests for petty offences during the period of the annual fair. Traffic wardens please note. Kingsbridge church has great charm, and has, on the south wall of the chancel, a splendid epitaph which the traveller must read for himself. This was for an old cooper named Richard 'Bones' Phillips: a philosopher even if he wasn't, as we are assured by his contemporaries, a teetotaller.

CHAPTER 7

Salcombe to the Tamar

✤

Sharpitor, a mile and a half south-south-west from Salcombe, is National Trust, has a youth hostel, a small museum and very fine gardens, always open. In **Starehole Bay** the famous four-masted barque *Hergozin Cecilie* was beached after being wrecked around the corner. She lay there for nearly a year and finally broke up and disappeared in a storm.

Bolt Head has a cavern called the Bull's Hole, into which a bull is said to have disappeared, and to have emerged a week later – its hair having turned snow white! The cliffs here are weird and unearthly in the extreme. Made of crumbling pre-Devonian mica-schist, most of it with a vertical strike or grain, they have fallen and crumbled into weird shapes: it is easy to imagine faces and birds and animals. There is a very good path cut along the cliff face, and it is a fine and easy walk to Hope Cove. As we get further along the cliffs the rocks get less weird but still impressive. Ravens, kestrels and shags nest along them.

Soar Mill Cove is a paradisial place, when there are not too many people there at least, but there is an hotel up the valley. You can see where a mill leet brought water down to drive the old mill (only a few foundations of which remain) which was down by the sea as many water mills once were. No doubt cutters and ketches used to beach below it to load flour or meal for away. It was on the Ham, or Hem, Stone that the *Hergozin Cecilie* struck in April 1836, and at Soar Mill Cove yet another tea clipper came ashore, the *Hallowe'en*, but this time the ridges of tea on the beach were only seven feet high. Less tea or more honest observers? If you see some rusty old boilers near Lantern Rock they come from the *Jane Rowe*, which went ashore here in 1913 loaded with Swedish iron ore.

Below **Bolberry Down** are strange clefts in the crumbling rock, and dangerous landslips. One of the clefts or caverns is called Ralph's Hole, for here a smuggler of that name was wont to hide. These cliffs are fascinating to explore. There is a car park on top of the Down where people practise what has come to be the favourite

75

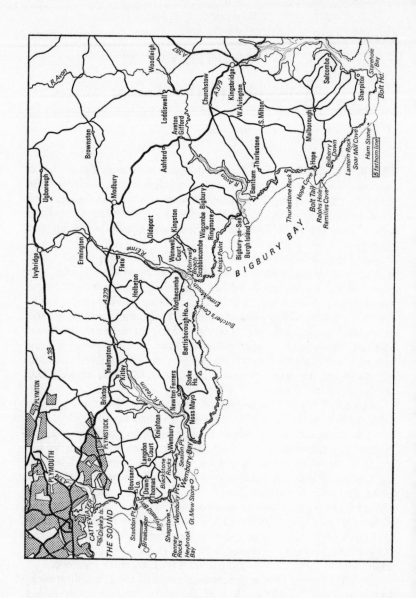

British pastime: sitting in their cars with the windows shut alternately gazing out to sea or reading the newspaper.

On **Bolt Tail** is a fine promontory fort. **Inner Hope** has a square of thatched houses straight out of Hans Andersen. It is infested with tourists and artists. There is a Fishermen's Reading Room, somewhat decayed but of strong period interest with some pictures inside. One of the immensely wealthy 'summer residents' who lives along this shore should untie his purse strings and find a few hundred pounds to put this place in order. There are still a few professional fishermen, who keep their gear in the disused Lifeboat House, but struggle to keep going. Here, as elsewhere along this coast, the lobster grounds have been much denuded by skin divers, who will soon be searching for the last lobster. They haven't taken seriously to crabs yet, and so these still yield half a living to the professional fishermen. Old people at Inner Hope can remember when there was a huge pilchard industry here – the local boats used to take up to £7000 worth a year and the village was given over to pressing the fish to extract the oil and salting them for export. Herring used to come here too in large numbers: the present Harbour Master once counted 150 Lowestoft Drifters in the bay together with perhaps a hundred local boats: 'it was like a floating city!'

The Armada ship *St Peter the Great*, 500 tons, was wrecked here, and gold coins have been discovered. But local people have found coins of the time of King John IV of Portugal, which makes them too late to have been in the Armada, so another ship must have been wrecked as well. Near here is **Ramillies Cove**, so called because H.M.S. *Ramillies*, 74 guns, went ashore here in 1760, and out of her 734 men only 26 were saved. The *Chantiloupe* was lost here too.

Outer Hope is a place of hotels. At **Thurlestone Rock** is an arch of red triassic conglomerate.

Thurlestone is much dominated by a golf links and many extremely wealthy houses. It is a place, we are told, where the rich go to be with each other. There is a fine church.

The **Avon**, pronounced 'Awn' by true Devon scrumpy-drinkers, is a pretty little estuary but doesn't take long to explore. At **Bantham** is a foot ferry, that sometimes works and sometimes doesn't. **Bantham Sands** are famous for surfing: you even see masochists doing this in the middle of the winter.

Burgh Island has the Pilchard Inn, which is too picturesque for words, and a huge 1920s period hotel of hideous aspect, where prime ministers once used to play and where there were four hotel servants for every guest. This has a strong period interest, and will be treasured in years to come. The figurehead and stern cabin of the old H.M.S. *Ganges* were acquired by the owners of the hotel when the old ship was broken up at Plymouth. The stern cabin has been formed into a bar. It would be a splendid gesture, surely, if the owners presented the figurehead to the present H.M.S. *Ganges* – which is a shore station for training boys at Shotley, in Suffolk. Surely the Admiralty could give a *quid pro quo*? At low tide you can walk across to Burgh Island, over clean sand: at high tide there is a splendid machine on huge rubber wheels that crawls through the water keeping the passengers dry. Herring gulls nest in such profusion on the cliffs of the island that their eggs have to be culled every year to prevent gross overpopulation.

Bigbury, inland, has, in its church, a 14th-century brass to Sir William Bigbury, who brought to an end his family's long occupation of this place by getting himself killed in a duel. The lectern has the head of an eagle on the body of an owl. It once had the head of an owl too, but the parishioners bought the head of the eagle from another parish, not deeming the owl a sufficiently noble bird. Wisdom, apparently, was not enough. **Bigbury-on-Sea** is a modern holiday resort.

Ringmore, a pretty village, had a fighting parson, William Lane, who set up a battery of cannon near Aveton Gifford to oppose the Roundheads. After fighting his guns to a standstill he spiked them and rolled them down into the river. He then fled and hid in a secret room in the tower of his church. Later he managed to get to London and obtain a pardon. There is a fine pub here, the Journey's End, early 14th century.

The cliffs beyond are of Lower Devonian red sandstone and blue slates. There is a good footpath all the way. At **Hoist Point**, on top of the cliffs, were once small holdings on common ground where local fishermen grew early potatoes. They fertilized these with seaweed which they hoisted up from below and carried on donkeys (is this where the name Hoist Point comes from?) and they carried the crop away on donkeys to sell. Now of course the common lands have all gone, together with the donkeys, and the enormous farm which centres on Scobbiscombe is beset with notices trying to keep people off.

The cliffs about here are of a shiny, satiny rock, very beautiful: a schist of some sort: all rock fiercely metamorphosed by the heat and pressure of the Dartmoor upheavals. There are the blue flowers of *Scilla verna* in the spring. The beach, and combe, just to the east of the Hoist is called **Wiscombe**. It is very beautiful. There is a strange little house here, now empty, in which we are told that Princess Margaret once had tea.

At **Kingston** is the Dolphin Inn, where Mr Bert Triggs is a mine of information about the locality if you can get him away from his Euchre. The inn has deeds of the 15th century.

The mouth of the **River Erme** is very beautiful. When it is not too crowded with people it is a very pleasant place to be. There is a fine beach at **Wonwell**, where are two old ruined cottages and the remains of the Pilot's House, which was occupied by a pilot until not long ago. The pilot got paid extra for keeping his house painted white so that it would act as a leading mark for shipping coming into the Erme. It was his job to pilot vessels in and up river to Clyng Mill or to Ermington.

You can walk, very pleasantly, all the way up the Erme to **Ermington** on the east bank. At **Oldaport** there is a wall said to be Roman. Ermington has a church with a crooked spire on its 13th-century tower, a 13th-century porch, a fine Elizabethan brass, three 17th-century screens and much modern carving done by Violet Pinwill, the daughter of the vicar.

Holbeton also has fine screens in its church although the one in front of the chancel is a modern copy. There are modern windows in the north wall which I for one find very embarrassing.

Beside the Erme is a big heronry, and purple herons, night herons and little egrets are sometimes to be seen.

Below **Mothecombe**, by the mouth of the Erme on the west side, is another nice sandy beach, and the shore from there on becomes rather inaccessible, being obstructed by the enclosed estate of Mothecombe House, a fine Queen Anne mansion wherein the Mildmay family now live having moved to here from their old home at **Flete**. The late Lord Mildmay, a great swimmer, was drowned in Erme Mouth fairly recently. **Battisborough House** is now a public school. There are some splendid little sandy-beached coves at the foot of the cliffs along here (if you can get to them – a boat is the best way). **Butcher's Cove** has a nice little mini-beach. Below **Stoke House** is a big caravan site, and a ruined church with an ancient, unkempt graveyard.

Rowden Farm, just inland, was built all in one piece in 1884, and is a splendid example of a purpose-built farmstead of the years of High Farming: a complex of buildings beautifully designed for their job (note the engine house and shafting), and still very much in use today.

Noss Mayo was once the property and plaything of Lord Revelstoke, and he built the church here in 1882 and filled it with carvings made by one 'Harry Hems and his Merry Men'. He used to entertain Edward VII and George V when the latter was a prince. He took an interest in the local fishermen, as decent squires always have done, and built the 'Baulking House' for them as a fish-curing shed. In 1900 there were thirty boats fishing from the Yealm.

The **Yealm** (pronounced 'Yam') is now an important and very select yachting harbour, and a commuting dormitory for Plymouth.

Newton Ferrers has large hotels, many villas with their gardens running down to the water's edge where their yachts lie moored in Edwardian splendour. If you wonder what a strange collection of water tanks is, with sea water being pumped through them, down by the riverside, it is not a place for purifying shellfish. It is a place for testing the under-water paints of Messrs International Paints Ltd.

The Yealm has twelve miles of lovely cruising waters, and was once quite a port because it sent two ships to the Siege of Calais and ships against the Armada. At **Yealmpton** (pronounced 'Yamton') is **Kitley Cave**, where cave bear, woolly elephant and rhino used to live. Old Mother Hubbard lived at Kitley House and the rhyme about her was written in 1805. In Yealmton church is the Toreus Stone, said to be Roman, and some good monuments.

Weast of the Yealm, **Thorn** has a fine sub-tropical garden. **Season Point** is National Trust and good walking. **Wembury** was the Wiegenbeorge of the Anglo-Saxon Chronicle, where the Danes were defeated in about 851. The place is now a sprawling bungalow plantation. The café was once a mill. At **Langdon Court** is a magnificent range of farm buildings, 18th century. The Court itself was built 1577 but rebuilt 1707 by Josias Calmady.

On the **Great Mew Stone** a man and his wife once lived in a cottage to look after the tame rabbits that were dumped on that place as a commercial enterprise. Now it is uninhabited, and I have never seen any rabbits there although that doesn't mean to say there aren't any. It is believed that monks once kept a lighthouse on the island.

Nasty rocks stick out half a mile at **Wembury Point**. The naval gunnery station H.M.S. *Cambridge* is here. **Heybrook Bay** and **Bovisand Bay** have bungalows and caravans: **Renney Rocks** need a good berth given them if you are afloat but the Shag Stone Beacon shows where they are.

Bovisand Fort is a most interesting place. It is one of the two great rings of forts built around Plymouth as a defence against a possible French invasion in Napoleon III's time. There were 9 forts in the inner ring and 22 in the outer. Bovisand was one of the most powerful of the system, mounting 23 muzzle-loading rifled guns of 10-inch calibre, each weighing 18 tons. The walls of the main battery are immensely thick and beautifully built, the embrasures were protected by armour plate hatches when not in use (one of the original hatches remains, in the most easterly embrasure), each two casemates share a common underground magazine. The hoists for lifting the shells and powder from the magazines, the hold-fasts for the tackles that trimmed and ran out the great guns, are still there. It would be nice if one of the guns could be discovered somewhere, or one like them, and installed *in situ* in one of the case-mates, with dummy ammunition and other stores and equipment, and the place opened to the public.

Above the main 1868 fort is an earlier building, of about 1800, with officers' quarters that look as if they have not long been vacated. Plymouth was the main base of the Royal Navy and sited in a most vulnerable and exposed part of the kingdom, and this fort was one of the three absolutely crucial ones for its defence. Therefore its defences and armament were the most sophisticated of their period. It was an extremely important fort. There are two ugly towers of the Second World War.

The use it is being put to now is a most excellent one, for it is the headquarters of Plymouth Ocean Projects, started in 1970 by a group of young enthusiasts and obviously most flourishing. Here, in one of the casemates, is air compressing machinery for the charging of air bottles, in another a gentleman perfecting his own self-built miniature submarine, there are dormitories, 'ablutions', mess rooms, bar and club room, drying room, lecture room: the whole place is being transformed as a school for under-water activities. Seventy people can be accommodated. Every branch of under-water work is being studied and taught. People go there for courses of a week or two, paying forty pounds a fortnight for tuition, board and lodging, and use of equipment extra. There are many weekend courses also. There is an extremely relaxed, enthusiastic and friendly atmosphere about the place. It is a most stimulating place to be.

The small harbour below the fort was obviously built as a harbour for the construction and supply of the fort. It is a useful harbour for the under-water centre, or for a night's refuge, but untenable in bad weather.

Plymouth Breakwater, which is less than a mile from this point out to sea, is one of the most notable structures of its kind in the world. Plymouth Sound was obviously a splendid anchorage for the ships of the Royal Navy in sailing ship days, because the mouth of it was wide enough for ships to beat (tack) out of it against a southerly wind, and with the wind from any other quarter the anchorage was both sheltered and easy to get out of. But if a southerly gale sprang up the Sound became untenable, and ships would have to slip their cables and scuttle for the Hamoaze or the Cattewater, which could be a great inconvenience. So, in 1812 it was decided to construct a breakwater which would convert the Sound into a more or less sheltered anchorage, and at the same time leave room on both sides of it for ships to beat in or out against the wind. John Rennie was the engineer in charge. Limestone was quarried by a labour force of four hundred men near the bank of the Cattewater at Oreston, taken to the waterside by a railway, and shot into specially made ships with trap doors in their bottoms. It was carried out to the breakwater and simply dumped: the *pierre perdue* technique. The inside of the breakwater was built of nine-ton limestone blocks set by crane; the seaward side just by dumping. In November 1824 a great storm overthrew most of the work, but by 1841 it was completed – four million tons of Oreston limestone having been used and three million tons of dressed granite. The breakwater is nearly a mile long, the channels left between it and the land at each end are about half a mile, forty feet deep at high tide and twenty-two at high springs. The wall is 133 feet wide at its base and fifteen feet at its top and it encloses a roadstead of 1120 acres. The fort behind the breakwater has an artesian well in it!

Staddon Point is a great place from which to view the Sound and Plymouth. Charles I is supposed to have sited his guns here for the bombardment of Plymouth. Plymouth stood firm for Parliament and became the only town in the South-West to hold out. The town was besieged from November 1642 to January 1646, off and on. On the 10th of September 1644 Charles himself led 15,000 men with 28 guns against the town but the attack was repulsed.

Mount Batten Point is R.A.F., was a seaplane station, and T. E. Lawrence was stationed here when he unfortunately met his death in a motor cycle accident.

Plymstock lays claim to Robinson Crusoe. Alexander Selkirk, the historical figure from whom Defoe took his character, sailed from here, and when he got home after his long exile married a widow lady named Frances Candis and retired to Oreston to spend the rest of his life. His Last Will and Testament was dated 12 December 1720.

CHAPTER 8

Plymouth

❦

Plymouth is now a very big city and growing very fast. In William the Conqueror's time it was a hamlet. By 1295 it was already chosen as a naval base of the first importance, for here Edward I assembled his fleet for the Bordeaux wars. The king spent a month with his expeditionary force in the spring of 1297, and sailed with 325 ships for France.

The French didn't take it all lying down though: in 1388 'certain Pyrats' 'brent' many 'great shippes' and part of the town, and in 1403 du Castel attacked the place and burnt 600 houses.

By then Plymouth was the chief port of pilgrimage for St James of Compostella, sharing the right to ship pilgrims with Exeter, Dartmouth and Weymouth. A fascinating glimpse into medieval shipping is given by the following list of 15th-century ships which followed this traffic: *Katherine* – 140 tons, *Galliote* – 150, *Marye Batte* – 100, *Little Nicholas* – 120, *Pylgryme* – 100, *Holye Ghoste* – 90, *Saynte Marye* – 110, *Adventurer* – 100 and *Dorcette* – 100.

In 1440 the town got its charter as a town.

In 1528 English exploration was getting under way. In that year William Hawkins sailed to Brazil in the *Paule*. He made three voyages.

In 1577 Drake set out to sail round the world, leaving Plymouth on the 15th of November. The account of his voyage was written by his chaplain – Francis Fletcher. Drake started with five ships: *Pelican* 100 tons, *Elizabeth* 80 tons, *Marigold* 30 tons, *Swanne* 50 tons and *Christopher* 15 tons. The *Pelican*, alone, got back to Plymouth two years and ten months afterwards, having circumnavigated. Drake, the greatest English seafarer of any time, had two houses in Plymouth, one at **Thornhill Park** and one at the corner of **Looe** and **Buckwell Streets**. Drake and Sir John Hawkins died at sea on the same voyage to Central America. They had sailed from Plymouth in 1595. The Hawkins family (to which Drake was related) had a fantastic history of privateering, slaving, and merchant adventuring.

The Armada sailed in 1588 (after spending years victualling – but the crews ate the victuals faster than they could be acquired). John Hawkins, the father of the slave trade, the son of the William who used to sail to Brazil, was Vice Admiral of the English fleet and Drake was Admiral of such of it as lay at Plymouth. The famous game of bowls could obviously be finished in perfect calm because Drake and his captains knew that they could not get their ships out of Plymouth Sound until the ebb tide. The shattering of the Armada by a much smaller fleet of smaller ships was due to the fact that the English had really mastered the art of sailing to windward. They managed to get the weather gauge of the Armada and keep it, and the great Spanish galleons, with their high fore and stern castles which made them so unweatherly, were unable to turn and attack them.

In 1606 Sir Walter Raleigh sailed for Virginia and planted a colony there. But it was not until 1620 that the first really serious attempt was made to form a lasting settlement in North America, when the Pilgrim Fathers sailed, on 6th September, in the *Mayflower*. They had only put into Plymouth because they were forced to because of damage to their ships (as so often the passage westwards down-Channel proved more punishing than the crossing of the Atlantic). Probably Boston in Lincolnshire (see *The Companion Guide to the Coast of North-East England*) can justly claim the Pilgrim Fathers better than Plymouth: the latter was just the last port of call, but it is nice to know that in Plymouth they were hospitably used.

After the trauma of the Civil War Charles II built the massive **Citadel** on the Hoe: whether to keep out an enemy or to intimidate the inhabitants of this very puritan town is not clear. Probably it did both. William of Orange, that champion of Protestantism and believer in constitutional monarchy, laid down the great Naval Dockyard on the **Hamoaze** in 1688: the year he arrived in England.

Captain Cook sailed from Plymouth in 1768. But Plymouth has mounted uncounted voyages of exploration since the earliest times. The fact that there are forty-three Plymouths about the world is some indication of this.

Other dockyards were built during the 18th century, Vanbrugh designing **Morrice Yard**. Many of the buildings which remain are very beautiful. **Millbay Dock** was mostly constructed after 1849, when the railway came. The dockyards are open to visitors of British nationality Mondays to Fridays at 9, 10 and 11 a.m. and 2 and 3 p.m. and on Saturdays 9, 10 and 11 a.m.

In 1941 the centre of Plymouth was practically flattened by German bombing. What had been a superbly beautiful ancient

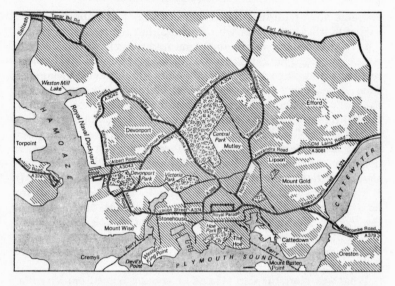

seaport city was laid in ruins, and now has been built up as a vast modern shopping centre and complex of housing estates.

The **Barbican** still gives a hint of the flavour of pre-bombing Plymouth. There are old houses here and old streets, it has the air of a seafaring place, there is a good fleet of big (rather old) trawlers: some engaged in white fish trawling, some in dredging for escallops, and others in potting and other activities. There is a succession of passenger boats leaving the Barbican in the summer for a tour of the Sound and Hamoaze ('See the battleships!').

The **Hoe** is justly famous, for here Drake played his game of bowls. It is a fine breezy place, it has the Royal Naval Memorial which whatever it is like aesthetically is very moving, and Smeaton's Eddystone lighthouse stands beside it. There is a good aquarium under the Citadel.

The story of the **Eddystone Lighthouse** is nothing if not dramatic. The Eddystone Shoal, thirteen miles off-shore, was a terrible claimer of ships: in thick weather there was no possible way by which a ship could know she was approaching it: soundings were no good – the first thing the ship knew she had struck. It became absolutely imperative to build a lighthouse on this terrible reef. One Henry Winstanley decided to have a go. During the building of it, in 1697, Winstanley and his builders were seized by a French ship, France then being at war with England. Louis XIV ordered the men to be released, and punished the privateers who had captured them, saying that he was at war with England, but not against mankind. The light first shone out in 1698, and immediately the incidence of wrecks ceased. The lighthouse was of wood, and was highly ornamented with ironwork. But several sailors and local men prophesied disaster, although Winstanley himself had complete confidence in the work and often expressed a desire that he should be himself in the lighthouse when a gale blew. He had his desire: in the words of Daniel Defoe: 'he happened at last to be in it once too often, when that dreadful tempest blew, November 27th 1703. This tempest began on the Wednesday before and blew with such violence, and shook the lighthouse so much, that, as they told me there, Mr Winstanley would fain have been ashore, and made signals for help: but no boat durst go off to him; and to finish the tragedy, on the Friday, November 26th, when the tempest was so redoubled that it became a terror to the whole nation, the first sight seaward that the people of Plymouth were presented with . . . was the bare Eddystone.'

What was more the ship *Winchelsea*, coming home from Virginia, was lost, for lack of the light, with all her lading and most of her seamen. And the gale which drowned Winstanley and his three assistants overthrew four hundred windmills throughout England (many of them were not blown down but set on fire by the heat caused by friction because of their unbridled speed), fifteen warships were lost from the Royal Navy and three hundred merchant ships, eight hundred houses were destroyed in London alone and the Bishop of Bath and Wells and his sister were killed by the collapse of their palace.

Anyway, in 1708 another lighthouse, this time a circular timber tower on masonry, was lit. This had been built by a London silk mercer, John Rudyerd. These were the days, before Trinity House automatically maintained all sea marks, when private venturers would build a lighthouse and maintain it for the money that they could make by levying a toll on shipping. Rudyerd's lighthouse stood well to the gales, but was finally set on fire by its own light. The crew was rescued but one man, who was just ninety-four years old, died soon afterwards and was found to have *swallowed* a large dollop of molten lead during the conflagration! It was during the existence of Rudyerd's lighthouse that one of the two keepers died, and the remaining one went mad, and after that it was decided never to have less than three keepers.

Smeaton was then called in for a third attempt, and he built in dovetailed stone. The tower was eighty-five feet high, and the light was lit in 1759. This tower would probably still have been serving if the sea had not started to undercut the stone on which it stood. Because of this the present lighthouse was built by Trinity House, by Sir James Douglass. In 1882 the lantern was lit, 133 feet above mean high water. The light had cost £80,000 to build, and taken three years and eight months. Smeaton's tower was demolished stone by stone and bought by Plymouth Corporation, and this is the tower we now see on the Hoe, where it was re-erected as a memorial.

Up the Tamar **Saltash** was once more important than Plymouth. It was a tin port and ship-owning place: the Slugge family was prominent in the Middle Ages owning many pilgrim ships and troop transports. Defoe found Saltash 'a little, poor, shattered town – the ruins of a larger place'. Brunel designed the very interesting Royal Albert Railway Bridge across the Tamar at this point, which was opened in 1859. It is 100 feet above the water and 2240 feet in length. Alongside it the Tamar Road Bridge was opened in 1961.

The **Tamar** is a long and fascinating estuary, with its big tributary the Tavy, and makes a delightful cruising ground. It is a great wildfowl area, with avocets in winter, thousands of golden plover, thousands of wigeon and such comparative rarities as black-tailed godwits. A most interesting place on the Tamar is **Morwellham** (pronounced morwell*ham* and not mor*well*'am), which was a very important river port in the late 18th and all through the 19th centuries. It was connected to a whole string of mines both by canal and railway, and a huge tonnage of metallic ores went through it: copper being the most copious, but tin, manganese, arsenic and other ores also being important. The place has now been turned into a recreation centre, there is a museum there, a café, nature trails and much to see. The whole area is of first interest to students of industrial archaeology.

Drake's Island, once a fort, once a prison, is now an adventure centre. Courses are held in sailing, climbing, expeditions and marine biology.

CHAPTER 9

The Tamar to Polruan

❧

Torpoint is just a dormitory town of Plymouth and growing all the time. The experiment is being made of dumping white sand from the china clay pits on the shore so as to establish a sandy beach. It seems to be working. **Anthony House**, inland, is Queen Anne and fine, with very good furniture. Open Bank Holidays, and, in the summer, Tuesdays, Wednesdays and Thursdays. There is another huge Victorian fort at Antony.

Back to the mouth of the Tamar, **Mount Edgcumbe** is a magnificent park, open all the year on Wednesdays and Sundays, also Bank Holidays. You can get to it easily by the foot ferry from Plymouth to **Cremyll**, which is a little forgotten-looking place with a flourishing boatyard. This district came to the Edgcumbe family in 1493 when Sir Piers married into it (having come from **Cotehele**, higher up the Tamar – also a house well worth visiting). Sir Richard was Comptroller of the King's Household for Henry VII. Mount Edgcumbe house was built in 1552, burned down by German bombing in 1941 (when so much of Plymouth went) and rebuilt in 1952. At **Picklecombe Point** is a fort of 1800: the next fort along is Hawkins Battery followed by Grenville.

Maker church has a seventy foot tower which can be seen for miles around and acts as a fine beacon for seafarers. It was for long used as an Admiralty signal station, in the 19th century being manned by a lieutenant, a midshipman and two seamen, and even now the vicar has the right to fly the Union Flag from it. There is a holy well towards the road – Cornwall has plenty of holy wells. The little chapel is 14th century. The word Maker comes from Macuir which is said to be Cornish for a wall or ruin, from the Latin *maceria*. Cornish, like Welsh which it resembles so closely as to be the same language, borrowed freely from the Latin. In about 705 King Geraint of Cornwall granted land here to Sherborne Abbey.

Down the hill into the twin villages of **Kingsand** and **Cawsand**. These charming places (or place because you can't tell where one ends and the other begins) enjoyed great prosperity before the

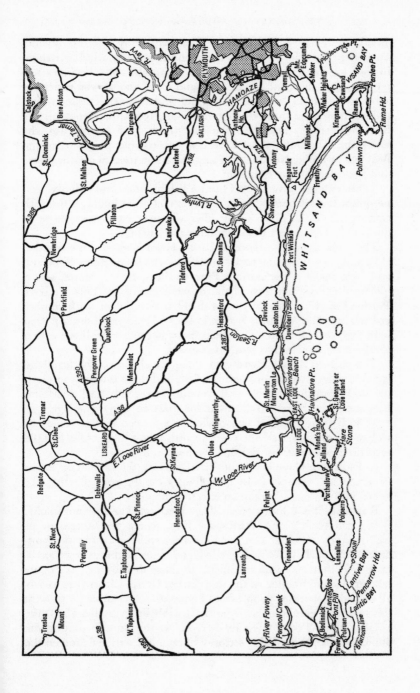

breakwater was built, because **Cawsand Bay** was an obvious anchorage for ships in a westerly or south-westerly wind: anything in fact except a south-easter, when it immediately becomes untenable. But the fleet lay in Cawsand Bay, and it was easier for ships to be victualled from Kingsand and Cawsand than to send pulling boats the three or four miles to Plymouth. Hence all the fine 18th-century houses in the two places, and hence, also, the fine pubs. The latter must have been rip-roaring places when the fleet was at home. Nelson and Lady Hamilton used to use the place and they slept in the Ship Inn.

These villages have always been a fishing port, and still are, and no doubt the pilchard fishery, in its time of great boom in the 19th century, kept the place going after the fleet had taken more to docking in Devonport than victualling at anchor.

The walk along the shore to Rame Head is good. Fine wooded cliffs and jagged-looking rocky inlets into which smugglers could run and hide make it fascinating. **Pier Cellars**, now a house, was a 'pilchard cellar' in which pilchards were cured (see Looe). Above **Penlee Point** is a huge fortress of the First World War, with another one towards Rame. From Penlee to Rame Head the shore is armed with jagged rock teeth – God help the vessel driven in there with a south-easter blowing, as many a one was.

The path to **Rame Head** goes along the cliff top. The headland is a marvellously sited promontory fort, and there is a most interesting and beautiful chapel on it, rebuilt by the 4th Earl of Mount Edgcumbe in 1882 but licensed for mass in 1397 and again in 1425 so it is not new. It was obviously a beacon or lighthouse, as well as an oratory, and there are records going back as far as 1488 recording payments for lighting the beacon in it.

At **Polhawn Cove** is yet another 1860s fort, the present occupant of which has sensibly built greenhouses on the roof. Beating the sword into a ploughshare in an effective manner.

Rame itself is a diminutive village, mentioned as a manor in 981.

We can walk along **Whitsand Bay**, where are bungalows as well as sandy beaches. The bungalows are sprinkled down the foundered cliffs, each with a little garden, and many people express horror at their existence. I find it difficult to share this dismay: they only take up a small fraction of the shoreline of Cornwall, and are nearly all owned by working people from Plymouth who can sorely do with this means of getting away from it all. Nobody grumbles about the hideous mock-Tudor villas further on. At the time of writing the bungalow people are being seriously threatened with eviction on the grounds that their sanitary arrangements (buckets) are a danger to health. This from authorities which dump thousands of tons of sewage straight into the sea.

Freathy has interesting cliffs of mica-schists, National Trust land beyond, but then a large area of cliff given over to rifle ranges, centred on the enormous **Tregantle Fort** which, with Antony Fort, cuts off the narrow neck of land of the Maker with Rame Peninsula from attack from the westward. This promontory had to be denied to the enemy: one gaining it could have commanded the whole of Plymouth Sound and the Hamoaze and have rendered Plymouth untenable as a naval base. Hence the importance of these two fortifications.

The coast path is non-existent from here on to **Portwrinkle**, the latter place much dominated by a golf course. There was actually a port at Portwrinkle, and it is a measure of the strong incentive there was in sailing ship days to make a port almost *anywhere* that this was so. But sea transport was so much cheaper than land that vessels would even take the risk of going into Portwrinkle! There is a stone beacon on the spit of half-tide rock which runs out in front of the village itself. Do *not*, if you are sailing a boat in, take this for a harbour mark. It is anything but, and whether you leave it to port or to starboard it will put you on the rocks. There are two white stone leading marks up on the cliff-top a few cables further west – these take you in to whatever beach there is to land on. The little artificial harbour is a non-harbour really. Just west there is a splendid amphitheatre in the cliffs where kestrels nest. If you are walking you have to take to the road from here west for a couple of miles.

Downderry, slipping into the sea somewhat and being reinforced with green plastic-covered pig wire, is a small and select resort with red flat rocks on the beach under the crumbling cliffs. **Seaton** has a beach and many bungalows.

And then we come to **Murrayton**, and the monkey paradise. If we must have zoos, or collections of wild animals in captivity, surely this is the way to do it. The Brazilian Woolly Monkeys who inhabit this place live in big open cages with trees growing in them, and a wonderful system of wire netting tunnels and conduits so that every part of the large system of cages is accessible to every monkey. Further, a high tower from one of the cages connects with the tops of a number of tall trees by rope gangways, and the monkeys can get into these treetops whenever they like. Further, if they really want to, they can climb down to the ground and go right away, but the point is they don't want to. They are all members of a community, and no individual would dream of leaving the rest. Either they would *all* have to climb down and run away or none of them would, and as they are perfectly happy where they are they don't want to. The cage fencing, as the people who run the place tell you, is to keep the humans from disturbing the monkeys – not *vice-versa*.

The monkeys feel perfectly free, at home in their own territory, and their relationships with each other are the natural and normal ones that they would have in the wild. Visitors are admitted, and further, at certain times of the day the monkeys are invited out (if they want to come) and introduced to the visitors. They are extremely clean (unlike the scruffy animals kept in zoo cages), very affectionate and engaging. The staff are charming with them, and very good with the public too: they have a kind of Quaker quietism and good manners. It is a place very well worth going to see. The birth rate among the monkeys is very high and the death rate so far nil, and this is in striking contrast to most zoos.

And so we work our way along the shore to **Millendreath Beach**, where is a swimming pool on the shore, to **Looe** (Cornish *lake* or *river*). If we are afloat Looe is easy enough to get into, although it can be exciting when a south-easter is blowing, both banks of the river are fairly crowded with boats but there is still room to tie up. Above the bridge (but you have to drop your mast) is plenty of room and two lovely wooded rivers, although only a couple of miles of readily navigable water. The first bridge here was completed in 1436 – the existing one in 1853, widened in 1960.

Looe is old: twenty ships and 325 men at the Siege of Calais 1346, and before that, in 1337, twelve ships and 234 sailors and 15 boys went with Edward III to the start of the Hundred Years' War. Early in the 19th century it became active as a port for shipping out copper and lead ores and also granite. Until 1832 the Looes, East and West, returned *four* members of Parliament to Westminster. In 1828 a canal was dug to Liskeard, which climbed up twenty-four locks in six miles from Tarras Pill to Moorwater. In 1860 a railway superseded it, and this faced gradient difficulties too, climbing 650 feet in six miles. The trucks ran down, loaded, free, and the empties were hauled up again by horses. Granite went out for the new Westminster Bridge, the Thames Embankment and the base of the Albert Memorial besides many other places, including the Channel Islands, Plymouth, Dover and Portland breakwaters. The big quays, on the East bank of the river, from which all this heavy stone was loaded, have now been turned into car parks.

Looe is still a busy fishing port. There is much long lining (which we shall discuss more fully under Mevagissey), some trawling and potting, but the main activities are mackerelling in the winter and sharking in the summer. The mackerel are caught with hand lines. When they are scarce, or shy to bite, the boats cruise slowly towing three lines astern with spinners on them, and this is called *plummeting*. One of these lines trails from the stern, and the other two from long rods which are fixed to each side. As soon as the fish appear in any quantity though the 'trolling' or 'plummeting' is discontinued, and 'feathering' takes place. The discovery of the art of mackerel feathering only occurred some fifteen years ago, and it completely revolutionised the fishery. The 'feathers' are actual feathers dyed pretty colours (to suit the whims more of the fishermen than of the fish which don't care a hoot what colour they are) attached to hooks. A man works one line with perhaps a dozen hooks on it and a lead on the end. He does this by the operation known as 'plonking'. The boat is stopped and the heavy lead takes line and hooks quickly down through the upper layers of water where the smaller mackerel lurk to the depths where the larger ones live. Often before the hooks have got down as far as they are going every hook has a fish on it. In the summer, when the fish swim shallow, the line only has to be in the water a few seconds to be full of fish. The skill is in clearing your line quickly enough – and without fouling it – to get it back into the water to catch more fish without waste of time. When the fish are shy then is when you have to 'plonk': you work the line up and down by lifting and dropping your arm. More and more, the feathers are being superseded by small spoon-shaped metal lures or small bits of rubber tube: anything bright and flashing in fact will attract the fish. You see boats coming into Looe, with perhaps four fishermen on board, laden with mackerel caught by this method.

But in the summer, although some men still go for mackerel (very plentiful but a poor price) the bulk of the Looe fishermen turn to the new and profitable industry of taking amateurs out sharking. Parties of enthusiasts are taken out (three is a fair number – if more go they are most unlikely all to get a turn) to a fair distance from the shore, bags of pilchard offal called 'rubby-dubby' bags are lowered into the water on short lines to attract the sharks, large single hooks are baited with whole mackerel and cast out. The line is eighty-pound breaking strain braided nylon and ends in a twelve or fifteen foot wire trace. A large float keeps the bait at a constant depth. Probably two lines are put out, at different depths. If a shark is struck it provides an exciting fight. If it is brought to the boat and gaffed and clubbed and got on board (the club for knocking fish on the head is called the *priest* – because it ministers the last rites) it is taken back to port, weighed, and then – if no one wants it for crab-pot bait, towed out to sea again and dumped. Which all seems a bit senseless. It would be a good thing if there were more fish-meal factories around. Blue Shark, Mako and Porbeagle are caught. If you catch one of 75 lb or over you qualify for membership of the Shark Angling Club of Great Britain. In May of 1971 a Mako shark of exactly 500 lb was landed at Looe: an all-time record for a shark caught in British waters.

But Looe was once primarily a pilchard port, and at one time the whole place was given over to the catching and curing and selling of these multitudinous fish. For some reason the pilchards seem to have deserted this part of the Channel. Whether for reasons of changing sea temperatures, or change in the habits of the pilchards' food, or from over-fishing, is not known, but now if you want reliable catches of pilchards you have to go much further west out into the Atlantic.

The pilchard is the adult sardine (or put more logically, the sardine is the juvenile pilchard), and pilchards were once to Cornwall what coals were to Newcastle. In Tudor times 'Pilchards and Tin!' was the Cornish toast: these two commodities were the mainstay of the Cornish economy.

In the middle of the 19th century drift nets of 190 fathoms length by eleven to thirteen fathoms deep were used from the typical Looe luggers, and each net then cost £170. The fishing was best on moonless nights. The fish were brought in and stacked five foot high with salt. Thus they were left for from five to six weeks, and the oil which ran out of them, because of the pressure, ran to the floor, and into channels, and down into sumps from which it was collected and sold to tanners for dressing leather, for lamp fuel, for medicine, and for making soap. It was a very important item of commerce, and thousands of tons of it were produced.

The fish were then either just packed into barrels, or pressed into the barrels with screw presses, and any extra oil thus pressed out added to the main supply. The barrels were exported to the Mediterranean, or to Spain, where the people have an appetite for that sort of thing and about 1850 they sold for 50/- a hogshead. East Looe was full of pilchard cellars, or pilchard 'palaces'. Even now there are several left, all put to different uses. One is now the Cornish

Museum, run and in fact owned by Mr William Paynter who is an authority on Looe and its district, and in this cellar one of the presses is preserved, in working order, the channels and sumps for the oil can be seen, and also a chimney for the smoking of pilchards for local use. This is, by the way, a fascinating little museum: one of the best for its size in the country, and it has many other things in it besides relics of the pilchard industry.

The traditional way of preserving pilchards for eating other than salting is to 'souse' them. You clean the fish, put a bay leaf in each one and some pepper and salt, cover with vinegar in an earthenware crock, and put in a slow oven overnight. In the morning take the crock out and cover it over with paper. The contents can be eaten, cold, at any time, and will keep indefinitely, hot they are disgusting. Mackerel, or herring, can be treated in the same way.

As for Looe today it is an absolutely charming place, except that too many of the old houses in its narrow and tortuous streets (I am now thinking of East Looe) are too 'tarted up' – made too consciously 'picturesque' – they are quite picturesque already and only need to be left alone, and there are far too many visitors. In the summer the place is absolutely *crammed*. There is a charming small sandy beach inside the Banjo Pier. There is an aquarium on the pier, and a shark museum. There are always fishing boats heading for sea or coming home, and plenty to watch. The small half-decked motor boats with sheltering glass 'canopies', so common here as in other places along this shore, are called in Looe *Quotters*. In other places they are called *Toshers*.

The hinterland of Looe, particularly between the two Looe Rivers, is very beautiful. Duloe, St Neot, St Cleer, St Ive are charming places. Herodsfoot is strange and interesting, and was once a roaring mining camp: over 800 men once worked in the silver-lead ore mines. There were then many pubs in the parish and the parson had to write a special prayer against drunkenness. By the 1860s the mines were worked out, however. An explosives factory continued working until 1963 when it unfortunately blew up.

Duloe (Cornish *Black Lake*, or *God's Lake*) has a very interesting church indeed: it is really very beautiful and unusual. There is a fine, and very old, stone circle in a field at Duloe: probably older than Stonehenge. At **St Keyne**, besides a notable church, is St Keyne's well. The husband or wife who drinks first of its waters rules for the remainder of their married life. The water doesn't taste very nice and it doesn't work.

At St Keyne's Mill is the **Paul Corin Musical Collection**: a most interesting collection of mechanical organs. These are played at various times during the day. Some of them are beautiful, others are vulgar to the point of utter hideousness, but all are of astonishing ingenuity, and one or two of them are extremely *loud*. It is somewhat uncanny to listen to Paderewski's recording on a perforated roll on a mechanical piano that he used to play himself: *and actually see the keys going up and down.*

Back at the shore, and **West Looe, Hannafore Point** does not appeal to me although the large houses there have a fine view. **Looe Island**, which has been variously called St Michael's, St Nicholas's and St George's Island, is owned by two charming ladies who allow people to land on it; you can get tea, and it is easy to get a boatman to take you out there. There are scanty remains of a chantry or chapel on it, it is known that two monks lived there in 1144 and it was dissolved in 1549. There are some strange carved stones on the island, thought to have been brought as ballast perhaps from the Mediterranean by ships coming back light for another load of salt pilchards or tin. There is a local legend that St Joseph of Arimathea sailed here in a boat with his nephew the boy Jesus. He left the latter on the island while he sailed into Looe to take on stores. A whale washed up on Looe Island before the war and had to be blown up.

Back on the mainland, **Monk's House**, now just a trace of foundations, was another religious foundation once called **Lammana**. This name has been variously interpreted as having been derived from *Lan Mynach* which is Cornish for 'Monk's Church' (*lan*, like the Welsh *llan*, actually means less a church than a sacred enclosure, generally a circular one such as one still finds on every other hill top in parts of Ethiopia) and *Lan Manac*, or the Church of St Manac. The place was closely connected with the other oratory on Looe Island, and both were cells of Glastonbury.

It is pleasant to walk up on **The Downs**, west of Looe, which really are like downs and provide magnificent views, and a path leads to **Talland** where is a beautiful and individual little church with a detached tower and many very fine bench ends. There is a small beach further down, too many cars in summer, and ice cream. The purple-greenish slate here is from the Dartmouth Beds. Up in **Porthallow** is a man who fires pottery in a wood-fired kiln: very unusual nowadays. He uses drift wood, and it takes nearly a quarter of a ton of it for a firing.

Polperro is just too pretty for words and is infested with piskies. There is even a shop which specializes in selling *Cornish ghoulies and ghosties* and that sets the tone of the place. Coach-load after coach-

Blackpool Sands.

Polperro.

load of people from the North of England and Midlands disgorge in the terribly congested coach park up above, and the people swarm down into the little village looking with apparent non-comprehension at what they see about them, while the anti-social try to penetrate through the milling crowd in the narrow and tortuous alleyways with motor cars, which are as out of place as Cadillacs in the *suks* of Baghdad and as big a nuisance. The place *could* be – and *was* – absolutely fine: a working village inhabited by honest fishermen and smugglers. There was even a man so honest – his name was Zephaniah Job – that the smugglers entrusted their finances to him and he used to lend them money for their expeditions and even printed his own currency. There were gentlemen over the other side of the Channel who used to provide brandy in four-and-a-half gallon anker barrels ready roped up for easy carrying.

It is not Polperro's fault that it is so absolutely overwhelmed with trippers in the summer, but is it really necessary for the inhabitants to cater always for the lowest tastes in the spectrum? The mobs from the industrial cities will buy whatever is offered them: offer them something decent and they will buy that too. The Office Holders of the Cornish Gorsedd of Bards should arm themselves with muskets loaded with silver bullets and forthwith shoot every *pisky* in Cornwall. The Duchy will be well rid of the tiresome little creatures. As for Ghoulies and Ghosties – they should be firmly exorcized, once and for all.

Polperro has a nice little harbour in which long-suffering fishermen struggle to keep their integrity as craftsmen among the milling and staring crowds – but incidentally make a pretty good thing in the summer time by taking people out to look at the caves. The little harbour is very crowded, it dries right out at low tide, and the bay leading into it can be very nasty in a south-easter. The harbour piers have been much damaged, in 1774 and again in 1817 and 1824 they were practically wiped away, in 1887 a public fund was raised to repair them and now there are collecting boxes into which people are asked to put money for this purpose. The little community of ageing fishermen is just not financially strong enough to maintain this splendid little working harbour unhelped.

In 1850 it was recorded that there were thirty fishing vessels about twenty-seven feet on the keel working at long lining part of the year and *driving*, or drift-netting for pilchards the rest. At long lining they employed two men per boat, at driving four. At long lining the catch was divided into fifths – the boat got one share and the men two each. At driving the catch was divided into eighths: the boat and nets taking four shares and the men one each: a measure of the difference in price of a set of drift nets and one of long lines. The gear came from Bridport where rope cables were being made in 1227 and where the firm of Bridport Gundry still supplies gear to most of the long-shore fishermen of England.

There is some National Trust cliff to follow, but then the path peters out and if you are anything like me you will get driven back to the road. There is a fine-looking house called **Raphael** by the road: it was the fortified manor house of the Hywysch family in the 14th century. West of the Shag Rock is a nasty shoal but marked with a bell buoy.

Lansallos has a very fine church: not to be missed even by non-church-lovers. There are fine benches of 1490 to 1520 with Renaissance scrollwork in a Gothic frame, except for the chancel roof the roofs are old and beautiful, there is a marvellous stone slab carved with an Elizabethan lady in full fig on the south wall, a Celtic cross, and the grave of a smuggler whom we are told was killed by a cannon ball near the gate outside.

The shore along **Lantivet Bay** and **Lantic Bay** is wild and lonely in the extreme, the cliffs very steep and beautiful, the jagged rocky beaches either inaccessible or only approached by steep paths. This is a connoisseur's shoreline. Much of it is National Trust.

And so we come to **Polruan**, which shares with Fowey the mouth of the beautiful River Fowey. Comparisons are odious, and I am not going to make any, I am merely going to admit that I am more of a Polruan man than a Fowey man myself, and that far more people (and motor cars) crowd into the latter than the former.

Approached by boat from the east the ruined wall of St Saviour's Chapel acts as a landmark. The river entrance is wide, deep and easy. It is a beautiful harbour and unobstructed by any bridges.

There is a strange wooden cross called Punches Cross set on a rock east of the mouth: not as a beacon for ships but for some religious or historical purpose. Some people say that it marked the limit of the harbour authority, which was vested in the Priory of Tywardreath. This seems very probable. But there is also a legend that at this spot the boy Jesus landed, with his uncle St Joseph of Arimathea, and from here walked up to the site of St Saviour's Chapel on the top of the cliff, and thence to Glastonbury. There is also a legend that Pontius Pilate, having blotted his copy book in Judea by the Crucifixion of Jesus, got banished to Britain by the Empire, landed here, got as far as Esse, where he was eaten alive by lice. In the new church of St Saviour in Polruan there is a little booklet on sale, by Mrs Frances Burdett, which describes all this. It also gives some far too short excerpts from a marvellous diary kept by one of the crew of Sir Richard Edgcumbe's ship the *Anne of Fowey*, when he sailed with a fleet and 500 men to force certain Irish chieftains to make an oath of allegiance to King Henry VII. They had a rough old time, with westerlies blowing when they wanted to go west, and easterlies when they wanted to come back again: '. . . it blew so much, and the Coasts were so jeopardous of Sands and Rocks, that that night the Mariners durst not take the Sea, but lay still at Anchor about the seyd Isle, and there he and his company vowed gret Pilgrimages that God would cease the Tempest, and send a fair and large wind.' This document is in the possession of Lord Mount Edgcumbe. If it hasn't been published it ought to be because it is of great interest.

Headlands Gardens, which run down the cliff at Polruan, are very charming. **St Saviour's Chapel**, so little of which remains, was a Celtic foundation, was substantially rebuilt by Sir Richard Edgcumbe in 1488, was a chapel of ease for Lanteglos, was a place of pilgrimage for sailors returned from voyages. It started to fall into disuse towards the end of the 16th century. The sad remains of it, and the open space around it, were saved from speculative building by the Polruan Town Trust, to which more strength.

People who drive cars down Polruan High Street are doing their fellow men a disservice. At the bottom of it is the Lugger Inn, which I like very much indeed. On the wall of the public bar are two pictures of local topsail schooners, now departed: the *Waterwitch* and the *Katie* – both of which were engaged in shipping china clay out of Par not so long ago. There is a foot ferry here over to Fowey. Polruan is a most attractive place.

Inland, up the little stream that runs into **Pont Pill**, are two very interesting watermills. One has just been bought by the National Trust and is a fine corn mill. The other belongs to Colonel Shackerley's estate and is that rare thing, a water-driven sawmill – still in working order and still working – it saws wood up for the estate.

Further inland yet **Lanteglos** has a church the interior of which is so movingly beautiful that anybody going anywhere near this part of Cornwall who does not go and see it is making a very bad mistake. I will not describe it here: there is a good guide book within: I will merely say *go and see it*, and savour something of the clean simplicity of an uncorrupted faith.

CHAPTER 10

Fowey to Pentuan

❦

Fowey as a port of course includes Polruan. It was important of old: eight ships in the Bordeaux wine trade in 1303, 19 ships and 547 men against the French in 1337, 29 ships and 720 men against the Scots in 1342. It was then, besides being a port which supplied ships and men for the king's service, nothing more nor less than a nest of pirates, although these generally went under the more respectable name of privateers. The harbour was well defended, with a block house each side and a chain across the mouth. A Fowey man, Mark Mixtow, owned three privateers which he used against the French. A relation of his did not stop at the king's official enemies – but brought a Genoese carrack into the port – an enormously rich prize. It was said that until the middle of the 15th century piracy was the most important trade. But in Tudor times more legitimate trade had taken its place, and it is known that Fowey ships traded to St Malo, Morlaix, Roscoff, Greece, Jamaica, Guernsey and Spain. During the 19th century one export trade began to push out all the others. This became so big that by the 1870s big improvements were made to the harbour so that ships of 10,000 tons could lie alongside, and they still do, and the trade is china clay. Big ships are coming and going through the harbour mouth with great frequency – coming in high out of the water and going out loaded down well to their marks. The old railway to St Austell has been remade as a private haulage road, so that clay can be carried direct to the port without too much congestion on the public highway.

Up the beautiful estuary you can take a shallow draughted boat to **Lostwithiel**, which, as it was a very important port, must be mentioned. After the accession of Henry II in 1154 the Cornish tin industry made very rapid growth, and Cornwall was about the only known source of this metal in the known world. Bodmin became the centre of the tin area, and Lostwithiel a very important stannary port. Strangely, the Isle of Oléron, off the Garonne in France, became the international market for tin, much as Amsterdam is the world market for diamonds now although no diamonds are produced there. The Cornish tin was shipped straight to Oléron where

it was bought by merchants from all over Europe. In the 13th
century the chief stannary town (town in which it was lawful to deal
in tin) became Lostwithiel, and the port soon had a greater foreign
trade than all the Cinque Ports put together. Edmund Plantagenet,
who 'owned' all the tin in Cornwall although he never actually dug
any himself, had a great range of stone buildings called the Hall of

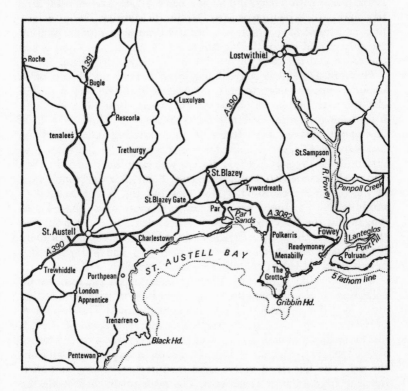

Stanners built in Lostwithiel. About this time the town became the
capital of the Duchy. But the tin mining, which made Lostwithiel
great, ultimately brought her down again. So much sediment was
discharged into the Fowey River from tin streaming works (alluvial
mining) that the river got shallower and shallower. This, added to
the fact that ships were getting deeper and deeper, drove the traffic
down-river to Fowey. By 1400 Lostwithiel itself had practically
ceased to be a sea port. Barges still traded to it from Fowey, however, until nearly 1900, and even after that timber was sometimes

rafted up the river from ships at anchor at Fowey. Small ketches, too, continued until about this period bringing limestone and coal up to the kilns a mile or two down the river.

A tiny wood on **Penpoll Creek** has a heronry in it.

There is a great cliff walk around **Readymoney Cove** and **Coombe Hawn** to **The Grotto**, where indeed is a grotto, and a storm beach with a beautiful lagoon behind it, and a beautiful little bay, and Lady Browning or Miss Daphne du Maurier. The latter lady lives at **Menabilly**, which is a beautiful house in a park (she has recently moved out of the big house into a smaller one) and it was this place that she used for the setting for her novel *Rebecca*.

Gribbin Head has a great big blind beacon up on top of it, useful for vessels trying to make St Austell Bay. The very beautiful cliff-top path brings the walker to **Polkerris**, which is a gem of a little fishing hamlet, and not *too* over-peopled. There is a little drying-out harbour here (there is an interesting painting in the pub showing a lugger running for it in a storm). The fine stone pier was built in 1735. A lifeboat station was established here in 1859 and in 1865 made two dramatic rescues. Soon after the launch most of the oars were smashed by the seas but the boat managed to scrabble into Par under sail and get some more oars. These lasted longer and the boat rescued twenty-one men and a cat from two stricken ships: the barque *Drydens* and the brig *Wearmouth*. Now there is no lifeboat and anyway nobody to man one. The fishing industry here is dead: killed by pollution by the china clay.

The pub is like a museum. There is the strangest and most exotic collection of objects hanging from every inch of wall and ceiling space in it that could possibly be brought together. The fine range of cannon outside it contains two rifled muzzle-loaders of 1876, a mortar with a primitive sight, or at least an elevation calibrator, of about 1790, and some other guns. One cannon was dredged up from the sea. The big rifled pieces were mounted at Fowey, and then taken to Menabilly as ornaments. The *white* turtle shell inside the pub is from a fresh-water turtle from the Amazon. Outside there is a fine and interesting double lime kiln, and the remains of a big Elizabethan 'pilchard palace' up aloft.

Par is the strangest little place and quite unlike anywhere else. An indication of its strangeness is that on the 2nd of July, 1971, a Welshman drank 62 pints of stout in the space of an hour at the Royal Hotel here, thus establishing a world record which, one feels, is likely to stand for a long time. *Stop press*. He beat it himself a month later.

The **Par Sands** (which we achieve after passing a part of the rocky cliff called Little Hell) are nearly as white as snow, and the reason for this, of course, is china clay. The sands are backed with a large caravan site for holidaymakers will have sand, white or black. The Par sands have a kind of sticky muddy consistency. Probably this will improve now that English China Clays Ltd has taken the momentous decision to stop polluting the ocean. Behind the caravans is a sprawling industrial housing area, mostly Victorian but with some modern housing too, which goes back to **Tywardreath**, once the site of an important abbey. *Ty* in Cornish means house, *Dreath* means beach. There is a railway junction and station at this place, lost in a marsh.

Everything at Par seems to be dusted with white, from, of course, the china clay. There are friendly working-class pubs and friendly Cornish clay workers. It is a very nice place. There are two entrancing little steam-driven locomotives shunting clay wagons on the railway leading to Par Harbour. It is hard to believe that any company would ever be crass enough to replace them. Par Harbour itself is small, surrounded by gigantic white buildings where china clay is subjected to its numerous processes, and where it is then loaded into ships with great speed and efficiency. Nothing much bigger than a thousand tonner can come into Par, but they are turned round once they get there so quickly that the tonnage that goes through the little harbour is very great, well over a million tons a year.

Par Harbour started as a copper ore port, shipping supplies in and ore out to South Wales, where it got smelted. It was in 1828 that John Thomas Austen, a mining adventurer, started building the harbour. In doing so he enclosed tidal flats and made a lot of new land, on which factories were built and industries started. He built an amazing aqueduct-cum-viaduct three miles inland from Par just before **Luxulyan** and this is 650 feet long, 98 feet high and it contains 200,000 cubic feet of granite. This brought china clay down to the little port, also granite which was used extensively in London and was also used for the monument placed on the field of the Battle of Waterloo. Into the port came plunger poles from Scandinavia (the long tree-trunks which, fastened together like giant rods, went down the mines from the great 'fire engines' to work the pumps that pumped the mines out), hemp, barrel staves (much china clay was exported in barrels, as were, of course, pilchards), iron, coal, mining machinery, tallow, salt, canvas, and general merchandise.

H. T. Treffry called in an engineer named Rendel to improve the harbour about 1840.

Permission to visit Par Harbour, and the complex of clay processing buildings around it, can readily be obtained from English China Clays Limited's very helpful public relations department in St Austell.

After a weird piece of coast, with a kind of a storm bar, a lagoon, hotels and a golf course, we come to **Charlestown**, another little artificial clay harbour, and another apparently lost and forgotten place – although lost and forgotten it is not, for it is currently being enlarged and improved for deeper draughted ships. There is here the headquarters of St Austell Divers, with a good shop selling under-water objects.

The harbour here was started in 1791, and the whole place – harbour and little village behind it – has a 1791 look about it. The place was called West Polmeare before the harbour was built, but renamed Charlestown afterwards. The adventurer who did it was Charles Rashleigh. At first copper ore was the chief export, but by 1850 15,000 wagon-loads of china clay were going out, brought down from the linhays by 150 full-time wagoners. A modern Dutch sluice gate is being fitted to the 'floating harbour'. It will lie down on the bottom for the ship to go over it instead of swinging to one side.

St Austell is an interesting and distinguished town, and the better for being a thriving and bustling commercial centre: the Johannesburg of the china clay fields. The carvings on the outside of the tower of Holy Trinity Church, including that of the Holy Trinity itself on the west face, are among the most distinguished pieces of sculpture in the West of England. The Pelican in Her Piety over the main door is a most sensitive piece, as are many of the gargoyles and other figures. Another fine building in St Austell is the Quaker Meeting House (1829) up the road to the station: there is something very satisfying about it.

St Austell flourishes on china clay, and so this industry must at least be briefly described. Whether we have walked or sailed to St Austell we will have for long been aware of a strange unearthly landscape, such as we imagined the Mountains of the Moon to be before men actually got to them: a kind of distant white fairyland, or magical country of sugar candy. No photograph ever gives a hint of the magical effect of this weird land when seen from a distance, and I personally have yet to see any really effective paintings of it either.

In the 8th century A.D. the manufacture of porcelain was discovered in China. The Chinese kept their secret for a thousand years, Many attempts were made in Europe to crack it, but nothing but stuff called 'artificial porcelain' was produced. In 1710 Johan Bottger discovered the secret in Saxony. It was – a mixture of kaolin ('china clay') and ground 'china-stone'. The secret quickly spread to Austria and Venice but not to England. By 1740, 'artificial' porcelain works were set up at Bow, Chelsea, Derby and Worcester, but there was no true English porcelain.

In 1768 though, the great breakthrough was made. William Cookworthy, a Quaker of Kingsbridge, Devon, found the way, independently, of making true porcelain from what was locally known as *moor stone, china-stone* or *growan* mixed with kaolin, locally known as *growan clay*. Thus was the English porcelain industry born, and also the great china clay industry of Cornwall and Devon.

The china clay, or kaolin, is a product of the decomposition of granite by hot acidic gasses or fluids forced up under great pressure from the earth's interior. The kaolin itself is the felspar constituent of the granite: the mica and quartz have to be separated out of it. Some of the mica is then removed from the resulting sand to make 'Muscovite mica', used for such purposes as making the 'glitter' for Christmas decorations, or extending paint, or in welding electrode coatings. The sand left, which is pure quartz, is known as 'silver sand'. The 'china-stone', which has to be ground up and mixed with the pure kaolin to make porcelain, is merely a kind of granite, which is found in the china clay areas. China clay is unsuitable for making porcelain by itself: the 'china-stone' acts as a filler, and a flux. melting in the firing and sticking the other ingredients together into a hard mass.

The original method of mining the china clay was by directing streams into the pits already formed while gangs of men dug up and dislodged the decomposed granite over which the streams ran, so that the water carried the clay away in suspension. Having got to the bottom of the pit the water was generally led through a tunnel to the bottom of a pump shaft, and pumped to the surface by a big 'Cornish engine'. It was then run into tanks and allowed to settle for several months until most of the water had evaporated away, the damp clay cut into lumps which were air dried, and what was left was kaolin.

The method now is to aim very high-pressure jets of water at the clay face by remote-controlled jets called monitors. The water, with the clay in suspension, runs down to a sump in the bottom of the pit, is pumped to the surface by centrifugal pumps, freed of water by big filter presses (the water is forced out by pressure through filters which retain the clay) then dried in big kilns. Ninety per cent of the kaolin goes to the paper and ceramic industries, the rest into rubber, paint, plastics, insecticides and fertilizers (as a binding agent). A great many people in the St Austell area work in the industry (some 7000 altogether). The deepest pits are now 400 feet deep. The clay occurs in funnel-shaped masses, for this is the shape made by the hot fluids as they were forced up from below through the granite.

A very welcome decision made recently is to pump the waste water into old clay pits and not into the sea. This will avoid the progressive silting up of St Austell Bay, the killing of large areas of fishing ground, and a general fouling of the shores and beaches. It will cost the company a lot to do and it is a triumph of the conservationist lobby that they are doing it.

A walk through the china clay area is an extraordinary experience. Again, E.C.C. Ltd are very willing to take people around, in parties, and their public relations office in St Austell will arrange this.

There is a slight recession in the industry at this time, owing to two factors. One is that chalk has been found, when treated properly, to be an acceptable substitute for china clay for many filling purposes. English China Clays are therefore diversifying by buying up chalk pits in the south-east of England, but this is no consolation to clay workers fearing for their jobs and wanting to go on living in Cornwall. The other is that china-stone, when used for certain industrial purposes, gives off deleterious hydrofluoric fumes, and so a stone is being imported from the Continent which doesn't, which reduces the market for china-stone. Again a blow at Cornish economy.

Back at the coast, south of Charlestown, we find a rocky shore, the only sandy beach here is the prerogative of the campers of **Duporth** Holiday Camp only (they reach it through a sunken pathway, and it is most effectively fenced off). At **Porthpean** is a small beach and a sailing club. There is a sort of cliff path along here, which can be followed by locating the kissing gates which have been erected along it, but it is very badly marked and it is terribly easy to lose it.

The headland beyond **Trenarren** is heathy, bosky and beautiful, and west of **Black Head** is a marvellous little south-facing beach nicely inaccessible. The path leads on to the splendid seafaring village of **Pentewan**.

I could wish that the *vast* (3000 standings) caravan site just to the south of this place were nearly anywhere else than where it is, for Pentewan is a perfect example of a real old schooner port and village. Most of the larger houses were the homes of schooner officers or owners, the smaller ones of forecastle hands, or of people engaged in the many trades and activities connected with keeping ships at sea and trading. The place would be of great interest to an industrial archaeologist. There is a long leet bringing water from higher up the Pentewan Stream, and supplying four big pounds, now empty and grown up with alder and willow, and the pounds were used for flushing the harbour out to keep it clear and also for driving two mills: one in later years a bone meal mill. There was also a gunpowder factory here until late 19th century. Some of the sluice gate mechanisms, etc. can still be discovered.

The harbour was built in the 1820s by Sir Christopher Hawkins, and it was connected to St Austell by a tramway, down which china clay was brought by gravity and the empty trucks taken up again by horses. There is one school of thought which says that the water leet was once a transport canal, antedating the tramway, but I have not found any local person who believes this. About 1860, steam loco-motives replaced horses on the railway. In ancient times a quarry for very good freestone was operated at Pentewan: the lovely church at Lanteglos was built of it. Pentewan's own church is contemporary with the harbour, and very unusual in that it is built, like a terraced council house, in the middle of a row of dwelling houses: putting God well in His place – just one of the neighbours. It is a distin-guished late Georgian building though, as are the houses of the neighbours.

The harbour now has its entrance completely silted up, and the basin is a lagoon cut off from the sea at all but very high tides. When I last saw it a pair of swans was nesting right in the entrance to the basin. Local people have photographs of schooners lying in the basin, and of one schooner cast up on the rocks to the north of the channel, from which she was never salvaged. The last cargo of china clay came out in the 1930s, in the schooner *Duchess*, but sand was still being sailed away from the beach (where was a large grading plant) up until the Second World War.

The place now has not been spoiled, although the pubs, which must have been splendid sailors' pubs, have been much tarted-up. The beach here is a wide sandy one which, because of the paucity of sandy beaches in Cornwall, is terribly crowded in the summer. Currently a lot of china clay sediment comes down the river, but this will cease, it is hoped, when the new non-pollution policy of E.C.C. Ltd gets working.

Up the pretty valley is a village called the **London Apprentice**, and near here, at **Trewhiddle**, the oldest chalice known was dug up in 1774. It is believed to be 8th century. It is in the British Museum.

CHAPTER 11

Mevagissey to the Fal

NOBODY could not like **Mevagissey**, and in the winter, when it is not too crowded, it is a marvellous place. In its beautiful harbour, which has an inner basin and an outer one and fine great breakwaters, is a fine fleet of fishing vessels which somehow has weathered the storms of centuries, for from its position Mevagissey had to be a fishing port. For one thing it has a good fishing ground sheltered from the west wind right at its front door, which means blow the wind high or blow it low as long as it stays in the prevailing quarter men can get out and fish. It was far enough west in the pilchard days to be right in the heart of the pilchard industry: in the 18th century it was the fourth largest centre in the Duchy and some 35 million pilchards were sent every year from this port alone to Italy! Inaccessibility by land from markets did not matter when the chief fishery sent all its produce abroad by water.

There was a harbour pier in the 16th century, it was rebuilt in 1775. After the Napoleonic wars there was a tremendous revival of the pilchard industry. By 1850 there were 80 big luggers here manned by about 300 men. By that time many trading schooners were being built in Mevagissey yards, and the place was a schooner-owning port too. Ships were needed to take pilchards away and barrel staves in: the latter from such places as Russia, Scandinavia, and North America.

In 1866 the outer pier was built, increasing the harbour from three-and-a-half to ten acres and making it a low tide harbour too: vessels could never get into the inner harbour at low tide. There was a lifeboat soon after that (called the *South Warwickshire*) and on her first mission, in 1869, to a Bordeaux sailing ship, she was flung right up on the beach by a wave but her crew managed to re-launch her, got themselves off the ship, and beach the boat on Par Sands. They were said to have been in a condition of complete exhaustion when they landed.

There is no lifeboat here now, as lifeboats became motorized and the range of them increased, each station could cover a much larger area. Hence the demise of so many stations. The lifeboat house at

Mevagissey has now been turned into an aquarium, run by the two brothers who run the aquarium at Fowey, and very well run too. Keepers of much larger and more ambitious aquaria could learn a lot about displaying and keeping sea fish by visiting the aquaria at Fowey and Mevagissey. They are both stocked entirely by the local fishermen: when I last saw Mevagissey aquarium there was a sturgeon in it: caught, unharmed, in a ray net.

The fishermen of Mevagissey, in their 'dandies', 'toshers' and 'luggers', engage in practically every known form of inshore fishing. There are a few small otter trawlers, there are crab potters, hand liners, long liners and ray netters. The latter engine, called in other places a tangle net, is simply a large-meshed (3½-inch 'bar') long net of very fine nylon, eight foot high, sunk to the bottom, on rocky ground as a rule, where its weighted foot line and moderately floated headline cause it to stand up like a wall in the water, and fish become tangled in its meshes. Crabs are caught like this in large numbers. As a rule they have to be sold as 'dressed crab' because it is hard not to break them when taking them out. Rays, and skate, turbot, plaice, brill, lobsters and many other fish are also taken, and for a man in a small boat (like a 'dandy boat') it can be a very profitable form of fishing. More about it under Newlyn.

Long lining takes two forms: true long lining or *boultering*, and *spiltering*. The spilter line is a fine line with small wire hooks (Mustad No. 10) on it: three good men may work up to 3000 hooks tied four-foot-six apart on the line – and the prey is chiefly whiting. It is a summer and autumn job, when the whiting are in, and is tending to be a dying trade as whiting are more easily caught in the trawl. It is extremely hard work: all the hooks have to be baited with bits of pilchard or mackerel or other fish (try baiting 3000 hooks if you are not a fisherman!), it is hard to pay the line out and get it back without snarling it, or getting a hook sunk into your hand, or even some other part of your anatomy.

True long lining is called boultering when the line is slightly shorter than the true long line which has maybe a thousand hooks on it. There is one lugger at Mevagissey which has a crew of five young men and which shoots a line nine miles long with 7000 hooks on it! It takes at least forty stone of bait to bait all these hooks. The difference between true long lining and spiltering is that in the former the line is much heavier and the hooks are much bigger (Alcock No. 5 swivels), and the quarry is not whiting but such big things as conger eel, hake, skate, cod, ling, dog fish and other large fish. Conger eel are the mainstay of the Cornish long liners, and it is nothing for a brace of men to haul in half a ton of them in a night. These, and dog fish, are sent to the Midland cities where they are sold as 'rock salmon' in fish and chip shops: a piece of salesmanship that surely it would be hard to beat!

To go long lining from Mevagissey is an exciting experience. You may spend the afternoon baiting lines. These lines are coiled down in baskets, each basket holding from three to four hundred hooks spaced nine foot apart (thus twice as far apart as spilter hooks). The hooks hang over the rim of the basket, and the bitter end of the line comes up from the bottom and hangs loose ready to be bent on to the top of the next line before the latter is shot. Your boat may put out in the evening: possibly soon enough for you to hope to snatch a pint or two before the pubs close on your return. Starting your motors (most of the luggers have two engines – a main engine and a 'winger' – the latter a smaller engine for pushing the vessel along very slowly while the line is being worked) you put out to sea, steam maybe a couple of hours, throw the *dahn* away (a buoy with a flag staff on it), the *dahn line*, the *buff* (another buoy but without a flag staff), the *creeper line* which is an anchor line, the *creeper* which is a little anchor with many flukes, and then the long line. The latter flies away at a great speed and it takes skill to fling it clear – a hook in your hand then can be a horrible experience and men have been dragged overboard and drowned by it. A knife is always kept handy for instant use. Basket after basket of line is shot away until you come to the last, then another *creeper* goes, its line, another buff and another *dahn*. You then head for port – and those pints.

You get up at perhaps four or five in the morning, walk sleepily down to the harbour, and steam off again in the darkness. Perhaps just as light is beginning to break you find your first *dahn*, pick it up, and start hauling.

Suddenly, down there in the clear water, you see what looks like a small eel coming up. It is not a small eel but a large conger, and as it gets nearer the surface you realize this. When it reaches the surface one man gaffs it with a large gaff, hauls it over the rail, wrenches the hook out of its mouth with a small hook mounted on a handle, and gaffs the fish into the fish hold. If it were left on deck it would either bite somebody or get overboard again. By then there is probably another conger coming up, and good timing and co-operation are needed between the two men – the line hauler and the gaffer – so that neither of them is overloaded and the fish keep coming in with an even rhythm. Every now and then a small shark called a rough dog comes in. This is useless (the only place where there is a sale for rough dogs is Brighton for some extraordinary reason – there it is absorbed into the 'rock salmon' scene – nowhere else will anybody touch it). The rough dog is given a bang on the side of the boat which both stuns it and gets the hook out of its mouth. Everything else is hauled in. If there are more than two hands the ones not engaged in fishing set to work and 'ready' the lines as they come in, paying them into other baskets with the line neatly coiled and the hooks over the edge ready for baiting. When the end of the line is reached, and the second *dahn* got aboard, the main engine is started again, and it's full speed ahead for home, all hands except the helmsman readying the lines for the evening. You get home for breakfast (which by God you enjoy!) and then go down to the boat again to unload the catch in baskets, weigh it, and clean the boat down. You then have the day off until the afternoon baiting session.

The fishermen of Mevagissey have formed themselves into Mevagissey Fisheries Limited, which is a co-operative society, and is doing extremely well with a turnover now of £100,000 per annum.

There is a very good book in preparation about Mevagissey fishing: *Inshore Fishing* by Stan Judd (Fishing News Ltd). Mr Judd is a local fisherman, currently engaged in long lining. Incidentally he runs, in the summer, a Fisheries Exhibition down by the harbour, in which actual fishing gear and wall charts are used to explain the esoteric arts of fishing to the layman. There is also a good museum by the harbour. The 'Pilchard Grill' was once a pilchard palace: i.e. a curing shed. Most of the little 'knick-knack' shops down by the harbour, selling curios, were once the offices of fish merchants. But the harbour is still a real fishing harbour and is expanding and not contracting. There are plenty of boats taking anglers out (mostly mackerelling, but to ground marks too), there are shark fishing boats, and anybody willing to work hard, who owns a good motor boat, can earn a living for himself for most of the year simply by plummeting and feathering for mackerel. It is an easy harbour for yachts to sail into, and there is plenty of room to lie in the Outer Harbour.

Portmellon, just south of Mevagissey, is being much attacked by the sea: so much so that a nice range of cottages down by the beach has been condemned. One feels it would not be beyond the wit of man to save them. The Rising Sun, though, seems unlikely to set yet, being slightly higher up the hill. Percy Mitchell and Sons run a big boatyard here, in this unlikely place with no vestige of a harbour, and they launch their quite large decked fishing boats and well built yachts straight into the sea. They will build up to fifty

On the Helford River.

Porthallow.

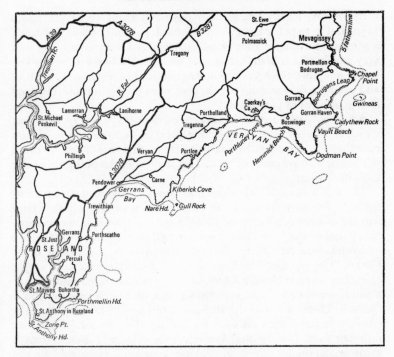

feet in length. Their big shed is on the site of an old pilchard palace. When a high tide coincides with a strong south-easter the place gets flooded. Mitchell's took over in 1925 from Roberts, a venerable builder of Cornish luggers.

Chapel Point is windy and exhilarating, and the monastic-looking buildings on it are the dwellings of wealthy – and fortunate – people. Near here is **Bodrugan's Leap**. Over this daunting cliff, the story goes, Sir Henry Bodrugan rode his horse – to arrive safely below and leap into a boat which was to take him to France. Sir Henry was a Yorkist, fought on the wrong side (or at least the losing one) at Bosworth, and joined in Lambert Simnel's rebellion against Henry VII. After this last unfortunate affair he saved his life by the afore-mentioned leap but lost all his estates, which were handed over to the Edgcumbe family by the king. The Edgcumbes knew which side their bread was buttered on, and did very well out of sequestered properties subsequently at the Reformation.

Bodrugan, which is a big farm, is behind the hill to the west (a footpath goes straight to it from Chapel Point). The Bodrugans were a rip-roaring family before their downfall, rising to wealth about 1250, and in 1475 Sir Henry was knighted. He built here at Bodrugan a splendid fortified manor house, acted (like his ancestors) the part very much of a robber baron, was continually being taken to law by his neighbours for various outrages but always got away with it, and owned a fleet of ships which, besides engaging in trade, engaged in a good deal of piracy too.

A fine footpath runs all the way round the cliffs to **Gorran Haven**, which is another very early fishing port: in fact one of the earliest references to the seine net, which was in this case a net to catch pilchards, was a *Taxatio* of 1272. This is proof of the antiquity of this form of fishing.

There is a strange little church at Gorran Haven, stuck up amid cottages almost overhanging the sea. It seems most likely that here was the oratory of a Celtic saint, although there is no direct evidence to say that it was. The dedication is to St Just St Just was associated in Wales with St Gwrin. Gorran Haven is in the parish of St Goran. The present building, though, is 15th century. It was a chapel of ease for Gorran Churchtown, was desecrated and used as a fish store, then as a non-conformist chapel, and is now back as a church. There are two mysterious recesses within: one thought possibly to have been an oven for baking Holy Bread (which was different from Consecrated Wafer). This subject is discussed with great erudition by Mr J. H. Adams in a little book sold in the church.

Gorran Haven has a harbour, or at least the vestige of one: a practicable harbour for beaching boats in. In 1585 it is known that there was a quay. The present structure was built in 1885 by the Williams family who lived at Caerhays 'Castle', just along the coast. By the harbour can be discerned a watch house, or water guard house, a lime kiln and pilchard cellars. The Watch House, as the house of the preventive men was called, was once used as a chapel. It is a very pleasant little village, of jumbled cottages up the hillside.

I have seen a pair of ravens who looked as though they were nesting above **Cadythew Rock**. **Bow** or **Vault Beach** is a super beach. **Dodman Point**, where is a promontory fort, is beautiful: a blaze of yellow gorse in spring time. There is a large granite cross on the end of it erected 'In firm hope of the Second Coming of our Lord.' The National Trust has managed to acquire a patchwork of bits of land here, like a jig-saw puzzle. **Hemmick Beach** is also super, particularly when the wind is east and the sun is west.

Boswinger has a youth hostel and a caravan site, inland and well sited.

The whole shore of **Veryan Bay** is wild, lonely and unspoiled. It is a vast sweep of beautiful coastline, mercifully cut-off and hard to get to by motor car.

Caerhays Castle is a Victorian-Gothic extravaganza to beat all. It was built by the Williams family, which had made a lot of money in mining, and is the centre still of a large and feudal-seeming estate. **Porthluney Cove** is sheltered and beautiful, the park and woodlands of Caerhays are English parkland at its best, and the valley that runs inland from here is superb countryside. One cannot but envy the occupants of Caerhays. **Portholland**, a mile further on, is equally enviable, although this little mini-hamlet has been called 'the graveyard' by cynical estate workers: only because of the enlightened policy of the estate in allowing elderly retired workers, principally widows, to live out their days here. The valley that runs inland from Portholland is idyllic.

Tregenna has pony riding and a caravan camp, again back from the coast, of a humane size, and well sited.

Portloe is another dreamy Cornish fishing village, and there are still real live fishermen here: five full-time boats, of the traditional and beautiful design of the South Cornish beach boat, each working about a hundred crab pots. Mr Fred Trevarden is the Uncrowned Mayor and Harbourmaster and knows more about the place than anybody else. The Lugger is a posh licensed restaurant but not an inn. The Ship, further up the street, is very much an inn, a very good one, and the landlady's home-made soup is something well worth experiencing.

Further on, round **Nare Head**, is mostly National Trust and very rugged and beautiful. **Kiberick Cove** is a nice rocky beach, with steps cut down the cliff to it: thank God very hard to get to by motor car.

Gerrans Bay is wild and unspoiled. It was too wild for the German four-masted barque *Hera* when, in February 1914, she struck the Whelps, a submerged reef off the Gull Rocks, and sank in ten minutes. Some of the crew got into the boats but were immediately capsized. Of the ones who clung to the rigging of the wreck, the First Mate, Second Mate and two seamen died of exhaustion, three men fell into the sea and were lost, and Falmouth lifeboat, which was towed to the scene by the tug *Perran*, took the handful of men who still clung on for their lives at 3.30 in the morning.

Pendower House is now an hotel, and one of the most attractive-looking ones from the outside that you could find. It has a veranda which gives it a stately colonial look, added to by the lush, almost tropical look of the little valley by which it stands. In front of it is a long and very good beach, and in the rockier parts of this a very good winkle can be found: a nice-sized winkle – not one of your mini-winkles that is not worth wielding a pin to.

Carne Beacon, just to the east, has a tumulus said to be the grave of one variously known as King Gerennius, St Gerrans, Geraint of the Round Table, Blarens or St Gerent. The tumulus was opened in 1855 and charred bones were revealed: the thing was a Bronze Age *kistvaen*, or tomb. **Gerrans Bay** is named after this saintly king, and the legend is that his body was rowed across the bay in a golden boat propelled by silver oars after he had 'crowned a happy life with a fair death'. He is supposed to have founded the church of **Gerrans**, which is dedicated to him. This is an interesting church, with a tower that is a good seamark, a fine Celtic cross outside (the cross was superimposed on a stone circle. It is sometimes supposed that these stone circles were Druidic – and crosses were cut on them after Christianity came). Inside are some fine bench ends. The parish registers are said to be very complete and of great interest, but I have not seen them.

Porthscatho, just down the hill by the sea, was once a fishing place but is now just a holiday resort.

St Anthony Head has a lighthouse of 1825 and is National Trust. **St Anthony in Roseland** has a beautiful little church, which was founded in 1124 by William Warlewast, Bishop of Exeter, and dedicated to St Anthony who was a 3rd-century Egyptian monk. The bishop also founded here a cell for two Augustinian monks, or canons. The little priory, or cell of the priory of Plympton which is what it was (in 1273 a monk here, Peter, became Prior of Plympton Priory), was, after the Dissolution, turned into the present mansion of Place (which means *palace* in Cornish) and which is now a beautifully sited hotel. The crests of Henry VIII and Anne Boleyn are carved on a front pew of the church, and it is said that this happy pair spent their honeymoon here. A Saxon arch was found in the outside wall of the church (covered with masonry), so William Warlewast's building wasn't the first here. Two skeletons were also unearthed, one on each side of the altar. These are thought to have been the remains of Peter, the monk who became Prior of Plympton, and David Bercley, who was also Prior and who died about 1507. The church, which has a spire put there at the request of seafarers to act as a seamark, has a fine Norman door, but is predominantly Early English.

Percuil, called **Porthcuel** on the Ordnance Survey map, is now the headquarters of Mr Jack Ward who repairs and maintains yachts, the Percuil Sailing Club, and an oyster laying of Mac-Fisheries. The river, although overcrowded with moored yachts (which never seem to take to the sea, winter or summer) is very beautiful.

The oyster layings are used for growing on and fattening seed oysters brought from Brittany, nowadays all the way by motor lorry. They are thrown down just below low water mark in the mud, 'worked' from time to time to keep them from becoming silted up, and, when fat, sent to the purifying plant in the Helford River to be cleaned. We will discuss the oyster farming more fully when we come to Helford. Mr Rowe, the manager of the oyster farm here, has a most engaging tame robin.

In spite of what the latest Ordnance Survey maps will tell you there is *no* ferry at Percuil or Porthcuel. But there is, if you can swim, or persuade somebody to put you over, or if you have your own boat, a pleasant footpath to St Mawes.

St Mawes was founded by, or at least named for, one St Mawe or St Mauditus, a 6th-century Welsh prince who turned monk, was driven from Wales by Saxons, and built himself an oratory at St Mawes here and carved himself a stone chair near a holy well. The well is just above the Victory Inn, but the stone chair is built into a house. These stone chairs of the early Celtic saints were presumably the forerunners of the modern *eisteddfodau*, and the Chairs awarded to the Welsh and Cornish bards. St Mawe is supposed to have left here and crossed to Brittany, where he settled on an island in the bay of St Malo. He became an abbot and is honoured as St Maudez in Brittany.

St Mawes Castle was built in 1542, one of the many artillery forts built round the coast by Henry VIII. St Mawes never saw shots fired in anger: when Fairfax led his army up to it on 12 March 1646 the governor, Hannibal Bonython, sensibly decided to surrender it without a blow. The Roundheads thus captured thirteen pieces of cannon and 160 small arms. A survey of 1609 says that the castle had two sakers and an iron minion on the roof, a culverin and six demi-culverins of iron and one of brass on the bastions, two culverins and a brass saker in the courtyard. The calibre of a minion was $3\frac{1}{4}$ inches and it weighed about half a ton, a saker was $3\frac{1}{2}$ inches and it weighed 1500 pounds, a culverin was $5\frac{1}{2}$ inch calibre and weighing nearly two tons. The fort is interesting in plan and construction: being of an unusual clover-leaf shape. It is highly defensible from the sea, but, as Hannibal Bonython so sensibly decided, no great shakes when attacked from the land.

There was a stone pier at St Mawes as early as 1536 (the place lies very exposed to southerlies), and in 1854 the St Mawes Pier and Harbour Company built the present harbour. It was almost washed away in 1872 but was rebuilt the next year. There are many boat-yards at St Mawes, many expensive houses in large bosky gardens, many yachts and sailing dinghies, a frequent ferry service over to Falmouth and all summer a constant coming and going of passenger launches. A large pig of tin was found in the sea near here, of a shape which indicated great antiquity. Until 1832 St Mawes sent two members to Parliament.

Roseland, which is the beautiful name of the peninsula on which St Mawes stands, was not called after roses, but from the word *rhos* which is Cornish, and Welsh, for heathy country. **St Just-in-Roseland** is much visited by tourists just because of its name, although it is, indeed, an attractive village, with a sub-tropical feel about it. The St Just part of the name may have come from St Jestyn, who was supposed to have been the son of Geraint of the Arthurian legend, and who carried his father's body over the bay in the golden boat.

CHAPTER 12

The Fal

❧

THE east bank of the Fal and the Truro River are mercifully inaccessible to motor cars. The steep banks are clad in woods of small sessile oaks, and the latter are cut down and stripped of their bark which is used for tanning, as the bark of oaks should be. **Malpas** is the low-tide port for Truro, for here the numerous motor boats which ply for hire on these estuaries embark and disembark their passengers. If you are in Falmouth and want to get to Truro, or in Truro and want to get to Falmouth, by far the pleasantest way to do it is in one of these motor launches.

Truro was built where so many county towns were built: at the highest point of navigation and the lowest point of fordability of a tidal river. It is still a port: Fyffes import bananas to it and Cornwall Farmers' Co-operative still bring in cattle food and fertilizer by water. As fuel oil gets scarcer and more expensive Truro will resume its old maritime importance.

Being in the heart of the tin country Truro had to be a port. Henry II gave it a charter in 1156 and at that time tin was being shipped to the Island of Oléron, off the Brittany coast, which for some reason had established itself as the tin-exchange of Europe, just as Amsterdam is now the diamond-exchange and London the fur-exchange. Merchants came from all over Western Europe to Oléron to buy tin. In 1296 Edward I started buying all the tin produced in Cornwall to re-sell at a profit to finance his wars. In 1377 and again in 1404 Truro was well looted by the French, who presumably sailed up the Fal to do it. By the 16th century the assaying and 'coining' of a third of the tin produced in Cornwall was being done in Truro. Coining consisted in cutting a corner off a block of tin for assay. When this had been done, and the heavy duty paid to the Duchy of Cornwall, the ingot was stamped and could then be exported.

But by the 17th century Truro began to dwindle in importance as an actual shipping place, for the deeper draughted ships then coming into vogue began to use places nearer the mouth of the Fal. Truro remained a very prosperous place, however, through the Georgian period, being the centre of commerce and also of elegance and culture of the Duchy, and this is why there is still much good architecture in the little town. The best view of the cathedral is from the Cattle Market. Yachts can still get up to Truro at high water, and more should.

Coming downstream again, on the west bank, **Coombe** would be a good place at which to study the main industry of the Fal system of estuaries: oysters. From the 1st of October to the 31st of March some thirty-two little sailing boats are to be seen sailing up-tide and dredging (still under sail) down, in most parts of the Truro River, Fal, Restronguet Creek, Tresillian River and Carrick Roads, after oysters. The reason why these boats still work under sail is very simple: they are not allowed to do anything else. The Duchy of Cornwall and the Truro City Council both insist that no oysters shall be dredged by any boat that has an engine in it, but within that restriction anybody can dredge, provided that he pays the licence fee which is £16 per dredge. This is certainly the most sensible and civilized arrangement that could possibly be made. If motors were allowed the oyster beds would be destroyed in a season. In order to protect them a monopoly would have to be given to one or two operators, who would then get rich while all the other oystermen were out of a living. As it is anybody who can get a boat and has the strength can do it, and everybody who does it makes a good living all winter, and is freed in summer to work on the pleasure boats, or go sea fishing, or otherwise engage in the summer seasonal jobs that are so easy to come by in Cornwall. Also, the sight of these beautiful sailing boats plying their trade all over the estuary is extremely pleasant.

The dredgermen use what are locally called 'work boats'. These, built locally, are half-decked boats from 24 to 30 feet long, and drawing from four-foot-six to five feet of water. This comparatively deep draught for estuary boats is necessary so that they can sail to windward well, for obviously they are having to do this much of the time. They draw most water aft, have fine and beautiful under-water lines, are transom sterned and cutter rigged. In the summer, when their owners use them for racing in numerous regattas, they set big jack-yard topsails, in the winter while working they usually dispense with these but set only their gaff mainsails, foresails and jibs. They cling to the gaff mainsail because they need the driving power that a bermuda mainsail would not give them. Some of the bigger ones tow up to six dredges, and it takes considerable power to drag these over the bottom, although of course much of the power comes from the tide and not from the wind.

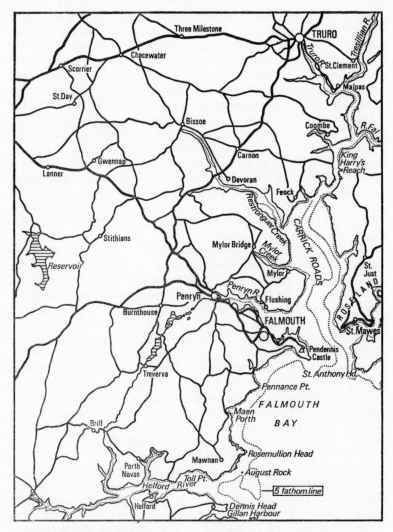

The dredges are heavy bag nets set on iron frames which keep their mouths open and which hold them as they are dragged along the bottom of the estuary. The foot bar of the frames has teeth which cut into the mud of the bottom and hook out the oysters. The bellies of the nets are protected by chain-link armour. One man can work two dredges. Most of the boats are worked single-handed, in which case two dredges are the limit. Some of the larger boats have two or even three men in them, however, and work more dredges. The dredging calls for great skill and experience. Either the tide or the wind, or both, are used for the motive power needed to haul the heavy dredges through the mud of the bottom: a boat pulling dredges is like a boat dragging heavy anchors. The dredges are seldom pulled from the stern, but more often over the side of the vessel, and the boat crabs sideways through the water, steering herself not with her rudder but by the placement of the dredge warps. The dredgerman has to play a little tune with his dredge warps, his rudder, his three sails, the wind, and the tide: when a perfect balance has been achieved between all these forces and agents then the boat is dredging effectively. At the beginning of the season a good man will get a thousand oysters a day. Towards the end he is pleased to get four hundred. The oysters when they come up cannot be sold immediately for eating.

The Fal waters are heavily loaded with copper from old mine workings, and the oysters that feed in it are a bright green colour and the copper content is too high for safety. The oysters must be sold to people who lay them down in copper-free waters elsewhere, such as the Helford River, or Penryn Harbour, or Porthcuel, and after they have voided their copper (and become 'white oysters') they are put into purifying tanks which clean them completely and remove all bacterial infection, and then they can be sold. There is strict government supervision at this stage. Hitherto the wild oysters were simply dumped on the bottom of the estuary somewhere and either dredged up, or picked up at low spring tide, as required after they had voided their copper content and also become fatter and bigger. Now experiments are being made with wooden frames covered with nylon fabric into which the oysters are put. This of course leads to much less loss of oysters.

Besides the sailing boats there are, in these waters, about the same number of boats called 'punts'. These are not punts at all, but boat-shaped boats, and each boat is fitted with a powerful hand-operated windlass in her bows. The punts are operated by the crew dropping a very heavy anchor, rowing stern-first for perhaps a hundred yards paying out anchor line from the windlass as they do so, dropping their dredges over the stern, and then winding the boat up to the anchor again by the use of the windlass. In other words it is all done by muscle-power. It works perfectly well and the 'punt' men do nearly as well as their brethren in the more expensive sailing boats, but whether they work under sail or under oar and windlass, the dredgermen of the Fal are a hardy lot, much stronger and tougher than most people are today and, as one of them told me, 'they ail nothing'. They are not allowed to kill themselves working though: the permitted hours for dredging are from nine in the morning to three in the afternoon. Mr F. A. Gunn, who lives right here at Coombe and who is the Bailiff for the City of Truro, watches every trick, and any man who contravenes the regulations immediately loses his licence. In particular no oyster that can be got through a ring of $2\frac{5}{8}$ inches diameter may be taken. The net result of all this control is that the oysters do not diminish, and the fishery goes on flourishing from year to year unlike so many other fisheries in other places.

Devoran was a tin exporting port such as Truro, although never so important. But in 1824 it was connected with the Redruth and Chacewater tin country by railway, and a lot of tin concentrate was exported to be smelted elsewhere. In 1830 55,000 tons of freight a year were going through Devoran. Its *raison d'être* was its undoing, however, for the river which fed it brought so much sediment down from the tin-streaming works that Restronguet Creek became silted up and Devoran died as a port. **Point** was also a busy little port.

Mylor Creek is now much used by yachtsmen, and very pleasant it is. There is a little privately-owned harbour and a large boat-hiring and sailing centre. St Mylor church is interesting and beautiful and in a marvellous setting. St Mylor was probably the Melor who is still honoured in Brittany, and who lived in the 5th century. He probably resided here for some time: the farm near the church is called Tawithic; it was once called Lanwythek and this means 'the Monastery among the trees'. There is a legend that St Melor was martyred at this spot in A.D. 411. Of course Cornwall, Brittany and Wales were practically one country with one culture in the 5th century. There is a fine Celtic cross near the south porch.

Mylor was fortunate in its epitaph writers of long ago: consider the following splendid piece of verse.

> Alass frend Joseph –
> His end war Allmost Sudden
> As tho' the mandate came
> Express from heaven –
> his foot, it slip and he did fall
> help help he cries – and that was all

This was Joseph Crapp, a shipwright, died 1770. Or the final lines of the inscription on the monument to Francis Trefusis within the church:

> Yett ere the welcome summons hee obeyed,
> 'Pardon my enemies', he calmly cried,
> 'As Jesus did pardon dear God' and died.

Or the gravestone to Thomas James, which tells us that he was shot by a 'Cus-toms officer':

> Officious zeal in luckless hour laid wait
> and wilful sent the murd'rous ball of fate
> James to his home (which late in health he left)
> Wounded returns – of life is soon bereft.

In 1866 the training ship H.M.S. *Ganges IV* was moored offshore here full of boys learning to be sailors. She was transferred to Shotley in Suffolk and her name eventually transferred to a shore station there which is still functioning. We have seen her figurehead and stern cabin at Burgh Island at Bigbury-on-Sea, in Devon.

There are pleasant walks from Mylor to Flushing, one of them a footpath past Trelew Farm, the other along the coast past Restronguet Sailing Club: either on top of the little cliff or, at low tide, rock-hopping below. If the latter route is taken you will see the stone obelisk standing on the foreshore with the letters 'T.B.' carved on it. This was placed there after a legal action in the 18th century whereby the Mayor of Truro lost his ancient jurisdiction over the whole of Falmouth Harbour as far down as Black Rock. The upstart Falmouth won its right to its own waters, and this obelisk was set up to mark the west end of the boundary between Truro waters and those of Falmouth. It is still jealously observed: particularly by the two authorities which control the oyster dredgings, and once every six years the Mayor of Truro 'traces' out the letters on the pillar in his beating of the bounds. Further on are the *gazonnes*, two rocky inlets caused by lines of weakness in the heavily striated rock. One of these was once connected by a tunnel to the Trefusis's mansion. This was foolishly closed in 1891.

Flushing was thus named by Dutch drainage engineers and *polderjongen*, or dykers, who came here in the 17th century to build sea walls and quays. When they did so Flushing was but a small place, but as Penryn and, later, Falmouth over the water, became more and more important and took the trade away from Truro, Flushing grew larger. Flushing's period of glory was in the heyday of the Packet ships. In 1688 the Post Office chose Falmouth for the base for a fleet of fast sailing ships which were to carry the mail between Britain and most of the countries bordering the Atlantic and Mediterranean. They were tiny ships, mostly of about 150 tons (smaller than a large Thames barge), some brigantine rigged (two-masted vessels with square sails on the foremast and fore-and-aft sails on the after), others ship-rigged (three masts all square-sail-rigged), privately owned and chartered to the Post Office, carrying from thirty men and boys to up to fifty in times of war. They were lightly armed with six-pounder guns, and relied upon their speed to save them from the numerous hostile vessels that they were sure to meet.

> Then up spake our Captain when the Pirate had gone
> 'Go down to your grog boys – go down every one!
> 'Go down to your grog boys – and be of good cheer
> 'For while we have sea room – my lads never fear!'

These little ships could outsail most vessels, and when they couldn't could still fight. In the Napoleonic wars they fought thirty-two actions against enemy warships and won seventeen of them. We don't hear what happened to the fifteen who did not win their actions, but we do hear that, at one time, there were a hundred widows of Packet men living in Flushing.

The Packet men lived in Flushing because, at that time, Falmouth hardly existed, and Flushing is situated in a most perfect place for living: kind and fertile land, sheltered from the easterlies (which Falmouth is not) and, further, although the Packets were officially based on Falmouth, as anybody who has lain in a vessel at anchor on the Falmouth side when a north-easter is blowing will know, the creek off Flushing is a much better anchorage. Without a doubt this is where most of the Packets would have anchored during their periods in port.

The Packet captains were, for sailors, extremely well off. Not only did they get very well paid (for Packet captains and crews were the pick of the Merchant Navy) but they were allowed to trade on their own account, and trade they did, and the Customs men let them pretty well alone. Both captains and crews would stock up with export goods when going away, and sell these and buy dutiable import goods to bring back, and, as the mails only took a negligible space on board, the ships had plenty of carrying capacity, and it would have been a very bold Customs officer who would have said a word to them when they were rolling back to Falmouth Harbour. There were a lot of them, and it is reasonable to suppose they were not timid men. There grew up in Flushing a small army of women called 'trosyers'. These were formidable characters who used to wait ashore for the returning Packet men and buy their merchandise from them, and carry it on donkeys or ponies inland where it would sell. Further, the captains used to carry passengers across the Atlantic for £54 to New York and £107 to Brazil.

Flushing, then, became a little place of great wealth for its size. Its society was led by the Trefusis family, and still is, and always has been since at least the time of William the Conqueror. The Packet captains vied with each other in building good-looking Queen Anne and Georgian mansions at Flushing, some of which still exist, and James Buckingham, who spent most of his life in Flushing, wrote, in his autobiography, that the place '... literally sparkled with gold epaulets, gold lace hats, and brilliant uniforms'. In his day, late 18th century, two squadrons of frigates of the Royal Navy were also stationed in Falmouth Harbour. Buckingham paints a vivid picture of the splendid social life that the place then enjoyed. There is, by the way, a little booklet called *The Story of Flushing* on sale at nearly every shop in the place and in the church, written by Ursula Redwood, which is a very model of what such a local guide book should be.

Flushing now is a pleasant residential village, with a frequent ferry service over to Falmouth and a small fishing fleet. Besides several of the oyster dredging fleet there are six sea-going crabbers, a few long-liners and ray-netters and one or two trawlers. Although on a river it is very much a place of the sea.

Just upstream, or west, of the Fish Cross, is an area of hard muddy ground on which are oyster layings belonging to the firm of H. Johns. Here oysters bought from the dredgermen are put down, some in the nylon-covered trays, to clean themselves and fatten, and thereafter taken ashore to a purifying tank for the final purging. The water of the purifying tank is cleansed by being passed over a small weir where it is subjected to ultra-violet rays. This method has recently supplanted the ozone-purifying method that was in practice. Further is **Little Falmouth** about which tiny place a worthwhile history could be written, firstly a pilchard palace was here, then a tidal dry dock, which was completed in 1820, the remains of which still resist the weather and neglect of the years, but our age cannot find anything better to do with it than turn it into a rubbish dump. It is built of splendid great blocks of granite. Near it is a covered slipway, built soon after the tidal dock, and still used for yacht storage and repairs. The dockyard was in use for slipping and repairing the Packet ships, and fell into disuse after these declined. The end of the Packet trade came, incidentally, soon after 1820, when the Admiralty took over control of the Packet service from the Post Office. Against all local seafaring advice their Lordships insisted on replacing the fast little brigantines and ships with heavily armed brigs. These rapidly came to be called the 'coffin ships', and six of them were lost in bad weather in the first six-and-a-half years of their service. But by 1850 the era of the sailing packets was over, and the new steam vessels were using Southampton, and the many retired Packet captains in Flushing could live with their memories.

A great seafaring family of Flushing was that of Pellew. Captain Humphrey Pellew, ship-owner and tobacco plantation owner in Maryland, built much of Flushing, and his son, Samuel, fathered four sons, three of whom entered the Royal Navy and won renown. Of these Edward earned great fame and was made first a baronet and then Lord Exmouth. It was he who commanded the frigate *Nymph* in her action against the *Cléopâtre* which we noticed when considering Prawle Point. When as a young commander of a sloop, or small warship, he captured a big French ship as a prize, he wrote home to his wife: 'My dear wife, No more pilchards and haggis!' and she threw her darning basket across the room.

On the Newquay, south-easterly point of Flushing, is the headquarters of the Flushing Sailing Club, which has the letter 'V' on its burgee, in honour of the fact that the name Flushing comes from Vlissingen, the town that we call Flushing on the island of Walcheren. At the main quay, in the centre of the village, not only does the motor ferry come and go to and from Falmouth, but a most delightful lady, who is past her first youth, carries passengers backwards and forwards across the wide and often windy water in a small rowing boat. She charges two new pennies for this service, which can hardly pay for the wear of the leathers on her oars. Besides getting you there she is courteous, pleasant, and very informative. On the fore-shore of Flushing are some of the fattest cockles I have ever seen: lying boldly on the surface of the hard mud, not cowering coyly beneath the sand as most cockles do. They are very good to eat. So are the large prawns that can be caught by small boys with baited ring-nets from the quay, or the shrimps that are caught in the shallow water with the traditional seaside shrimping net. But do not wander on to the oyster layings, or you will arouse ire.

Penryn, at the head of the little estuary, is a much more venerable place than Falmouth and I find it very attractive. I think the steep main street of Penryn is one of the most pleasing main streets I know: it is amazing that nobody has yet got round to destroying it and replacing its comely Georgian houses with pebble-dashed rubbish.

Penryn may well have been started by St Gluvias, one of the obscurer Celtic saints, thought to have been the son of the Welsh Prince Gwynllyw. The church he founded is still there, although 'thoroughly' restored by the Victorians. Penryn itself was founded by Simon de Apulia, the Italian Bishop of Exeter, and in 1236 got its charter, although it had another one in 1275. Bishop Bronescombe founded the Glasney Collegiate College there, and this became a very important place. Nothing remains of it now.

By 1308 Penryn was obviously a victualling port, because it by then had four corn mills. There was also a fulling mill, an important market, and we hear that cheese and tin were exported (the latter illegally – it is nice to think of the Duchy of Cornwall being cheated of some of its unearned revenue) and barley, wheat, garlic, tallow, wine and salt came in. In 1536 Leland wrote that there was a defensive boom 'Sette in the creke at Penrine, afore the toun, a little lower than wher it brekith into armes.'

In the Tudor period Penryn saw more trade than any other port in England except London. It was a great victualling port, and an entrepot port for the Americas. An example of its trade is the ship that sailed, in 1696, for Maryland with woollen stockings, 2880 tobacco pipes, pewter, woollen rugs, linen, fustians, painted calicoes, Spanish wine, salt conger and herrings. In the same year a ship sailed for Spain with: coal, lead, tin, pewter, beeswax, butter and tobacco. Of course few of the commodities carried by either of these ships had originated in Cornwall: they were brought here from many places, and then shipped off as one cargo. There was a big trade in charcoal from the New Forest for the smelting of tin, and smelted tin out.

In the 19th century the silting up of Restronguet Creek brought more trade to Penryn, and about this time the big export of granite began. Granite went from here to the new Fastnet lighthouse, old Waterloo Bridge, Lambeth, Putney and Southwark Bridges, the Old Bailey and New Scotland Yard, the pedestal of a Turin monument, the monument to the Crimean War at Scutari, Billingsgate Market and Waterford Cathedral. At this time there were six Penryn sailing ships running a regular 'packet' service to London, two to Plymouth and two to the Isle of Wight. There were fifty quarries in the district, flour mills, paper mills, saw mills, a tannery, a chemical manure works, engineering works making mining equipment, and big ship-building yards. There was also the import of live cattle from Corunna in Spain. Penryn was a hive of commerce and industry. Now there is very little going on there at all but it is a very pleasant little place to be.

Falmouth is an upstart of a place, and didn't exist before the 17th century, when Sir John Killigrew got permission to build a town there. It wasn't until 20th August 1660 that the name of the almost non-existent little place that had been there before and which was called Smithwick was changed to Falmouth.

But the growth in importance of Falmouth was inevitable as ships became deeper in draught and could no longer get to places like Truro and Penryn. Defoe described Carrick Roads as 'next to Milford Haven in the South West the fairest and best road for shipping that is in the whole of Britain', and, as it was then, it is now. The standard instructions to the captains of sailing ships bound to Britain from any part of the world were: 'Falmouth for orders'. In the far south-west, this harbour could be entered by any ship in practically any weather conditions and at any state of the tide, and returning merchantmen would sail in here and drop anchor and wait for orders to come to them from their owners as to where to sail to discharge their cargo. In the 1850s we read that it was nothing to see 320 ocean-going sailing ships at anchor here at one time, and, earlier, in 1815 there were once 350 ships anchored in the Roads. In 1872 3945 ships sailed into Falmouth Harbour. Needless to say the town became crowded with trades connected with shipping: victuallers, chandlers, riggers and sailmakers, pilots and hobellers, and the little boats, which evolved for running backwards and forwards between ships and land in the multitudinous errands that such vast concourses of shipping required, famous for their sea-worthiness and handiness, were called 'Falmouth Quay Punts' and still any yachtsman who can lay his hands on one (now sure to have been converted many years ago into a yacht) considers himself lucky indeed. There are, alas, very few left.

In 1859 an Act of Parliament was obtained to convert 150 acres of land to build a series of docks. Two big dry docks were built, and in the First World War the Admiralty took over the dockyard and built another. In the Second World War Falmouth was of the very first importance, the docks, in spite of very heavy bombardment, being used to repair countless vessels and the port being used as a base for the Normandy landings of 1944. Falmouth was the head-quarters of the Netherlands Navy, and from here the exiled Dutch sailed to attack St Nazaire. Since the war ended there have been big extensions, and there is now a dry dock (the 'Queen Elizabeth Dock') that can take ships up to 90,000 tons deadweight. Practically any repair work can be carried out, and of course Falmouth, being the furthest west of all the big repair ports of the country, is always chosen for Atlantic Ocean casualties.

As a yachting centre Falmouth has become famous. The Royal Cornwall Yacht Club is here, and I have counted over two hundred sail in Carrick Roads myself and have heard that it is not uncommon to count three hundred.

And so we come to **Pendennis Castle**. The citadel of this was built as part of Henry VIII's great scheme to keep the French out, forced on him by the fact that the French and the Spaniards had sunk their differences and the Pope was preaching a crusade against the excommunicated English king. The central tower of Pendennis was begun in 1539, and finished in 1540. It was in Elizabeth's time (for she suffered from the same unpopularity with Papist Europe) that the great outer enclosure was made, transforming the fort into a very strong place indeed capable of containing a large force The place was never attacked until the Civil War, when it was held for the king by Colonel John Arundell of Trerice, called 'Jack-for-the-King' for obvious reasons and also 'Old Tilbury' because he was old enough to have been at the famous review of the troops by Queen Elizabeth at Tilbury in 1588. Fairfax arrived on the scene in March 1646 and summoned poor old Arundell to surrender. The latter replied 'I will bury myself before I deliver up this castle to such as fight against his Majesty.' He did in fact hold out until 17th of August when he hauled down his flag and he and twenty-four officers and about 900 men marched out, being accorded full honours of war, which in fact they deserved, for they had held out against the Parliamentary forces longer than any other castle but Raglan.

Before the siege Charles I's queen spent a night here as she was fleeing towards France, and Charles II hid here, as Prince of Wales, on his way to the Scilly Islands. The castle, in the care of the Ministry of Works, is in very good repair, and a fine example of a fortification of its period. There is a good guide on sale within.

CHAPTER 13

Helford River to Loe Bar. The Lizard

⚓

THE **Helford River** is one of the most beautiful anchorages in Britain, and easy to get into, but beware the August Rock. If you keep the bold headland at Helford Village open of Toll Point you will be clear of this obstruction. The Helford Sailing Club stands among trees south of the river a couple of miles inside, and the clubhouse has a grass turf roof, in the Scandinavian manner, and the grass is supposed to be of a kind that never grows more than nine inches long. In fact, when I last measured it, it was twelve inches.

Over the river, connected by foot ferry, is **Helford Passage**, where is a pub much used by sailing people; **Porth Navas** is up a creek just round the corner and here MacFisheries has an oyster laying, and the Ministry of Agriculture and Fisheries conducts experiments. One of them is the introduction of the Shaiga oyster from Japan, which is supposed to be a better animal than either the Native or the Portuguese breeds. There is a little club at Porth Navas with a bar, to which visitors are welcome.

Gweek, to which a boat can get at high tide, became the port for Helston when that town was cut off from its own river by the silting up of Loe Bar. The usual timber, coal and lime came in here, and also charcoal from Hampshire for tin-smelting. The place was important enough to have a custom house. Coal still does come in here: an enlightened coal merchant has 250-ton coasters in on spring tides to unload coal for the surrounding district. Would that more coal merchants would do this, and relieve the terrible congestion on the roads. Gweek is a lost little place now, with the mouldering remains of a quay system, and a very nice and friendly inn.

Helford is a little village of quite overwhelming charm, with thatch galore, bosky dells, the charming thatched Shipwright's Arms, and the Helford Sailing Club just over the creek. In the summer the place is humming with yachting activity. There are the remains of a quay here which once used to accommodate ships up to 300 tons, and granite used to be exported.

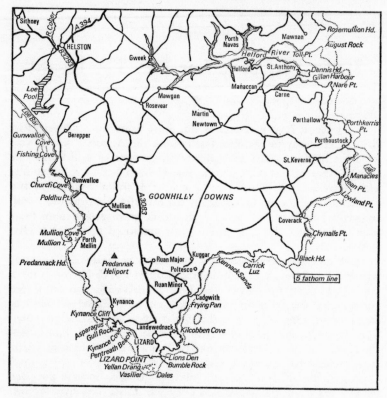

St Anthony, like **Mawnan** over the river, has a little church right down by the water. Dennis Head beyond it had a fort which the Roundheads took before they attacked Pendennis.

Manaccan is an example of how a Cornish village can be unspoiled, and unaffected by the tourist crowds, so long as it is even a mile or two from the sea.

Gillan Harbour is a tiny version of Helford River. **Carne** once had a tucking mill in it. Tucking mill is the local term for a fulling mill: a mill in which cloth from the loom was washed and shrunk and subjected to other processes (including being treated with 'fuller's earth'). The many people in Devon and Cornwall with the surname Tucker are no doubt descended from tuckers, or fullers, of old. In Wales these same mills were called *pandies*, thus Pandy is a very common place name there. Between Carne and Helford is a farm with a tall grain tower, and as enjoyment of coast or countryside depends very much on knowing what things are, and as these grain silos are becoming more and more one of our most distinctive modern agricultural buildings, I might here describe what they are for. They represent a return to Iron Age agricultural methods. Ancient man found that he could not store grain satisfactorily in a damp climate unless he either dried it thoroughly (which was difficult for him to do) or stored it in a hermetically sealed compartment so that it could get no oxygen. The latter was easy for him in well-drained rock such as chalk, for he could excavate a pit, line it with basket-work, dump his damp grain into it, seal the top with wickerwork and mud, and know that the grain would last until harvest came again. The reason why it lasted was that the carbon dioxide generated by the grain itself was toxic to any moulds, mites, or other organisms that would damage it. The medieval farmer adopted the method of drying the grain in the stook, and afterwards stacking it in the straw in ricks which the air could penetrate, and then threshing it out when he needed it. The modern farmer, however, has discovered the Iron Age secret again. He cuts corn with the combine harvester which threshes it out as it cuts it, presenting him with a bulk of damp grain. Tired of the expensive process of artificially drying it farmers are going back to the age-old method, keeping it damp in hermetically sealed aluminium silos instead of underground pits. Carne, besides its Iron Age, Aluminium Age grain silo and its fulling mill, had two corn mills, both (like the fulling mill) water driven, and the wheel of one of which is still there to see. The method of building cottages and farm buildings around here is to build the lower half of the walls with big blocks of granite and the upper half with cobb, or mud and straw. The result is that when a house is deserted the roof goes and then the cobb quickly washes away and the granite is carried off for use elsewhere. Nine cottages in this tiny hamlet of Carne have, within living memory, thus passed away. Carne was once a port, and until recently ketches with coal used to unload here.

Gillan Harbour is a pleasant anchorage if there is not an easterly gale blowing, and if there is you can wait for water and then drop down-wind up-river to a more sheltered anchorage. There are a couple of part-time crabbers. Men-aver Beach has caves and is fine for bathing. We soon come to **Porthallow**, with the Five Pilchards Inn, and a pleasant little harbour and beach for bathing. Just off here the *Bay of Panama* was wrecked in the terrible blizzard of March 1891. An idea of the remoteness and inaccessibility of this tiny place can be gained from the fact that a young farmer named

James rode off for help for the stricken ship from Falmouth, his horse foundered in the snow, he then spent some fifteen hours dragging himself through snowdrifts and reached Falmouth in a state of almost complete exhaustion. He gave the alarm however and help was sent. Stories, which can be paralleled many times around the Cornish coast, of people on shore going to the extremes of danger and sacrifice to help wrecked mariners, contrast strangely with the legends of 'Wreckers' so beloved of Victorian melodramatic novelists, with miscreants tying lanterns on to donkeys' tails and other incredible rubbish. The story of 'Wreckers' will die hard but it will die, for there is practically no historical evidence to support more than one or two cases of the wanton luring of ships to their destruction by men ashore around the whole coast of Britain, but hundreds of well documented stories of devotion and heroism of people trying to help the shipwrecked. That the local people helped themselves to the cargoes and materials of ships *after* they were wrecked is of course true: what fools they would have been if they hadn't.

We are coming now to a new sort of country altogether, for here the sedimentary Devonian kilns rock changes abruptly, first to the metamorphic, then to the igneous rocks which make up that wild and lonely land – wild and lonely through most of its history and in the winter even now, but pretty flooded with holidaymakers in the summer – of the Lizard.

East of here is a huge quarry, up until about fifteen years ago worked for roadstone which was shot straight down into the holds of ships which lay against the rocks in the open sea. It was called Porth Kerris. The stone is locally known as blue elvan, but is a kind of schist or hornblende. North of Porthoustock is another great abandoned quarry, with many remains of light railways and other equipment to interest the industrial archaeologist.

Porthoustock (pronounced Proustock) is a very interesting little place, and still a fishing village and a port. The rock changes here once again, to gabbro in the south with dykes of quartzite, and this is still quarried extensively for roadstone by Amalgamated Roadstone Corporation; small ships come in and lie below the quarry and the rock is shot into their holds. The gabbro is locally called 'Crousa'. North of the harbour is a massive concrete loading pier, no longer used, but excellent for small boys to sit on and haul tiny crabs from the depths below. Behind the shelter of this pier the fishing boats land and are hauled up the beach by winches. There are four or five full-timers, and much long-lining. Porthoustock had a lifeboat up to 1942. Since its inception in 1869 it had saved lives off the Manacles – that absolutely deadly collection of half-tide rocks which stretch a mile or more off the shore just to the south into the shipping channel towards Falmouth. Only one of the Manacles rocks is exposed at high tide, but the rest lie below hidden and ready to grab the ship that is unwary. They grabbed the emigrant ship *John* in 1855 and drowned two hundred people, and the *Mohegan* and another hundred and six in 1898. The dead from the *Mohegan* were buried in a mass grave at St Keverne, and there is a monument there to them. In 1636 seven fishing vessels were captured by Barbary pirates off the Manacles and 240 men carried off into slavery in North Africa.

There is a most charming footpath from Porthallow running inland to St Keverne. It goes along a valley of tropical lushness, in which, amongst other tropical and sub-tropical vegetation, are some impressive specimens of *Gunnera*. **St Keverne** has over four hundred drowned sailors buried in its churchyard: nearly all of them from the Manacles. There are fine bench ends in the church, three sets of rood stairs (showing that the church has been enlarged eastward that many times) and a mural of St Christopher. A mile inland, as the crow flies, is a place with the improbable name of Touch-me-pipes. Here a man with the improbable name of Captain Cooke makes very fine little model boats, which shoot along in the water propelled by the magical powers of a piece of camphor. The great Polkinghorne was born at St Keverne, but this piece of information would interest nobody but devotees of bare-fist boxing.

From St Keverne south there is a footpath through lonely country to Coverack, or you can walk, laboriously, along the coast, past Lowland Point – a raised beach on which the big passenger liner *Paris* was wrecked in 1899. **Dean Point** has a big still-worked quarry and loading quay.

Coverack is a splendid little place, which seems to keep its integrity against the holiday invasions and in which there is a refreshing absence of *piskies*. There has been a lifeboat since 1901. The old custom has been revived of holding a meeting in the harbour of Coverack in which Methodist choirs come and sing hymns to the music of a large brass band one Sunday every August. The harbour makes a perfect setting for this, for it has the aspect of a great amphitheatre, and people crowd the quay, the fishing boats at moorings, the lifeboat slip, and the hillsides up above. The Cornish sing, but the English don't.

Chynalls Point brings us into the serpentine country. This extraordinary rock, metamorphosed magnesium limestone or olivine (that is sedimentary rocks that have been subjected to great heat and pressure by earth movements), is a great feature of the Lizard Peninsula, and of very few other places. We shall discuss it more fully further on. There is an Iron Age camp at Chynalls Point. We happily assume that these great fortifications are all 'Iron Age' but it may well be wondered how we are so sure. There is a fine walk along the cliff path to **Black Head**. Around it we find an intrusion of a rock which I am told is called Flasser Gabbro, which is a basic (i.e. anti-acid) rock composed of big black and white crystals. For the student of igneous and metamorphic rocks all this coast, from Porthallow round to Mullion, is one of the most interesting in the world. There must have been a series of injections of boiling rocks from the interior, the heat and pressure of which formed the mile-wide band of schist which cuts off the geological zone of the Lizard and which runs from about Porthallow to about Mullion. These schists were metamorphosed from igneous rocks which are thought by some geologists to have boiled up from the depths in pre-Cambrian times: thus making them some of the oldest rocks of the earth. South of this zone the great intrusions occurred, first of serpentine, then of gabbro, then of granite. The red granite of the Lizard ('Kennack granite') doesn't cleave like the 'Cornish granite' further north, and is not so good for building stone. The serpentine is of little use for building stone as it is apt to cleave diagonally, giving it an irregular pyramidal structure (which can be very well seen at Green Saddle, a little further along the coast from where we are). Near Beagles Point are old mine shafts, which were for copper, but there is very little mineralization in the Lizard Peninsula, and no tin. St Keverne cursed the tin miners and 'no metal will run within the sound of St Keverne's bells'. The Cornish found it strange that there should be an area of their duchy where no metal could be found, and therefore had to discover a supernatural reason for it, and St Keverne got the blame.

Inland from us, as we go westwards past the beautiful little bay of Lankidden which hardly anybody knows, and the bold promontory of Carrick Luz with its 'Iron Age castle' (a Bronze Age sword was dug up by Miss Bush of Carnbesseck, a mile inland) is the typical Goonhilly country: a level table-land (levelled by the sea) of shallow coarse clay overlying the serpentine rock: infertile, impossible to drain or to cultivate, peppered all over with prehistoric remains. Ancient man seemed to favour the barren parts of the earth – or is it simply that in such places his remains have been undisturbed? The Caerverracks Reef runs seaward from the middle of the Kennack Sands, and is pure serpentine. These **Kennack Sands** are a favourite with such bathers as have discovered them, and caravans spread to the west of them. The beacon which says 'Cable' on the sands marks the Cornish end of a Post Office cable which goes to Spain and Portugal. It was recently renewed, when the Goonhilly Earth Station was built. The iron manhole covers in the road leading up towards Kuggar cover a tunnel which has been driven to contain the cable on its journey inland to Goonhilly.

Poltesco is a minuscule place which could rate nine out of ten for bosky charm, and it is also of great interest. There was a large factory there, down by the sea, the purpose of which was to work the serpentine rock into components for shop fronts and other architectural features. One is told that several Poltesco shop fronts are still to be seen in Oxford Street and New Bond Street, but short of actually going to the length of travelling to the Metropolis to verify this I can only pass the information on. Much of the stuff went to France. Small sailing ships landed on the beach to load it, and an enormous water wheel, nothing of which remains, supplied the power for the machinery. The ruins which remain are extensive, but hard to interpret. The place should be studied by a competent industrial archaeologist. Further up the path (past a farmhouse which looks as if it is being held up by its ivy – and about to be overwhelmed by the vigour of its surrounding vegetation) is the ruin of a little watermill which ground corn. The two pairs of mill stones are still inside, alas vandalized, and the place is being used by a farmer to store hay. In the wall on the north side, low down, is a stone with a crucifixion carved on it. This reminds me very much of similar carved stones in the Thomian Christian area of the Malabar Coast, which are dated at about A.D. 300. My own guess is that it is Celtic, but it should be examined by a competent archaeologist. So far as I can discover, it never has been. This little mill should be restored – and as quickly as possible! In the little Poltesco vale there are dense thickets of bamboo, and you expect to be attacked by tigers. There are nice trout in the stream but the water is very polluted, which is a disgrace.

Ruan Minor has a tiny church, much restored, the piers of the nave of which are made of such coarse-grained granite that they glitter with mica crystals like diamonds. Mr Hollyer, the vicar, is a very good geologist. Ruan Major is even more minor than Ruan Minor.

Cadgwith is a small and pretty, and very typical, Cornish expilchard village, now with a few fishing boats and more holiday-makers. In 1867 a lifeboat was established here rejoicing in the name of the *Western Commercial Traveller*. This little boat sailed seven miles out to sea in a WSW gale to the Black Ball Line iron sailing ship *Calcutta* which had been in collision and was sinking rapidly. Some members of the latter's crew had taken to their boats, but eight remained on board and were taken off by the *Western Commercial Traveller* with great difficulty, as there was every chance of the lifeboat being stove in against the iron counter of the sinking ship. The lifeboat then, not being able to point high enough to get home, had to run for Falmouth. One of the ship's own boats managed to reach Mullion but was driven ashore there and all of her twenty-one occupants drowned. In all, thirty-three of the ship's complement of sixty-four were lost. In the Second World War a lifeboat just completed for this station, having been paid for by the Girl Guides, was diverted to Dunkirk instead, where she did good service taking men off the beaches. She afterwards came to Cadgwith, but the station was finally closed down in 1963. Just under 400 lives had been saved in eighty launches from this station. The Devil's Frying Pan, just south-west of Cadgwith, is an awesome place, where the roof of an enormous sea-carved cavern collapsed in 1868. It makes you dizzy to look down into it. Cadgwith is in a stream valley which, like most of the stream valleys of this coast, is in one of the granite intrusions: the granite being easier for water to erode than the enveloping serpentine. There are old pilchard cellars here and a huer's house. The latter was a shelter for the man who stood on watch for the pilchard shoals.

Landewednack had a tiny port at a place near the Landmark, where is a pilchard palace beautifully converted into a private house, a slipway, a landing beach and a winch. At Church Cove the Lizard lifeboat was once kept, but the new boat, which calls itself the Lizard-Cadgwith Lifeboat, was moved in 1966 to Kilcobben Cove a little to the south. There are no full-time fishermen on this harbourless piece of coast and it is a marvel that a crew can be found for this important lifeboat, but one is: shopkeepers and carpenters and electricians racing for the Cove when the maroon goes off. Landewednack has the most southerly church in Britain, with a solid tower of granite and serpentine containing very old bells: one of them having been removed and plonked down on the ground outside the south porch. This latter is said to be 600 years old: one of the oldest bells in the country. The church, like most Cornish churches and most Welsh Anglican ones, was ruined in the

19th century, during the rearguard action of the Anglican establishment to woo the natives back from non-conformism.

There is still the stump of a windmill standing at Landewednack. It was advertised to be sold in the *Royal Cornwall Gazette* of 11th October 1828 in these terms: 'To be sold by private contract, determinable on the death of three lives of the purchaser's nomination; the mill, a house, barn and stable, and twenty-eight acres of enclosed land'.

Lizard Town is a strange little village, subsisting on the industry of the serpentine carvers. There are many small workshops in which men carve this strange and beautiful stone, gouging it with steel bits on small electric lathes, polishing it until it looks as if it has been dipped in molten glass, and making such objects as lamp stands, stone eggs, miniature lighthouses and the rest of it. The men work winter and summer at this activity and their wives it is, generally, who sell the objects to the tourists who simply flood this place all summer long. Some of the things they make are beautiful: the eggs are delightful if perhaps not strictly utilitarian (a millionaire poultry keeper might use them as 'china eggs') and the lamp stands can be well shaped and pleasant, but for my part you can have the lighthouses. Some of the craftsmen have relics handed down from their forefathers, who practised this craft in Victorian and earlier times. These have far more style and panache, but are not for sale. It is sad that the serpentine carvers suffer from the contemporary debasement of taste but not, of course, unnatural. We can, thank God, see an improvement coming about here, as though the nadir has been reached and passed, and perhaps there are better things to come. And so far I have not, and hope I never will, seen a serpentine 'pisky'.

Serpentine is a hydrated magnesium silicate ($3MgO.2SiO_2.2H_2O$) formed by the metamorphosis of olivine, augite or hornblende by heat and pressure. The serpentine that we see here at the Lizard being carved has veins in it of the minerals olivine, augite and hornblende which have not been so altered, and it is this mixing-up of minerals in different stages of metamorphosis that gives it such an astonishing appearance. It does, indeed, when polished, look like serpent's skin. It is extremely interesting and beautiful, and will stand a lot of gazing into: the more you look at it the more you seem to see. The carvers get it by prying bits of it out of the ground from small pits scattered around the Goonhilly country. Unfortunately the National Trust has made their work more difficult by banning this ancient enterprise on its holdings beyond Pentreath. The serpentine diggers are as much a part of the ancient ecology of this area as the sparrow-hawks and it is quite wrong to disturb them. In any case, the little scratching about they do in tiny pits causes no harm to the landscape whatever.

East of the lighthouse is the Lion's Den, another great fallen cave such as the Devil's Frying Pan. **Lizard Point** is as much a goal of agnostic pilgrims as Meshed is of Shia Muslims. Buses, thank goodness, cannot get there, the lanes being too narrow, but hundreds of cars do, forcing the more than hundreds of pedestrians to creep into the side of the dusty road to avoid them. What they see when they get there is the most southerly tip of England, if England is taken to include Cornwall, the lighthouse up which they are allowed to climb at certain hours when the foghorn is not blowing, Bumble Rock, the Yellan Drang rocks out to sea, the Enoch Rock, the Dales and the Vasilier. All rocks which have claimed ships but which harbour lobsters. Beyond is an impressive overfall or tidal race. Pre-Cambrian hornblende schist makes up this southerly tip of Britain, further west, by the Coastguard lookout, it is mica schist. This tip of the Lizard, not being on the barren serpentine, has small fertile fields on it, mostly growing barley and oats but some growing wheat, the latter apparently a martyr to the disease called smut in wet seasons.

Kynance Cove is in the National Trust land, and is very beautiful, guarded from the Atlantic breakers by Gull Rock and Asparagus Island. The serpentine here is a chromite serpentine, called tremolite; there is also epidiorite here in black dykes and a medium-grain banded gneiss. We can see here, on the path down from the cove, the teeth-like outcrops of rock which are caused by the diagonal jointing of the serpentine.

Kynance Cliff has a fine cliff path and fine views. From the Rill here the Armada was first sighted. Gew-graze, or Soap Rock, has soapstone in it. This soft grey stuff was quarried here once by the Worcester Pottery, and ground up to help make china body. It has since been superseded. The Botany Department of Bristol University have, incidentally, found nine plants here on this coast that are to be found nowhere else in Britain. Up above is the lonely barren moor, which is horrible to walk over because you slip continually in steep little holes hidden by the heather. The farm called Kynance is a non-farm. Two cottages were built, and a big barn, and the landlord thought better of it and the farmhouse itself was never built. The only way the occupants of the two cottages can get there by car is across the big Predannack airfield, now used by the navy for helicopters. It is sad that this large wild area should be spoiled and defaced by such a vast establishment for the exercising of a few flying machines, which surely don't require all this amount of space. The heathland out of the airfield area is grazed by store cattle. There are no sheep – people say because of liver fluke and this well may be the reason because the place is boggy enough in all reason – and the little ponies once called goonhillies, from which the Moor – and the Earth Station – got their names. It is not hard, when roaming about this desolate landscape, to imagine that it was, as it was, once the bed of the sea; and that the resistant serpentine rock has remained little affected by weather erosion since it rose up out of the waters.

Porth Mellin (mellin means mill, in Cornish as in Welsh) is more generally known as **Mullion Cove** for in this cove it lies. There is one full-time fisherman here now – the other gave up last year and moved to Hayle. The tiny artificial harbour dries out of course, and Mullion Island does not give it the protection you might expect from the westerlies, which drive their combers crashing over its breakwater and the little boats have to be hauled out.

In the 18th century Mullion was a great pilchard port, and the fish were sailed across the bay to Newlyn where they were cured and exported. A record exists of some details of the pilchard industry here in the 1880s. Men took turn to be *huer*. The huer stood up on the cliffs watching the sea for pilchard shoals. When a shoal approached the shore the huer would 'cry hevva!' and every man, woman and child would leap into action. The huer got seventeen shillings a week and every twentieth dozen of the fish caught. The two *net shooters* – skilled men on whom the whole operation depended for they were the men in the boat who paid the net out over the stern to encircle the fish – got 10/6d a week each plus one-and-a-quarter shares each of a quarter of the gross catch, and they also got twopence a hogshead each of the *owner's* share of the catch. A hogshead held 3000 fish. The *Master* of the cock-boat (the net-boat shot the line – the cock-boat hung on the shot end of it and waited for the net-boat to come full circle) and his *Bowman* got 9/- a week each and each one-and-a-quarter shares of a quarter of the gross catch and a penny each out of each hogshead of the owner's share. The ordinary crew members got 9/- a week and a share each of the gross catch. The *owner* need not be a simple entity, for many men might own the boats and net in company, each taking so many sixty-fourths of the whole.

Mullion Cliff is of serpentine but the cliffs to the north, and around the village of Mullion, are of schist, which makes the earth above it rich. The steep-sided valley that Porth Mellin lies in is granite, hence the water has been able to cut down through it. The stacks of Henscath and Scovard are serpentine. And here the serpentine ends: we will see it no more in our progression round the coasts.

Mullion has a little church with some of the finest bench ends in the country. To enter this building is to have the same sort of shocked feeling that one has slipped five hundred years that one has on entering the church of Wiggenhall St Mary in the Norfolk marshland.

Just south of Poldhu Point is a monument to Guglielmo Marconi, who transmitted the first wireless message to cross the Atlantic from this very point on the 12th of December 1901. Marconi came to England from Italy in 1896 and shortly afterwards built Poldhu Wireless Station. This was not closed down until 1934, and from it much of the pioneering of radio was done.

Winnianton, or **Gunwalloe** church is a strange and lonely little place, threatened by the sea which may well engulf it. Its little cove is charming and it is a place well worth going to see. Unfortunately there is a legend that somebody buried a coffin-full of treasure in its churchyard instead of the more usual deceased relative, and in 1971 some adventurer dug up half the graves in an abortive search for it.

At Gunwalloe Fishing Cove starts the three-mile-long **Loe Bar**, which is made of finely graded very fine shingle mostly composed of flint. It is a dangerous place to bathe from, for the shingle is steep and one cannot easily get a foothold on it, and it is easy to be drawn backwards by the undertow. It was on here that the frigate H.M.S. *Anson* was wrecked in 1807 with the loss of a hundred lives. Henry Trengrouse, of Helston near by, stood on the shore, with hundreds of other people, watching helplessly as the seas pounded the ship to pieces and nobody could get to her, either by land or by sea, and he went home to invent the rocket life-saving apparatus. He devoted his entire fortune of £3500 and most of the rest of his life to this, but he was rewarded by a £50 grant from the government, thirty guineas from the Royal Society and a diamond ring from the Czar of the Russias. In what relation Trengrouse stands to Manby, of Norfolk, who also invented a rocket saving apparatus, I leave their respective protagonists to decide. I only know that in 1966 the staff of Helston Museum let off one of Trengrouse's original rockets – and it went two hundred yards! Trengrouse died in 1834.

CHAPTER 14

Helston to Mousehole

✤

Loe Pool is beset about with a private estate. By Loe Pool the Wild Service Tree grows; King Arthur's sword *Excalibur* was flung into it at least in Tennyson's poem (or so people hold); the Pool is said to claim a life every seven years (it sadly did claim one in 1971), and there is good (but private) trout fishing and white water lilies. There is a culvert under the shingle bar which allows the head of fresh water coming down the Cober River to run into the sea, but in days of old this used to build up in heavy rains until the many millers along the banks of the river higher up (there were several tucking – or fulling – mills) used to plague the Mayor of Helston to do something about it, and he used to fee the Lord of the Manor at Penrose with a purse of gold to give him permission to cut the bar. This done the impounded water would surge out and after two ebb tides the people of the Scilly Islands would be catching fresh-water trout far out in the Atlantic. After mining had polluted the waters the Scillonians would know that the bar had been cut because the sea would turn ochreous about them. Or at any rate, this is the story that everybody believes.

Helston has its Furry Dance on the 8th of May every year, and a great old event it is too. The museum at Helston is well worth visiting, for it has a good collection of things really of local interest. It has Henry Trengrouse's rocket apparatus, a magnificent cider press of the kind that worked by gravity aided by enormous hand-cut wooden screws (it is easy enough to see how a good craftsman could have cut the threads on the male components – but what about the female?) and all the things that the County Museum in Truro *should* have but has not. It is refreshing that a generation of museum curators is growing up that does not believe that history stopped at 1750. In the middle of Coinagel Street is an old building, once a chapel, but then the Coinage Hall. This is where the corners (i.e. *coins*) which had been cut off the 320 pound blocks of tin were brought to be assayed, so that the tin could be stamped with the arms of the Duchy. *After*, of course, the heavy unearned duty had been paid. Helston was an important mining town until the middle of the 19th century. Wheal Vor, near by, was said to have been the richest tin mine in the world, and £10,000 a week was coming into Helston brought by the hundreds of roistering miners. The nicest thing about Helston today is the pub called the Blue Anchor near the main bus stop, which still brews its own beer called *Spingo*. This beer knocks all the factory beer you can find into a cocked hat and Helston should be proud of it.

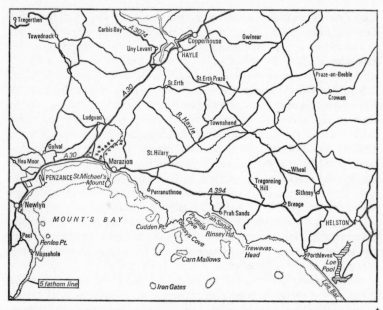

This might be the place to discuss the tin mining industry as it existed in Cornwall from the earliest times. We shall consider modern tin mining when we come to Pendeen.

It wasn't the Phoenicians, we are now told, but the Carthaginians, who came to Cornwall to get tin. Diodorus Siculus of Sicily, in the 1st century B.C., wrote about a man called Pytheas, a Greek, who in the 4th century B.C. had shadowed Carthaginians to find where they got their tin and followed them to a country called Belerion, where they landed on an island called Iktin and traded for tin. Belerion may have been Cornwall: Iktin may have been St Michael's Mount. Iktin may just as easily have been Oléron off the coast of Brittany, which later was the entrepot for tin and may have been then. But whatever the facts the *tin* almost certainly came from

144

Cornwall, because that is where the tin could be got. All we can be sure of is that seafarers from the Mediterranean, by one means or another, traded for Cornish tin.

Tin must have been very easy to get in Cornwall in Bronze Age days (when the metal was so needed to mix with copper to make the harder but still malleable bronze), because every stream that stemmed from tin-bearing country would have had alluvial tin in its sandy bed. The miners merely had to pan this (swish the sand around in a large pot or pan so that the heavier tin stayed behind and the lighter sand was washed away) and they had tin, or at least cassiterite, or tin oxide – SnO_2. The name cassiterite, incidentally, comes from the Mediterranean name for Cornwall – Cassiterides. The cassiterite could then be smelted by heating it whereupon the metal would run out. The furnaces used for this, and which were left dotting the countryside, afterwards came to be known as Jews' houses.

As time went on the alluvial tin became harder to find, and then men began breaking off the outcrops of tin-bearing rock itself, whence the alluvial tin had itself broken off, and this rock they smelted in the same way as the cassiterite. When the outcrops had gone there was nothing to do but to start following the lodes underground. At first they worked the cliff mines – driving tunnels called adits in from the cliff sides.

A *lode* of ore is mineralized rock which has been forced up from the molten depths of the earth into fissures and cracks and lines of weakness in the overlying rocks. This mineralized matter may come up in the form of vapour or molten liquid, but by whatever method it comes it solidifies and forms long narrow bodies in the 'country rock' as the surrounding rock is called, which bodies stretch for yards or for miles, and may go down into great depths or else peter out a yard or two below the surface. They may be inches thick or yards. The early miners, having no explosives, broke into these seams or lodes by lighting fires on the rock and then – when the rock was very hot – quenching it with water or, better still, vinegar. This heating and quenching process shattered the rock, for a few inches at least, and enabled it to be broken out with a pinch bar. When gunpowder was invented holes were drilled in the rock face, filled with gunpowder, which was ignited by means of such devices as rushes soaked in saltpetre or goose quills filled with gunpowder which – generally – gave the miner time to get out of the way before the charge went off. Gunpowder gave them more power and deeper they went, first following the lodes down from the surface – then sinking vertical or inclined shafts, often in the country rock, and putting out cross cuts (tunnels across the grain of the rock) until they struck the rock and then driving along it at right angles. The drive having been extended some way they would then 'stope' – that is mine the lode out, either above their heads or below their feet: in hand drilling days frequently the latter. In this way, eventually, all the material of the lode would be extracted. Then, maybe, crosscuts would be driven across the grain of the rock to search for more lodes which, if found, would be mined out in their turn. Cornish mining was (and is) as skilful as any mining in the world, for the ore is not in one great continuous body like the gold-bearing reef of the Rand or the ore of the Copperbelt, but cut up into hundreds of penny parcels, scattered about down below, some rich and some too poor to work, and the miner has got to use all his skill and instinct to find them. As for the old miners: 'their toyle is extreme, as they cannot endure it above four hours a day . . . the residue of the time they weare out at coytes, kayles, or like idle exercises. Their kalendar also alloweth them more holy-dayes than are warranted by the church, our lawes, or their own profit.' A mine was called a *huel* in Cornish, now corrupted to *wheal*. The smelting houses had thatched roofs which were burnt every so often to recover the tin in the thatch. This paid for a new roof 'with a gainful overplus'. In 1600 a tinner was earning four shillings a week, the Cornish pasty is said to have been evolved for the Cornish miners (miners are tough chaps); food underground was called *crowst*, a shift was called a *core*. Cornish mines, like windmills and ships, are 'she' – not 'it'. As mines got deeper (as soon, in fact, as they got 'below adit') it was necessary to bale or pump the water out of them. A great variety of fantastic contrivances were invented for doing this, some driven by man-power, some by horse gins, some by water wheels and some by windmills, until in the 18th century the 'fire engine' was invented and this enabled mining to go on at far greater depths, in fact it came in time to save Cornish mining from decline. Men descended the mines down ladderways, and up again at the end of the shift, and it was nothing for men to have to climb 1500 feet or more at the end of an exhausting day's rock drilling. Then the 'man engine' was invented: an adaptation whereby the old pumping fire engine or steam engine operated a series of alternating lifts underground up or down which men could travel. Eventually, of course, came the modern hoist which will lower or raise men, rock or material at high speeds in cages at the end of wire ropes.

Marvellous machines were developed for crushing the ore, and washing the tin out of it when it was crushed. Huge water wheels were built, and the power from them taken many hundreds of yards by ingenious systems of rods along the hillsides.

Some mines went to considerable depths: Great Dolcoath was 3300 feet deep, and in two hundred years six million pounds' worth of copper and tin were taken from this one mine, also arsenic, silver and cobalt. For Cornish mines produced not only tin but copper also in great abundance, lead, antimony, iron, zinc, silver, cobalt, manganese, bismuth, wolfram, arsenic, uranium and gold. Of these only tin, copper, lead, arsenic and a little bit of silver and cobalt were of any great importance.

But alas, alluvial tin was discovered in Malaya in the 1870s in huge quantities, and in Australia in 1875 and then in Tasmania, and as each successive discovery was made another blow was struck at Cornish mining. Copper was found in enormous quantities in central Africa in easily worked ore bodies and there were Africans ready to work it at colonial wages. In the 1870s there was a great copper depression and many Cornish copper mines went under. There was a recovery of tin about then owing to troubled times in Malaya but Tasmania came to tumble prices again. In the late 1870s hundreds of mines were abandoned, and thousands of 'Cousin Jack' miners (Cousin Jack is the name abroad for Cornishmen) went abroad to every country in the world with a mine in it. All the new and emerging countries in the world learnt their mining from Cornishmen. If you see a hole in the ground anywhere in the world, the old saying went, you will find a Cornishman at the bottom of it. Cornishmen have mined for so long (perhaps for hundreds of generations) and in such intricate and difficult country that they almost seem to have an inborn instinct for this skill or art: they are as much at home underground as a sailor is on the sea.

In the First World War there was a revival, for obvious reasons, but the miners 'picked the eyes out of the mines' – in other words they stoped without developing. They grabbed what was already blocked out and thought not of the future for to win the war was essential. In the Second World War some effort was put into prospecting, mostly by drilling, with little result. Now there is a modest beginning again. South Crofty, an old mine, is still going, as are Geevor and Levant which we shall look at when we come to Pendeen, and a big new mine, Wheal Jane, has just been opened near Truro.

Porthleven, back at the coast, is a pretty little harbour, in fact quite a big harbour, but as it faces south-west – where the big gales come from – it has had its difficulties. It was of very old a fishing village, but in 1811 some London adventurers obtained an Act of Parliament to build a harbour of refuge there operating under the title Porthleven Harbour Company. They were to claim dues from shipping. By 1818 the harbour was complete – but a storm in 1824 completely washed it away. In 1825 it was rebuilt. The intention had been to export copper from nearby mines, soapstone which came, as we have seen, from Soap Rock at Gew Graze and china stone from Tregonning Hill. The harbour was too difficult and dangerous, though, and was given over to fishing boats. By 1850 there were forty-six of these registered in the port. Then in 1855 Harvey and Company, from Hayle, bought the harbour and greatly improved it, building lock gates to the inner harbour. Porthleven is now an interesting and beautiful place. There is still a large fishing community here, but as the harbour is so bad the boats are inclined to work from Newlyn. There is a big privately owned canning factory here, Porthleven Fisheries, and quite a hefty boatbuilding yard. This, besides building wooden ships – many of them beautifully built with diagonal planking – is currently turning out highly specialized steel vessels too: when I was last there a very strange-looking steel power-driven twin-hulled vessel for Belgian ocean research. They will build up to a hundred feet long.

Now do not miss **Breage**, inland and off the beaten track a bit, for the astonishing wall paintings. These, which hit you in the eye the moment you walk in the door, are the usual St Christopher, also St Hilary, St Corentine and either St Ambrose or St Gregory, and a most beautiful and impressive Christ of the Trades. In the latter weird allegorical picture a naked Christ stands surrounded by the tools of various trades and professions – and he squeezes blood out of his heart to bespatter them. **Godolphin House**, inland yet again, is 15th century, its north front set on huge Doric columns of 1635. It was the seat of the Godolphin family who were great tin masters. I have not seen it.

Trewavas Head is granite, with an old mine the workings of which run out under the sea. **Rinsey Head**, also solid granite, has an old engine house on it which is going to be preserved for posterity. These tall old engine houses that are such a feature of the Cornish scenery were to house the great steam engines that either pumped the mines out or drove the hoists that hauled things up or down them. **Tregoning** or **Tregonning Hill**, inland, is part of this same granite boss (Cornwall has been described as islands of granite floating in a sea of shale and slate) and in it is some of the decom-

posed granite known as china clay and it is here that William Cookworthy first discovered the stuff, or at least discovered its applica-
tion – on which was founded the English porcelain industry. There
were important mines around here, such as Great Wheal Vor which
yielded fabulous riches until about 1847 when she was closed down.
After 1851 over a quarter of a million pounds was spent in opening
her again but it all came to nothing. Great Work was another big
mine in this area.

Praa or **Prah Sands** has caravans galore. After the caravan
country comes the broccoli country, where the Cornish plant
broccoli late in the summer so that it survives the mild Cornish
winter and can get to the London market in the hungry gap after
Christmas. The Common Market will kill all this. Spring flowers are
also cultivated from here on westward.

Prussia Cove is a cleft in the rock where a doughty smuggler
used to live, and he called himself the King of Prussia to mark himself
off from other smugglers. His name was Henry Carter, and he had
the temerity to mount a battery of guns on the cliffs commanding
Prussia Cove, and nearby Bessy's Cove (Bessy kept an inn, or
kiddleywink as it is called in Cornwall – what the Welsh call a
'pub smuggling' – meaning an unlicensed pub) to keep the revenue
men away and, when the latter captured any smuggled goods of
his, he used to raid their storeroom and get it back again. On such
occasions he never took any *other* smuggler's goods – only his own.
There are a few little boats there now, hauled up a steep cliff path.
In April 1947 the old H.M.S. *Warspite* was being towed from Ports-
mouth to Clydeside for breaking up when she broke adrift and went
ashore at Prussia Cove.

Marazion has, according to the guide book: 'the complete
world of Celtic charm and legend, plus firm golden sands, and safe
bathing.' The legend is there all right, and the Celtic charm is there
in the off-season but apt to be a bit overlaid in the summer time.
The place was of importance of old for several reasons. One was that
it was the resting place for pilgrims bound for St Michael's Mount.
The other that it was at one end of the land-route between the
English Channel and the Severn Sea. Mariners wishing to go from
the one to the other would even drag their boats overland here
(after all it isn't quite four miles) rather than face the hazards of
Land's End. Also, this place was in the heart of the tin country,
St Michael's Mount was almost certainly a market and export place
for tin in very early times. It has been linked with the Iktin which
the 'Phoenicians' are supposed to have come to to buy tin. It would

have been a fairly obvious place to have been a centre of this trade, conspicuous from the sea, easily defendable so that stores of tin there could have been secure, a place where foreigners of doubtful trustworthiness could be admitted without letting them actually set foot on the mainland.

As for St Michael's Mount it really is a most splendid-looking place, and if there weren't all sorts of romantic legends connected with it some would have to be invented. It is every child's dream of a fairy castle. You can walk there at low tide, and see part of it, though not the private part of the mansion of Lord St Levan. The mansion is built on the site of the Benedictine priory that was established on this so obvious spot by Edward the Confessor, and which became a cell of the St Michael's Mount in Brittany, which is so astonishingly like the Cornish version of it but so much bigger. Before the Benedictine priory was founded St Michael is said to have visited the place in the 5th century, St Keyne came here from Ireland, and without a doubt it must have been an important and busy link in the chain of mysticism and Christianity which bound together the scattered and beleaguered citadels which were trying to hold out against the pagan tide of the Dark Ages on the western fringes of Europe.

The Chapel Rock on the mainland, on which used to stand a chapel in which the pilgrims could have an hors d'oeuvre as it were while they waited for the tide to uncover the causeway so they could get to the island for the main course, is made of greenstone, while the island itself is made of granite. This greenstone was brought here in her apron by Cormelian, the wife of the giant Cormoran, to help her husband who was busy building St Michael's Mount of granite. When he saw that she had brought the wrong kind of rock he not unnaturally slew her, and she dropped her load where it still rests and the giantess is said to be buried under the rock. The theory that certain unexpected outcrops of rock originated in much this manner is widespread about the country: one finds the same story in Yorkshire for example.

In 1425 an attempt was made to build an artificial harbour inside the island but nothing much came of it. In the days when boats were small enough to be hove up the beach harbours were less necessary, but as even fifteen and twenty tonners came into vogue the pressure to build harbours began. In 1549 the sequestered Mount was given to the Basset family. In the Civil War it was held for some time for the king. By 1727 it was in the hands of the St Aubyn family, as it is now, for in that year they were busy extending the quays and building the little harbour, which was subsequently used for exporting copper ore (to the smelters in Bristol and South Wales), refined tin and cured fish.

The island is open to the public on Wednesday and Friday all the year, and on Monday too from June to September. There is much to see: rich armour, the Chevy Chase Hall with its fine stucco frieze of a hunt, much old furniture, the church, St Michael's Chair in the lantern tower that will reverse the order of 'who wears the trousers' between man and wife (that is, in most cases, in favour of the man) and there is a strange ambience about this place.

The name Marazion has been popularly supposed to have come from some strange derivative of Jews' Town, but nowadays everybody believes that it simply meant Thursday Market. Pity.

Marazion Marsh, inland, is a nice small bird haunt. **Ludgvan** was the home of William Borlase (although see Pendeed), who published his *Natural History of Cornwall* in 1758, and was also the home of the parents of Humphry Davys, the inventor of the Davys Safety Lamp. Ludgvan was a tin-smelting place in the middle ages, the ore being brought downhill on pack animals from the upland mines.

The railway spoils the shore to Penzance, although on the long clean beach you can ignore it.

Penzance had an annual fair and a Wednesday market in 1332 so it is not an upstart place. In the 15th century there was a busy export of woollen cloth from here to Gascony. In 1451 it is known that three ships were employed in carrying troops to Gascony in the final throes of the English attempt to hang on to the place. By that time trade was growing with Ireland. In 1614 Penzance got a charter giving her borough status. By then tin mining was moving westward: the more easterly alluvial deposits, such as those on Dartmoor, having been worked out, and in 1663 Penzance was made a coinage, or stannary, town for the West of Cornwall and much tin was exported from here for the Continent. Penzance probably became of importance in the first place because it was on that important communication route which ran right along the spine of Cornwall. Penzance got sacked and burnt by the Spaniards in 1595, and badly beaten up by the Parliamentary troops in the Civil War.

Penzance remained a coinage town until 1838. After this the town must have subsisted chiefly on the pilchard industry, and also on the fact that it was the market town for West Penwith. Then the railway came, and Messrs Gilbert and Sullivan, and

Penzance began to become the considerable holiday resort that it is now.

Penzance had a lifeboat as early as 1803, and the station was finally closed in 1917 after having had a magnificent record. On the 5th of January 1867 the boat went out twice in a terrific gale and saved seventeen men off three different ships, and two days later, the gale having got up to the point of fury when men were saying that they had seen nothing like it in their lives a ship went ashore near St Michael's Mount. The boat managed to get alongside her and thirteen men leapt into her, but the captain refused to leave the ship and ordered five men to stay with him – threatening them with a revolver to force them to stay. The lifeboat had to leave them, and in the morning all six were dead. On Boxing Day of 1912, in a gale officially measured as ninety miles an hour the sailing lifeboat *Janet Hoyle* was launched to go to the assistance of the Italian steamer *Tripolitania* which was ashore on Loe Bar. Conditions were so bad that signal was made by rocket from Porthleven for the boat to return, but before she could do so her stemhead had been split away from her strakes by the terrific pounding into the seas and two of her crew died from the experience.

Now Penzance Harbour is still a port. Potash comes in from Germany for fertilizer, and timber for the broccoli crates from Portugal. Yachtsmen sail in, many flying the French flag, and lie in wait tied up to the inside of the big breakwater until there is enough tide for the Harbourmaster to open the lock gates and admit them into the floating harbour. On this tide-ridden coast it is delightful to be able to lie, for a few days, afloat all the time, tied up to a nice stone wall, without worrying about warps, legs, dinghies, mud, or the other hazards and encumbrances of tidal waters. There is a large and busy dry dock and a local diversion is watching the intricate business of getting ships in or out of it. This dry dock was built about 1884. The Old Pier was started in 1766 and extended in 1785 and in 1810 the first dry dock was opened. About 1811 the Pier was extended to 600 feet. The Northern Pier was started in 1845 and more improvements were made in the 1870s. Which all goes to indicate that Penzance was, in the 18th and 19th centuries, a considerable port for such a remote part of these islands. Trinity House is here, with their servicing depot for lighthouses and navigation buoys, this is the terminus for the Royal Mail Motor Vessel *Scillonian* which sails on Mondays, Wednesdays and Fridays in the winter and every day except Sundays in the summer. In February and March the *Scillonian* comes back loaded with flowers. You can also get to the islands from the heliport, to which buses go from the railway station.

Penzance is now not important as a fishing port. The harbour, in fact, seems to be under-used. Part of it in fact was filled in and turned into a car park and this is a tragedy, because who knows the trend of traffic in the future? The small ports seem to be slowly coming into their own again.

Newlyn is a larger and expanding fishing port, and is likely to expand far more as the Channel waters are fished out and boats are driven more and more to exploit the further reaches of the Atlantic Shelf. It has now been found that there are plenty of pilchards still – if you look far enough west for them. There are also tuna in western waters. Newlyn is well placed to exploit these fisheries.

At the moment there are about thirty biggish trawlers (biggish that is for Channel trawlers: there is nothing anywhere in the South of England remotely like the huge deep-water trawlers that fish from Hull and Grimsby), most of them old wooden ships, and there are some dozen large liners. Also several scores of small open boats – toshers and the like, which go lining, or tangle-netting, or potting, or taking trippers. There are some fourteen big boats here which belong to Porthleven but which fish from Newlyn. The tangle-netting is becoming perhaps the main trade here. A decked boat will shoot from ten to twelve *tiers* of nets, and there are some eight to ten nets in a tier. This may add up to about 800 fathoms of net in all. The tangle net, or ray net as most of the men call it here, is of very fine man-made fibre, with a very large mesh (maybe a foot across diagonals), enough lead in the footrope to sink it but enough buoyant plastic in the headrope to make at least some of it stand up like a wall in the water. Everything that crawls or swims near the bottom is apt to get tangled in it. It is a killer for lobsters, crabs and crayfish, is superseding the pot, and many fishermen – including those who use it – believe it will destroy the grounds. But fishermen are forced by economic circumstances to use the most destructive methods for taking fish – no matter how much long-term harm they do to the fisheries. Of course this net is entirely unselective, and very little that goes into it survives.

Newlyn is old: in 1340 there are records of it as Niwelyn. The name has been derived from Old English *niew*, new, and *hlynn*, torrent. Personally I would derive it from Brythonic *newydd*, new, and *llyn*, court, or great man's house. In 1435 Bishop Lacy gave forty days' indulgence (and you can do a lot in forty days) to people who helped build a pier. This old pier is still in existence inside the new piers. By 1800 Newlyn had the biggest drifter fleet in Cornwall. When the Bristol to London railway was opened in 1841 Newlyn fresh fish could be sent to Hayle, by steamer to Bristol, and thence to London, and this gave a boost to trawling, and Mounts Bay was a good trawling ground, also the premier mackerel waters. In 1866 and 1873 there were acts to extend the harbour. In 1888 the North, or Victoria, Pier was completed. Now ships of up to 2000 tons come in to load roadstone from the great Amalgamated Roadstone quarries at Carn Gwavas.

Newlyn anticipated St Ives as a centre for artists in the 19th century. The Newlyn School was founded about 1884, Walter Langley, Edward Harris and T. C. Gotch being the leaders. J. Passmore Edwards, in 1895, financed the building of a large art gallery, which is still there, and which is owned by the Newlyn Society of Arts: Forbes, Branley, Crooke, Chevellier, Tayler and Craft are names associated with it. Many of the artists eventually moved to St Ives, but Newlyn is still a lively centre of the arts.

Newlyn was the scene of two classic cases of Celtic assertion of independence. The first was the Great Sunday Fishing Controversy of 1896. At that time East Coast men, most of them Suffolk men from Lowestoft, were coming to the West Country in large numbers in their big sailing drifters for what they called the Western, or Mackerel, Voyage. In fair competition with the St Ives and Newlyn men they would shoot their drift nets – some of the big Lowestoft boats putting out five miles of net. But what the Cornishmen thought was unfair competition was that the 'Yorkies' as they called the East Coast men also landed fish on Sundays. The Cornish fishermen at that time were Wesleyans to a man and made an absolute point of not being at sea between midnight on Saturday and one a.m. on Monday. The East Coast men, after the quick penny in *this* life and not so concerned about the next, had none of these scruples. St Ives reacted first and the 'Yorkies' began to land at Newlyn but Newlyn quickly followed suit. In May 1896 the Newlyn and Porthleven men threw over a hundred thousand East Coasters' mackerels into the sea, and when a Lowestoft man complained he was severely beaten up. The next Tuesday six more Lowestoft boats came into the harbour with their Sunday catches and their fish were thrown into the sea after the first lot. Serious riots developed, the police could not cope with the situation, and two companies of the Royal Berkshires were called in and a torpedo-boat destroyer. Things got worse then and not better, and the soldiers had to warn more

Lowestoft boats to keep off by firing into the water. More warships were sent until four were anchored in the bay. In the end the matter was settled with typical British compromise, it being agreed that nobody should fish on Saturday night but they could on Sunday night. As late as 1929 a pleasure-boat operator got thrown into the harbour at St Ives for breaking the Sabbath and still Cornish fishermen are inclined to keep the Sabbath day if they can.

The other great drama was in 1937 when Penzance Town Council made, in their lack of wisdom, a clearance order for most of the fishermen's houses in Newlyn. Town Councils and other planning bodies just do not seem to be able to *take* 'fishermen's quarters' in English towns: the coast around these most beautiful and picturesque corners of our fishing ports have been ruthlessly bulldozed – always on the misconception that 'the fishermen would really rather live in nice clean council houses'. The fishing community of King's Lynn was practically destroyed when the North End was bulldozed a few years ago, while the desert that has been created in the fine old town of Hartlepool by the same kind of vandalism has to be seen to be believed, and the death of the Claddagh at Galway is an Irish tragedy. Nowadays, too late, it is being realized that these fishing quarters are 'picturesque' and at least they are not pulled down. The fishermen are forced out of them (*not* because they prefer living in 'nice clean council houses' as folklore has it – but because, when the houses come up for sale, they just cannot compete with the prices offered by city people). The fishing communities are dispersed, but at least the buildings are preserved.

When this threat hung over Newlyn the fishermen were so keen to leave their squalid dwellings and go to the 'nice clean council houses' that they sent a petition to Parliament which began:

'We, the undersigned inhabitants of Newlyn and district, wish to protest respectfully and strongly against the wholesale destruction of our village . . .'

Over a thousand people signed it. It produced, of course, no effect, and so the fishermen banded together and sent the Sailing Lugger *Rosebud* to London (460 miles) and when she got there her crew presented a petition direct to the Minister of Health. Another typical British compromise was effected: out of 157 houses 23 were to be reprieved and at least the fishermen were to get some very limited compensation for some of the others which were to be destroyed. At least a little was accomplished, but the resultant clearances destroyed Newlyn for ever as a 'picturesque fishing village'.

At **Penlee Point** a lifeboat station was established in 1913 to replace the stations at Penzance and Newlyn.

Mousehole was once of more importance than Newlyn, but now its fishing fleet has dwindled to nearly nothing. Its little artificial harbour was improved in 1861 when the New Pier was built, but thereafter, as Newlyn came up, Mousehole went down. In on-shore gales the mouth of the harbour has to be closed by a door, which is very nice when you are inside looking out, but not so nice if you are outside trying to get in. The village is very picturesque, very crowded, and motor cars should not be allowed to enter its narrow streets at all. It was burnt by the Spaniards in 1595 when Penzance and Newlyn were. Dolly Pentreath was buried at **Paul** just up the hill in 1777 and she is supposed to have been the last real Cornish speaker but there are plenty of people who will argue with that. Against the gate opposite the south-east corner of the church is a stone with an inscription on it for Dolly, with a verse in English and one in Cornish.

It might be useful here to consider very briefly the Cornish language. It is one of the Brythonic Celtic languages, the other existing ones being spoken in Wales and Brittany. Cornish is so like Welsh that it is really a dialect of the same language; the Breton onion sellers who come to Wales to sell their onions find themselves talking Welsh much more quickly than English. Unlike Welsh, Cornish has practically no literature, a few miracle plays being all that remain, but in 1902 the Celtic-Cornish Society was formed to try to revive the language and it has had some success: there are now said to be some seven hundred Cornish speakers, which is seven hundred more than there were in 1902, and they are increasing. In 1928 the first Gorsedd of Cornish Bards was held in the stone circle of Boscawen Un, which is only a few miles from the grave of Dolly Pentreath. A Cornish separatist movement is in existence, and growing quickly, to match the separatist movements in Wales and in Brittany. The Old Cornish Societies up and down the Duchy are not political, but try to stimulate interest in Cornish culture and language.

To return to Mousehole – it is strange, when contemplating Mousehole's insignificance today, to realize that it was once an important port for the shipping of pilgrims to Santiago and the Holy Land, and that in 1337 the Duchy of Cornwall decreed that Mousehole should be the most important fishery harbour in West Cornwall. The Duchy laid down various rules connected with it – one – a most excellent one and one that should be copied today in many places – was that the local peasantry should have the first option in buying their requirements of all fish landed at a reasonable price.

Mousehole was a trading port too: salt came in from Guérande in South Brittany and salt pilchards and pilchard oil went out. Maritime courts were held in Mousehole. The idea and form of these is said to have come to England from the classical Mediterranean world via the Isle de Oléron via Mousehole. An artificial harbour was started in 1393 but as Penzance rose, Newlyn declined.

In 1849 there were 425 fishermen in Mousehole and 370 fish packers, 45 fish curers and four cooperages. The name has nothing to do with vermin, there is a theory that it came from Old English *maew* – a gull, and *holh* – a basin. I feel though that the greater probability of a Celtic derivation should be examined, although there seems to have been a Cornish name which has since died out – Porth Enys, meaning port of the island – after the little island of St Clement's just off-shore. A hermit once had a chapel here.

CHAPTER 15

Lamorna to St Erth

❧

THERE is a fine cliff walk to **Lamorna**, where was a granite quarry and where ketches used to load. Much of it though was carted to Penzance in blocks and shipped from there, in ships too large to beach in the rather perilous Lamorna Cove. No vessel which is too big to be actually dragged bodily up the beach by her crew beaches on an open sea beach without a small element of risk. No weather forecaster in the world can be absolutely *sure* that an on-shore gale won't spring up during the period of low tide during which the ship cannot get off. If it does the big sea formed will most probably smash the ship before she can be hauled off to her kedges. But all round the coasts of the South-West and of Wales there are places like Lamorna Cove into which vessels did sail, drop some anchors (kedges) off-shore as they came in – and beach themselves at high tide for loading and unloading. The casualties among the ketches and sloops and small schooners that engaged in this sort of trade were always high. At Lamorna a small harbour was eventually built to try to lessen this risk, and ease the work of loading granite, but it wasn't much used. Up the valley from the Cove is a pub called The Wink. The derivation of this is obvious when it is remembered that a place like Lamorna was an ideal smuggling harbour. A man going into the pub and wanting some illicit brandy would not ask for it verbally, thus giving things away to any copper's nark who happened to be hanging around, but would merely give the landlord a wink. Further up the hill, at **Boleigh**, are two standing stones, or menhirs. There are also the Merry Maidens, which form a very fine stone circle (the maidens were dancing on the Sabbath and therefore quite rightly, many think, turned into stone), and, in a private garden, a fogou. There are several fogous in the Land's End peninsula, and the probability is that they were meat larders, exactly like the Iron Age meat larders on Skomer Island, or the similar constructions that are said to have been used on remote Scottish islands until very recent times. They are trenches which have been lined with stones and then covered over with big stone slabs so as to form a stone-lined tunnel. The Hebrideans and Skomer

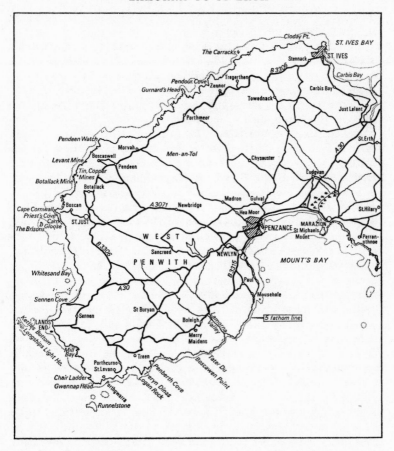

Islanders used to hang the young seabirds which they took from the nests in such large quantities to dry so that they could be stored until the winter. Fish, too, were dried by this means, and probably mutton, and from what I have seen myself in Africa I would guess that a small smoky fire would be kept going during the day – not to smoke the meat – but to keep the blow-flies away from it. Local legend has a quite different explanation for this fogou. It was, according to it, the entrance to the underground home of the wicked witch Buccabara. This lady held captive a hare, which, on being caught by the squire of Trewoofe when that gentleman was out hunting, promptly turned into a beautiful girl named Lamorna.

The happy outcome of this happening may be imagined. Lamorna itself was once called Nasmorna.

The cliff path is good from here, and progress very exhilarating. **Tater Du** has an unmanned lighthouse and foghorn on it, put there as late as 1965 after many a good ship had been wrecked on this coast, culminating in the Spanish S.S. *Juan Ferrer* in 1963.

Treen is a hamlet with a pub and a coastguard station. Phoenician merchants are supposed to have come to Penberth Cove below to barter for tin. **Treryn Dinas** (*tre* is inhabited place, *ryn* is fight, *dinas* is fort or fortified place) is a romantic place, marvellously situated, with an easily discernible triple line of defence across the narrow neck that joins the fort to the mainland.

The **Logan Rock** near here is the famous one that everybody goes to see. It got pushed over the cliff by the too exuberant Lieutenant Goldsmith, the commander of the local coastguard cutter, who, on hearing that the Cornish antiquarian Borlase had pronounced the feat impossible, went and did it. The local people, not unnaturally incensed, put pressure on the Admiralty, which put pressure on Lieutenant Goldsmith (who was a nephew of the poet, incidentally), and this gentleman, with a large body of bluejackets and an elaborate array of block tackles, hauled the rock – which weighs well over sixty tons! – up the cliff again and "in the presence of thousands, amidst ladies waving their handkerchiefs and universal shouts, Mr Goldsmith had the glory of placing the immense rock in its natural position uninjured in its discriminatory proportions.'

Porthcurno is chiefly distinguished by an enormous and hideously ugly car park. All car parks are ugly but somehow few of them are as overwhelmingly ugly as this one. Perhaps it is something to do with the setting, in what once must have been a beautiful cwm, or glen, running down to the sea. And beside the car park is the equally ugly engineering school and other offices of Messrs Cable and Wireless. Submarine cables go from here across the oceans. There is a grand little sandy cove here with some rare shells, in a fine setting, and hard by is the **Minack Theatre** which is something very beautiful and unique, for it is a natural amphitheatre half way down the most splendid cliffs, with the Atlantic as a back-drop. Here plays are performed all summer; details can be got from The Treasurer, Minack Theatre Society, Barclays Bank, Truro.

St Levan has a lost little church, with 'no parking' lines running down the lane towards it apparently for miles. There are two good crosses in the churchyard. Porth Chapel is very small ruins. **Porthgwarra** is said to have two tunnels connecting the *porth*, or cove,

Above, Kynance Cove; *below*, Mullion Cove.

Above, St Michael's Mount; *below*, Godrevy Lighthouse, near St Ives.

to the hamlet above, but I have not seen them. If you want the *good* part of the experience of standing at the Land's End without the attendant *bad* experiences that nowadays go with this then go to **Gwennap Head** which, although perhaps two miles further east than Land's End, is just as much a final outpost of England. Its local name is **Tol-Pedn-Penwith**, or the Holed Headland of Penwith, the hole being a great collapsed cave like the Devil's Frying Pan near the Lizard. The cliffs here are superb: showing very marked mural jointing: that is the granite seems to be cut up into fairly regular cubes. This happened when the rock was contracting after it had come up from the belly of the earth. The famous Chair Ladder is formed by this cuboidal fracturing of the granite that we have noticed, or mural jointing, and on it Madgy Figgy, a malevolent witch, used to sit and hope for wrecks. She did not always hope in vain, for the **Runnelstone**, about a mile off-shore, was a killer, standing, as it does, right in the track of shipping. Unsuccessful attempts at buoying this rock were made from 1795 onward, even the reprehensible Lieutenant Goldsmith had a go at it, but now it seems securely buoyed and has a light, a bell and a whistle.

Land's End must have been a very grand place before this age of motor cars, when Turner painted a great picture of it. It is still impressive to sail past it in a small boat (but what with the Kettle's Bottom, Tal-y-Maen – forehead of the rock – and the Shark's Fin you want to watch what you are doing. It is a very dangerous place to be indeed). To walk to Land's End, or otherwise approach it from the landward side, is most unpleasant and for my part you can have the 20th-century Land's End. There is a vast car park before the parking place in front of the big hotel and one of its several uniformed attendants actually runs out into the road and tries physically to stop cars to force them to go into the car park. As cars are larger and harder than car park attendants the thing to do is to hoot and drive on, when the attendant invariably gets out of the way. There is an air of catchpenny commercialism about the place that personally I find extremely distasteful. Incidentally the whole car park industry on the Cornish coast should be subjected to the scrutiny of a good accountant in the public interest.

The **Longships**, a couple of miles to sea, are of a porphyritic greenstone with masses of quartz in it. A Lieutenant Smith built a lighthouse there in 1795 but it has since been replaced with a light sixty feet high and on a fifty-two foot high rock. Six miles to the south is the Wolf, with another vital lighthouse, which was built by James Walker in 1870. To be seen far out on a clear day are the

Scillies: 140 islands, five of them inhabited. Between them and the mainland is said to have been the land of Lyonesse. The Seven Stones, of *Torrey Canyon* fame, only recently submerged in geological terms, were supposed to have been the site of a city. When Lyonesse was submerged a man named Trevilian is supposed to have escaped on a fast horse to the mainland: the sole survivor of the disaster.

Sennen Church Town is where King Arthur is supposed to have given thanks, after defeating the last Viking invasion of Britain to such effect that the mill wheel of the Vellan-drucher (velin means mill) was driven by the blood of the defeated enemy. King Arthur and his knights sat down to feast at a big flat rock called Table-men, which is about a quarter of a mile north of the church. On it ritual fires have been lit for divination purposes in the last century.

Sennen Cove is a splendid place. Before the breakwater was built it was just a terribly exposed beach from which boats could put off – absolutely unapproachable in an on-shore breeze. Even the lifeboat could not be launched, and after the wreck of the sailing ship *Khyber* at Land's End in February 1905 the breakwater was built so that the lifeboat could get out on these occasions. Twenty-three men aboard the *Khyber* lost their lives.

The lifeboat station was established at Sennen in 1853, after the local fishermen and the revenue officers, sinking their differences as seafaring men always do on this sort of occasion, ran the most terrible risks in the local boats trying, unsuccessfully, to save the captain and his wife and the crew of the *New Commercial* which went ashore on the Brisons in January 1851. One gold medal and eleven silver medals were awarded to the would-be rescuers by the R.N.L.I.: an almost unprecedented recognition of valour, for the R.N.L.I.'s silver medals are awarded with the greatest parsimony – let alone the almost non-existent gold one. All this contrasts strangely with stories of lanterns tied to donkeys' tails. This most exposed and dangerous station perhaps in the British Isles has saved to date 188 lives and won 21 silver and bronze medals. In the Second World War the boat was almost constantly in use. She can't be launched for an hour or two each side of low water, so pick your time carefully if you do intend to be wrecked on this coast.

As for Sennen as a fishing port, in 1850 there were eighteen fishing boats and 84 fishermen. At least once a winter (not generally more) a huge shoal of grey mullet used to swim into this shore, and the Sennen men tried to enclose it in their seine nets. The value of this catch, if they were successful, could be as much as a thousand pounds and so the incentive was considerable. The custom was that any Sennen male person – be he only a babe in arms – who was on the beach at the time of the haul had his share of the catch. Of course the main fishery then was pilchards. Now mullet and pilchards are of far less importance, but there are some rugged little boats which shoot pots around the numerous reefs and rocks of this rocky coast, a large number of small dories which are hired out to anglers, and a handful of men still earning a living from the sea.

Whitesand Bay, once called Porgowethan, is very popular with bathers and surfers, and also with beach anglers who catch plenty of bass and turbot besides other fish.

Land's End or St Just's airfield is just to the north and inland. It is privately run, and from here go flights to the Scillies and other places.

St Just is a peaceful little town, but once was a roaring mining camp. For it was very much the capital of the tin and copper belt that existed between Cape Cornwall and Pendeen Watch. It is beginning, it is pleasant to record, to derive some trade from tin mining again. In the church are some murals, one of St George and his dragon, and one of Christ blessing the Trades – the same theme as the more sophisticated mural at Breage. This fresco of Christ has extraordinary power. It will be seen that, as at Breage, the Christ is not only blessing the tools of the trades but also squirting his heart's blood over them. The paintings are thought to be about 1500. In St Just is a huge grand Wesleyan chapel that can be seen for miles. There is a pub at St Just called The Wink, so Lamorna is not unique in this respect.

The Priest's Cove at **Cape Cornwall** is the port of St Just, and here there is a concrete ramp up which boats can be dragged with windlasses, and some of those little tarred sheds in which fishermen keep their gear and get away from their wives when the weather is too bad to put to sea. There is a regatta, or water sports, here each year, in July, and local enthusiasts compete in a swimming race from the Brisons to the mainland. At **Carn Glouse**, **Gluze** or **Gloose** is a complex double-walled cairn surrounded by another double wall. This is an entrance grave, probably of early or middle Bronze Age. It is surrounded by mine dumps and remains. It was first excavated in 1874 by William Borlase and some miners, who found a huge dome within and seven burial cysts. Under it was a big pit, presumed by the diggers to have been the entrance to the underworld. Among greasy mould Borlase found an amulet, bits of pottery and lamb bones. Some people date it as late Bronze Age – I shouldn't think anybody really knows.

We are now right into the far west mining district of Cornwall. On the hill just north of Priest's Cove stands an isolated chimney stack which may well defy the efforts of the curious to guess what its purpose is. It was at the top of a shaft (now closed) which connected with underground workings and a fire was kept going at the base of the chimney which forced a draught of air up the chimney thus sucking air from the mine below and aiding in ventilation. This was Cape Cornwall Mine: near by was Wheal Owles where nineteen men and a boy were drowned when water rushed in from adjoining flooded mine workings, Boscean Mine, Wheal Edward, Carnyworth, Botallack, Levant and Geevor. Botallack was a large and famous mine. The Crowns Mine, right down near the coast near Botallack, which was closed in 1886 and the workings of Botallack itself (this shut down in 1912) are still interesting in the ruins that they have left on the surface. To help interpret these complex structures it may help to say that the circular stone or brick tables were the bases of buddles or buddle-frames, which were the large revolving frames down which water trickled to wash the lighter sands from the heavier cassiterite or tin oxide. Tall isolated chimneys connected by tunnels to furnaces are calciners. In the furnaces the ore was burnt to drive off the arsenic. The latter collected in the tunnel and chimney and from time to time was scraped off and sold for sheep dips, sprays for American cotton boll weevil, and doing away with mothers-in-law.

In 1919 one of these mines – the Levant – supplied a man-engine disaster. The man-engine was a device by which two series of platforms connected by rods to an engine on the surface reciprocated up and down – one series going up while the other went down. By this means men could get up the shaft by alternately moving from one series to the other, and thus spare themselves the fatiguing and time-wasting climb up endless ladders at the end of the shift. The rods broke at Levant when the day shift was coming out and thirty-one men were killed. There is still at least one man living in Pendeen today, who, as a boy, should have been on the man-engine, but was saved because he and some other boys had decided to race each other up the ladderways for a bet.

Levant is now part of Geevor Mine, and the two of them are one of the more successful tin mines now working in Cornwall. As Geevor is a working mine it is natural that its management does not encourage too many members of the public either wandering around their surface works, or clamouring to be taken underground. To anyone used to African copper or gold mines a Cornish mine seems

to be on a very small scale, also the complexity of the underground
workings is very great, for the tin-bearing lodes are scattered about in
the country rock in penny packets all over the place – often inter-
secting each other, often just petering out. Briefly the method of
mining at Geevor is this. Tunnels called *levels* are driven along the
lode (which is a nearly vertical slice of ore in the granite) at about
100-foot vertical intervals. Above one of these levels a sub-level is
driven – a smaller tunnel. This is connected to the main level just
below it by *rock-raises* which are steeply sloping tunnels with shoots
on their bottom ends. Miners go into the sub-levels and, using
pneumatic drills called pom-poms, drill holes into the ore above
their heads. These holes they charge with 'powder' (gelignite), the
rock is blown down, and some of the broken rock – but only some of
it – is drawn through the rock-raises into little tipping trucks (30
cubic feet at Geevor) drawn by battery locomotives, taken to the
shaft, shot into the skip and hoisted to the surface.

Only some of the broken rock is drawn out so that enough is left
for the miners to go in and comfortably stand on to drill the rock
above their heads again. Broken rock takes up more room than
unbroken, so that after every shift enough and enough only broken
rock is drawn away from below – and the miners stand on a floor of
broken rock to drill the next lot. At the end, when all the ore has
been blasted out, it is all drawn away down below to leave an open
gash in the granite rock – to stay deserted and empty until some
earthquake or cataclysm in future ages fills it in. This system of
mining is known as *shrinkage-stoping*, and when it can be done it is
ideal, being safe and labour saving. The ore bodies, or lodes, at
Geevor are narrow, the average width being about eighteen inches
although some are only four inches and some as much as six feet.
When the lodes are narrow the miners must break out some *country
rock* too – that is, in the case of Geevor, granite. This has to be
blasted out and got to the surface, otherwise the miners would not
have room to work, and it represents a heavy charge on the cost of
mining the ore. The almost-vertical stopes of Geevor (a *stope* is the
cavity left by the miners after they have blasted out the ore),
particularly after they have been emptied of broken ore and abandoned, and the intricate network of tunnels (a word miners never
use – there are drives, levels, crosscuts, adits, winzes and raises,
but never tunnels), these are very strange and beautiful. One can
easily see the fascination that has kept men going underground, in
spite of bad wages, hard and dangerous work, and – worst of all –
the ever-present danger of silicosis. Most old hard-rock miners con-

tracted this disease of the lungs to a greater or lesser degree: most of them died of it. Nowadays with wet drilling (water is forced down the bits of the drills to lay the dust) and other dust-laying techniques the danger is less, but it is still there. A man going underground is like a man going out to sea. He can never be quite sure that he will come back.

The great victory won at Geevor recently was the holing-through into Levant Mine. Levant was closed in 1930. After the man-engine disaster the deeper levels were never worked, and with the price of tin at a low level the mine simply could not afford the cost of new hoisting gear and other development. This mine had been worked a mile out under the sea and to a depth of 2000 feet below sea-level, and furthermore stoping had been carried out very close to the sea-bottom. A particularly rich lode of ore was found to get richer and richer as it was stoped out upwards nearer and nearer to the floor of the sea, until the miners – unable to curb their cupidity – could hear 'Davey Jones dragging his furniture about' in gales of wind above their heads. In other words, they could actually hear rocks being churned about by the waves at the bottom of the sea. They had sufficient restraint not actually to hole through into Davey Jones's locker and let the sea *in*, but when the mine was examined by the resuscitated Geevor mine in 1959 it was observed that the water in the flooded workings rose and fell with the tides. Thus it was realized that during the years in which the mine had been closed the sea had, in fact, broken through. Thereafter followed a unique and terribly difficult engineering operation, as aqualung divers explored the breach in the sea floor, and cleared it of débris. They fitted a reinforcing iron cover, and thousands of tons of cement were pumped from the cliffs above, and eventually, after many failures, the breach was closed. Then it was possible to de-water the mine, then go down it and pump more concrete into the levels nearest the breach to make quite sure the sea would not break through again, and then it was considered safe – to hole through from the adjoining Geevor Mine. The rich ore reserves of Levant are now being worked again, and so are the lodes in the old mines to the north of Geevor: Boscaswell Down Mine, Pendeen Consols and the newly discovered Simms Lode. The mine is not a 'gold mine' in the sense that any quick fortunes are at present being made from it. A third of the gross output that the miners have to extract with such difficulty and danger from under the ground has to go to the owners of the land overhead (under the sea this is not Davey Jones – but the Crown gets the money; under the beach the

Duchy of Cornwall; under dry land the landowners). And this makes it very hard to compete with foreign producers. But the mine is *working*, and is the biggest employer of labour for miles around (it would be devastating to the economy of the region if it closed down), and development is three years ahead of stoping (meaning that three years of productive mining can be carried out from the unproductive development work that has already been done) – which is a very healthy position. And who knows what reserves of tin, or of copper, may still be discovered under land or sea? The treatment of the ore on the surface, incidentally, is complicated in the extreme; and even when it has been reduced to pure fine cassiterite at the mine it still has to be sent to the North of England to be smelted.

It is a good walk to **Pendeen Watch**, where is a lighthouse, and an old mine (Pendeen Consuls). From here to St Ives is a magnificent cliff walk which it would be tedious to describe in detail. Pendeen Watch itself is a killas outcrop, there are others at Gurnard's Head and the Carracks (at Gurnard's Head the killas takes the form of a hard schist), after Gurnard's Head is an outcrop of greenstone and east of the Carracks another. St Ives is on the greenstone. All the rest is solid granite, for this has been called 'the granite land'.

High spots on this coast are **Porthmeor**, which is a lovely group of granite farm buildings, which supersede a settlement of seven round huts, two courtyard houses in which were found coins of A.D. 160 to 180, and a fogou or underground storage and drying trench. Remains of early iron and tin smelting have been found here too. Two miles south is the extraordinary **Men-an-Tol** or the Crickstone. This is a circular stone with a big hole in it between two pillars. No one really knows what it was, but until recently children used to be passed through the hole to cure them of rickets. Maybe they still are, although adequate supplies of vitamin D are said to be more effective.

Zennor has a fine and impressive quoit, cromlech, or chamber tomb, with a chequered history. In the 18th century William Borlase drew it as it had been for many centuries. After this the local farmer removed the supporters of it to make a cart shed. In 1881 a farmer named Grenfell went so far as to blow it up. He found under it a perforated whetstone of a kind found in other early Bronze Age graves – estimated to have been made in from 1600 to 1500 B.C. The quoit has now been more or less put back as it was. These quoits, of which there are many in Cornwall (at least four in West Penwith – or the 'toe' of Cornwall – alone), consisted of a capstone held up by a number of vertical stone pillars, and were originally covered over with earth so that they formed the entrance to a chamber tomb in the earth which was extended to one end of them. They are thought now to be tombs because they had graves in them. Most of our churches have graves in them too.

In Zennor church is the 'Mermaid of Zennor' carved on a bench end in the small south chapel. She is very beautiful. Her original swam to the little stream that runs into Pendour Cove to listen to the singing of a chorister named Matthew Trewhella. She enticed him into the sea and he was never seen again, but for many years afterwards the sound of his singing could be heard coming up from under the waves.

At Higher Tregerthen, towards St Ives, D. H. Lawrence lived for some time with his Frieda, but because she was an Austrian and he wore a beard they were suspected of being German spies and had to leave.

Zennor also has Mr Wigley and his **Folk Museum**, the latter a most admirable enterprise. Mr Wigley's garden and outhouses (he lives in an old mill) are crammed with old mining tools, domestic tools, furniture and equipment, farm implements, and a marvellous series of models representing the surface workings of an old tin mine. This is a collection of great interest. Mr Wigley, a school-master at Hayle County Secondary School, charges nothing for admission but there are collecting boxes, but too many people put nothing in them and the whole thing is a labour of love, and could be even better if the public were more generous. It is here that we find that the lower of two millstones is called the *harp* and that the upper should revolve at 200 revolutions per minute.

St Ives could be a book in itself, for it is a place of much interest and history. St Ia is said to have founded it back in the 5th century, sailing across from Ireland on a leaf. It was of little importance at first, for Lelant, inland, was the port of the area, but by 1377 Lelant had gone down and St Ives had come up. In 1408 there was a papal mandate for the consecration of a church at St Ives. In 1487 borough status was given and Lord Willoughby de Broke had the first stone pier built here. In 1770 John Smeaton, of Eddystone Lighthouse fame, built a pier here.

Perkin Warbeck landed at St Ives with 150 men from Ireland in August 1497 to try to conquer England. He lodged his wife at St Michael's Mount, marched on to Bodmin Moor, and was hanged at Tyburn two years later.

St Ives was early a port of embarkation for Ireland, serving the purpose that Fishguard now does. It was once a considerable port.

Leland wrote in 1538 that the sailors maintained a 'pharos' or light-house on Pendinas which is what is now called the Island. The former name of Pendinas indicates that this was once a promontory fort.

In 1844 we read that 165 coasting vessels came into St Ives, and at that time the port had 400 fishing boats and 735 men employed in the fishing industry. And St Ives was a ship-owning port too: owning 8994 tons of sailing vessels and 498 tons of steam.

In about 1885 the overcrowding of the harbour was such that the fishermen actually rioted in protest at it. In 1890 a big addition was made to Smeaton's Pier, and the West Pier was built in 1894 as a loading jetty for roadstone. At that time St Ives was packed with pilchard cellars, smoke kilns (for herrings were kippered here) a net factory and net tanneries. Alas, it is all gone. The St Ives fishing fleet is almost non-existent. The uncompromising stand that St Ives took in the Sunday Fishing Controversy was one of the factors that proved its undoing as a fishing port, for Newlyn eventually weakened, all the 'foreign' (i.e. East Coast) boats began to use that port, the fish merchants went there, and there the trade was established and has remained. The arrival of the railway from London to St Ives in 1877 could have given this port an enormous advantage but it is an advantage that it did not keep. It was Wesley, of course, who was initially responsible for the uncompromising sabbatarian attitude. Such an attitude can certainly be defended in trawling or drifting or the sort of fishery in which one day is very much the same as another; but in a fishery such as pilchard seining it can hardly be defended at all. The fishermen may stand idle on the shore for week after week – waiting for the one shoal of pilchards to come that will make up most of their income for the year. And if God sends the shoal on a Sunday . . .

At the base of Smeaton's Pier is the little chapel of St Leonard's and in days of old a friar was stationed here to bless the fishermen before they put to sea. In the chapel now is a plaque recording the names of fishermen drowned at sea between 1833 and 1940, and it is a long list. For if the South Cornwall coast is a dangerous one for small fishing boats it is as nothing compared to the North Cornwall one. Such coast place names as Hell's Mouth and Dead Man's Cove tell their own tales.

As fishing declined so holidaymaking came, in the case of St Ives led by the very strong group of artists who settled there from the 1880s onwards and came to be known as the St Ives' School. Sickert and Whistler came here but there were many others, some famous enough in their time but now perhaps dated. The St Ives Society of Artists was founded in 1927, and in 1949 the breakaway Penwith Society of Arts, which seems to have all the trump hands now.

It was natural that 19th-century artists, preoccupied with their search for the 'picturesque' as an antidote for the horrors of industrialism, should have sought St Ives: with its narrow alleyways, fishermen's cottages built of huge blocks of granite, great fleet of beautiful wooden sailing boats. Now St Ives is only very marginally a fishing port, it is crowded with holidaymakers to suffocation in the summer (they *must* stop those cars down by the harbour – and there are just far too many people). But people like Barbara Hepworth and Bernard Leach still cling on here, presumably finding strength in each other's company. Writers perhaps do not flock together as much as painters do, but as we have seen Lawrence spent some time at Zennor during the First World War, and in St Ives itself Virginia Woolf lived, merely because her father lived there.

Besides being a fishing port and trading port and ship-owning place St Ives was a considerable mining town. St Ives Consols Mine was a great producer, its ore-bodies being much wider than most in Cornwall. The method of stoping these required timber supports for the hanging wall ('roof'). Shrinkage stoping, as we have seen, does not require timber. A disastrous fire broke out in the timbering underground in the 1840s and put the mine out of action. The present Pednolva Hotel stands where the engine house of a mine once stood, and it is said that steps may be seen cut in the rock inside the hotel which were once part of this mine. Part of St Ives is called Stennack, and this itself means tin workings. No doubt tin streaming occurred in very ancient times in the Stennack Valley. This whole area was dotted with mines at one time, and there were several right in the town itself.

Things to see now are the little fishermen's chapel already mentioned, at the base of Smeaton's Pier, the St Ives Museum at Wheal Dream, which is housed in an old Seamen's Mission building and which contains, among other things, an interesting collection of pilchard pressing and curing equipment, Knill's Monument, up behind Carbis Bay where, on 25th July every five years (next one due 1976), ten little girls have to dance to the sound of a fiddle and then sing the Hundredth Psalm. There are then the various old pubs down by the waterfront, particularly the Sloop, and there are plenty of exhibitions of the work of the local artists: the Penwith Society holding theirs in a pilchard cellar in Porthmeor Road, the

St Ives Society theirs in the Mariner's Church by the harbour car park and the St Ives Art Club in a building at Westcott's Quay.

There is an important lifeboat station here too, and one with a splendid record, if it has been at times a tragic one. On the last day of January 1938 the motor lifeboat *Caroline Parsons* went out in a terrible blow to try to save the crew of the Panamanian steamer *Alba* which had gone on the rocks north of the Island. The coxswain ordered the lifeboat's anchor away to windward of the wreck, intending to use the anchor to kedge the boat up to windward again after the men had been taken off the stricken ship. Twenty-two men were taken off the steamer but when the lifeboat's crew began to haul away on their anchor cable the anchor 'came home' – i.e. dragged along the sea-bottom. The result was that the boat could not get clear and was turned over by a huge breaking sea. The local rocket crew got all but five men ashore alive, including all the lifeboat crew, but the boat was a total wreck. The very next year, on the 23rd of January 1939, the *John and Sarah Vliza Stych* was launched in another very bad gale to go and stand by a ship in distress off Cape Cornwall. As the boat rounded Clodgy Point, and met the full fury of the westerly, a sea hit her and she capsized. Four of her crew of eight men including the coxswain were washed away and were drowned. Being a self-righter she recovered but her propeller was fouled, and she drifted to leeward across St Ives Bay. She was capsized a second time and the motor mechanic went and yet a third time and two more of the crew went, leaving only one man, William Freeman, alive. Finally she went on the rocks at Godrevy Point and, by one of those miracles that sometimes happens at sea, Freeman was able to crawl to shore, the sole survivor. Earlier, on the 2nd of February 1873, the lifeboat *Covent Garden* was launched to go to three sailing ships which were in distress. Being only under oars (the gale was too strong for canvas) she was driven back to the beach, having failed to reach the ships and with her crew completely exhausted. A second crew immediately volunteered and they managed to get out to one of the wrecks and save six men. When they got back they, too, were exhausted, and a third crew launched the boat again and managed to save one man, a fourth crew then made the attempt and were driven back defeated – and yet a fifth crew took over and this time managed to get to one of the wrecks and bring back six men. Anybody who has ever pulled at a heavy oar in a ferocious sea will have some idea of the killing nature of this work: it feels like trying to hang on to the leg of a bucking bronco. From its foundation in 1840 up to 1955 the St Ives station has made

250 launches, has saved 475 lives, and earned thirty-one silver and bronze medals. Lanterns tied on donkeys?

In 1820 the vicar of St Ives told the diarist Rev. Francis Kilvert that the stink of fish stopped the parish clock.

Proceeding round the bay, **Lelant**, which was the parent of St Ives, is picturesque and not so crowded, and the estuary in front of it is a bird sanctuary. Lelant was at one time in danger of being overwhelmed by blown sand, and it was probably the silting up of its estuary with this same sand that caused its decline and the rise of St Ives. The north coast of Cornwall is prone to drifting sand. This is because the predominant westerlies cause the sea to fling its suspended sand up on any possible beaches, and then, when the sand has dried, it gets blown inland to come to rest on the first convenient dune.

Right inland, and not on the coast at all, do not miss **Chysauster**. This is a most important and interesting Iron Age settlement, and very much worth going to see, for it is not hard here to imagine what it must have been like to have lived in an Iron Age village. Anyone who has lived in a central African village will not even have to use his imagination.

CHAPTER 16

Hayle to Padstow

꧋

Hayle comes from the Cornish word for estuary: *eyl*. Helford is
from the same source. It was originally part of the Port of Lelant.
It may not seem a very delightful place at the moment, having
rather the air of a *passé* industrial town, and being much congested
by traffic, but it is of great interest to the industrial archaeologist.

In the early 18th century it had at least two tin smelting houses,
using Welsh coal. Then some Bristol copper merchants came and
set up **Copperhouse**, still called by that name, where they smelted
copper also with Welsh coal. About the middle of the 18th century
the manager of Copperhouse, a young man named John Edwards,
had much work done on the port, which included a system of
scouring the harbour out with a flood gate: a technique much in
vogue in the 18th century, before dredgers were of much use. It is
interesting to compare the harbour-scouring arrangements of Hayle
with those of Seaton Sluice in Northumberland or, nearer at home,
Porlock Weir and Bridgwater. The walls of the lock pounds and
wharves are built of copper slag.

Hayle became the chief port serving the mines of the Camborne
and Redruth area, and it is said that in 1750 there were six hundred
mules employed in carrying coal inland to the mining area, and
refined tin and steatite, or soapstone, out. The steatite went first to
the Potteries, being shipped to Runcorn and carried overland to
Stoke on Trent until the Trent and Mersey Canal was built when it
went by water, and later to Worcester.

About this time a young blacksmith named Harvey set up a
foundry to cast machinery for the mines. Harvey's firm grew very
quickly and Harvey was a brilliant man, building his own dock at
Hayle which adjoined that of Copperhouse, and competing with the
latter firm to such an extent that a terrible rivalry grew up between
the two firms and there were violent scenes when workers of the
two groups actually came to blows. Harvey's won in the end and
swallowed up its rival of Copperhouse. The fact was that the latter,
as a copper house, was uneconomic. It required three tons of coal to
smelt a ton of copper and it was cheaper to ship the ore to Neath,

or Swansea, or Chepstow, where the coal came from. The wharf and buildings at Copperhouse were incorporated in the foundry.

Meanwhile the latter waxed great, making ore crushing, winding and pumping machinery, steam engines, and ultimately ships. When the great Haarlem Lake in Holland – known as the Wolf because its raging waters were swallowing up villages – was drained in 1844 Harvey's built the biggest pump in the world – a cylinder with a bore of 144 inches – to be shipped out for the purpose. To make this pump it was necessary to melt twenty-five tons of iron in not more than six minutes. In that same year, incidentally, 856 ships cleared in and out of the port of Hayle, which gives some idea of its importance. Ships of up to 4000 tons were built at Hayle, and one of the most interesting was a 43-ton iron screw steamship, the *Patmos*, built for Wedge of St Ives. There is a half model of this vessel in St Ives Museum. She carried cargo, running backwards and forwards across to France and also to Bristol. But she was designed as a trawler, and fished in Cornish and later Irish waters. In the latter she met resistance, from sailing fishermen who felt that steam was most unsporting. She was never a success, and was eventually sold for £800 to go to London River, and from there she went to South America, where she still may be.

But Harvey's, the yard in which the *Patmos* was built, went from strength to strength, and in 1860 was employing a thousand men. In the early 1900s, however, it all came to naught. Competition from the giant yards and foundries of the North was too much for it. In 1908 the foundry was wound up and the buildings turned into a builder's merchant's premises, which they still are.

In the early 1800s there was a regular steamer service to Bristol from Hayle, but in 1841 the railway came from London and killed all this. Before this even Hayle had had a railway: one to Redruth, and this was a most important factor in keeping Hayle a port: the mules couldn't go on for ever.

And Hayle is still a port, surprisingly in this age of the all-conquering motor lorry. Coal comes in for a power station that looks as if it ought to be scheduled as an ancient monument. Sulphur comes in for the I.C.I. works near by, and petrol and oil for the Esso depot. Rowes of Redruth have a huge shed, into which Irish and Scottish seed potatoes come by ship for the Cornish early potato growers. Scrap iron goes out in some quantity. Ships of a thousand tons can get into the port, and there is 14 feet over the bar at springs.

There is also some fishing activity. St Ives is not a good harbour

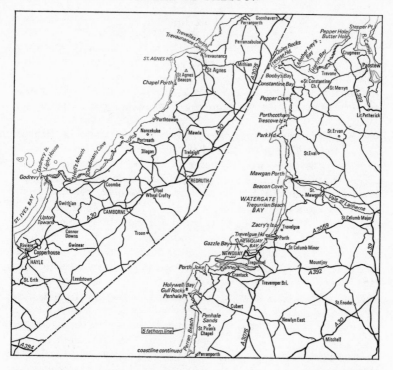

for boats of any size. The *Girl Renée*, a fifty-foot trawler, operates from Hayle. The family that owns her also owns a big 'skin diving' boat. There is much skin diving for lobsters and crayfish from Hayle. One boat here has a compressor on board, but there is a compressor ashore too, and boats without compressors can charge their air bottles there. The divers have practically denuded the coast for many miles of shellfish, and in fact have started moving across the Bristol Channel to base themselves in Wales and denude that coast too. The traditional fishermen hate them. They have claimed that the divers rob their pots. This is almost certainly untrue, because it would be too difficult for a diver to take a lobster out of a pot, but they certainly do dive right next to pots and clear up the lobsters that have been attracted by the smell of the bait. Undoubtedly, if something is not done very quickly to control this form of fishing, first the crayfish and then the lobster will become extinct around our coasts. The Irish have already had the sense to ban it in their territorial waters. When fishermen become too efficient fish become

175

extinct. There are only two logical courses to take about this skin diving for shellfish. One is to ban it, and allow the limited efficiency of surface methods of fishing (i.e. hoop nets, pots, and tangle nets) to preserve the fish from extinction, the other is to accept it but farm the bottom of the sea as the land is farmed. This would entail letting each diver, or firm of divers, 'own' an area of rocky ground on the bottom of the sea, and fish it to their heart's content but allow nobody else to fish it. The result of this would be that the owners, or concessionaires, would preserve their stocks of shellfish, just as the gulls' egg hunters of the Yorkshire cliffs used jealously to preserve the stocks of gulls along their private stretches of cliff.

The crayfish divers, though, are skilled and courageous young men. Most of them fish from boats owned by other people – about four divers to a boat as a rule – and give a third share of their catch to the boat. When fishing fresh ground it is nothing for a diver to earn £250 in a week, but of course bad weather prevents them from going out at all. Crayfish are the chief quarry, and when a team of divers is fishing ground which is not being fished by rival divers a certain conservation is exercised: notably the conservation of the cock crayfish, as it has been found that the cocks draw hens in from surrounding waters, and that as long as a cock is left on a piece of ground the hens will be drawn to him. If the cock is removed then that piece of ground will become barren. The divers freely admit that they have denuded the Cornish coast, and nearly all of them intend to move north to Wales to join their brethren there who are doing exceedingly well. What they will do then is doubtful, as crayfish do not extend any further north around the British coast than Strumble Head.

Hayle has a claim to fame in that the famous Trevithick's wife kept, first the Freemason's Hall, which was then a pub, then the White Hart Hotel, but more of Trevithick under Camborne.

Hayle Secondary Modern School, incidentally, has built up a good collection of models of old mines and of old implements, and anyone who is really interested can get permission to visit it. In fact, as I write, the possibility is being discussed of opening it to the public.

At **Riviere**, over the river, the tyrant Teudar kept his fortress back in the 6th century. He set upon a group of Irish missionaries who had just landed at Hayle and killed St Gothian, or Gwythian, and others of his party. He is thought to have been a Christian himself, albeit not a very exemplary one, for his name may have been Theodore, although it is not unlike the Brythonic name Tudur

Armed Knight and Longships Lighthouse, Land's End.

Above, St Ives; *below*, the coast near Chapel Porth, St Agnes.

so maybe this proves nothing. In any case he was an important figure in Cornish legend.

Upton Towans is a large area of blown sand, which tends to increase as more and more sand blows in from the fine beach of St Ives Bay. Dredgers, incidentally, were working in this bay until 1969 looking for tin. There were many mines in this area: one, Wheal Emily, on the Towans itself, then Nanterrow Mine, Wheal Nancemellin (*nans* = valley, *mellin* = mill), Silver Valley, Wheal Lilly, Wheal St Andrew being some of them. On the top of Prosper Hill was Wheal Prosper, the site of Trevithick's first condensing engine. The Towans were notable for a special breed of sheep up into the 18th century, which were said to have been unimproved descendants of the Bronze Age sheep whose bones are to be dug up in the same area. There is a story that once they were blown out by a great gale into St Ives Bay, and caught by the St Ives fishermen, who thought they were a new kind of fish.

At **Gwithian** was found a most important Bronze Age settlement, buried in the blown sand, and showing three levels of occupation, each separated by sand. The settlement is thought to have occurred between 1400 and 1200 B.C. There are lynchets, or small square fields, some of which had been fenced not by stone walls but by thorn hedges of the sort still so commonly used in Africa, plough marks of the *ard* or wooden scratch-plough can be seen (the plough still used by most of the peasants of Asia) showing the cross-ploughing recommended by Virgil in the *Georgics*. The plough furrows, or scratches rather, were from four to five inches deep and from a foot to two apart. Near the hedges, where the plough could not get, are spade marks similar to those made by the 'Celtic shovel', that heart-shaped tool in use all over the Celtic lands today. There was also at Gwithian a permanent settlement of the 7th century, including the remains of St Gothian's Chapel, which may have been built by the saint himself before he was martyred by the reprehensible Teudar, or may have been built in his honour by his converts afterwards. It spent many centuries preserved by the blown sand, but was most unfortunately uncovered by a Mr Richards Hockin, who, being a farmer and a Methodist, could find nothing better to do with it than to turn it into a cow shed. Nothing can be seen of it now. It was still visible in Leland's time (1540), not yet having been quite overwhelmed by the sand. Mr Charles Thomas (bardic name *'Gwas Godhyan'*) writes most learnedly about it in the little church guide on sale in Gwithian church.

Off **Godrevy Point** is **Godrevy Island**, on which stands the lighthouse that the characters in Mrs Virginia Woolf's book *To the Lighthouse* made such a meal of getting to. Mrs Woolf's lighthouse was ostensibly set in Scotland, but in fact it was here. The submarine reef which runs out north-west from the island (which is in fact several islands) and which should be avoided by mariners is called by St Ives fishermen as 'Plenty-to-come-yet' referring to the lobsters which used to proliferate in its rocky crannies. The skin divers have done for them now. In 1649 a ship which contained the wardrobe and other effects of the late King Charles the First struck the island, and of a crew of sixty only a man, a boy and a dog survived. They managed to clamber on the rock and spent two days living on rain and seawater, while his late Majesty's effects were washed up on nearby beaches. The steamer *Nile* hit in 1854, and so Virginia Woolf's lighthouse was built, and first lit in 1859. The lighthouse is now unmanned. Part of its original dioptic lens can be seen in Truro Museum.

The steep and rocky cliffs to Portreath have many old mine adits driven into them, some of which pour muddy water into the sea.

Camborne, inland, is the capital of the Cornish mining country, as Johannesburg is of the Rand. It is a place of first interest to hard rock miners. Here is the most famous School of Mines in the world, the Holman Mining Museum and Permanent Exhibition, which has in it a wealth of mining machinery (perhaps the best collection of rock drills in the world), some splendid early mining photographs, and a Rostowrack rotative beam engine which still works and fills the high building from floor to roof. (Holmans has now been taken over by another firm, and there is talk locally of the museum being closed. If it is it will be a disgrace.)

On Station Road there is a memorial to Richard Trevithick on his birthplace, and his statue stands outside the public library. Trevithick of Illogan was one of the great engineering geniuses of the 18th century. He built the first ever carriage to move over land by steam power, and he designed and built a great variety of pumps for mines, rock drills, dredging equipment and crushing and other milling machinery. His pumping machinery saved Cornish mining from eclipse. He died penniless, and Parliament turned down a request to give him a pension, but, after all, Cornwall is a long way from London. There is now a flourishing Trevithic Society in Cornwall, dedicated to the object of keeping his memory alive and of encouraging research into engineering history and the preservation of ancient industrial monuments.

Beacon Hill, near the station, is the road along which the first steam road locomotive made her maiden voyage. On the road to Redruth there are three ancient pumping engines, two of them (on the old East Pool Mine) owned by the National Trust. There is also one at the still very active South Crofty Mine which is preserved, but not generally open to the public. There is a monument also to William Bickford, of Tuckinmill, who was the inventor of the safety fuse. In 1830 his factory turned out forty-five miles of fuse. His safety fuse superseded the goose-quill or the rush filled with black powder, two hazardous devices. The idea of safety fuse is to allow the miner to provide for the lighting of his gunpowder, or in more modern times the detonating of his gelignite or other high explosive, without actually getting blown up himself. William Bickford's invention has saved countless lives.

But back to the coast. **Portreath** was a little port serving the mines around Camborne, and is a place of the first interest archaeologically. Alas, the fine little harbour is now in the hands of a company which is ripping up such things as one of the first railway lines in the world: a line laid on granite blocks, and which has fenced off the Pier, and tried to fence off the harbour, and is packing holiday houses into what was the harbour area as tightly as it can get them. The whole character of the place is being changed, and in my opinion for the worse.

The railway which is so ruthlessly being ripped up as I write was laid down in 1809, to the St Day and Gwennap mines, and an observer said that it was a way: '. . . over which the wheels of the carriages, which were constructed on purpose, run on cast iron: which facilitates in an extraordinary manner the progress of the vehicles, and greatly lessens the force of animal exertion.' By 1840 100,000 tons of ore a year were coming down this railway, to be shipped to South Wales ports in 700 shiploads. There were huge dumps of ore where the 'housing development' is now going on, waiting to go out, and huge dumps of coal having come in. The firm of D. W. Bain and Co. owned eighteen schooners in the port. It is a great pity that this fine little harbour should be so misused, particularly at a time when it looks as if small coastal shipping may be going to make a come-back.

The little bay to the east of Portreath can be got down into by a steep path, and it is a super bay, with sand among the rocks. The rocks are of a very shiny, crumbly, schist, rather beautiful. On top of the cliffs the cliff path takes you to Porthtowan, past the grim barbed wire of Nancekuke bacterial warfare experimental station. Just before you get to the fenced area there is a mine shaft on the cliff top and an adit down below in the cliff which pours out a great volume of reddy-brown water which colours the sea for some distance. I have been unable to locate the mouth of the mighty level which was known as the Great Adit, and was thirty miles long, discharging the waters of many of the mines in the Gwennap and Redruth areas. Maybe this is it, but I am writing here from ignorance.

Do not, on any account, miss Mr Morse's splendid farm museum at **Mawla** (it is on the coast road from Portreath to Porthtowan). Mr Morse, who is a road foreman, has here amassed a large and very comprehensive collection of farming implements: as good a collection as there is to be seen. Mr Morse charges nothing for a visit to this museum, and the collecting box that is there for such people as are honest enough to use it is for hospitals and other charities. It is sad that a vast number of the machines on view are open to the skies. It would cost five thousand pounds to build a building large enough to house them and Mr Morse hasn't got five thousand pounds, and is out at work on the roads all day. This is one of the most important collections of 'bygones' in the British Isles and badly needs assistance from somebody. Among the thousands of items of interest I like particularly the 'flop-jack' which works in the tiny stream by the house and pumps all Mr Morse's water, the ox cart, which is in the long shelter by the house, and the butcher's van. The latter, a splendid four-wheeled vehicle, was so built as to enable the butcher to do all his driving and selling without getting out of his seat. Mr Morse tells a story of how the owner outwitted two robbers. There is a cider press which is probably quite unique at the present day, worked by the weight of an enormous beam, with a very cunning device for levering the beam up again after it has come down to press the apples. There is a machine for beating the grain out of straw without breaking the straw, and thus leaving the straw in a condition suitable for thatching a roof. But it would take a long day to examine all the exhibits.

At **Redruth** is the Gladiator Club, which owns one of the most splendid self-driven steam engines in existence: the *Gladiator*, enormous and resplendent with polished brass. It tows astern of it an equally splendid steam organ, the voice of which can be heard from afar, and the two tour the country collecting money for charity. The *Gladiator* was built by Charles Burrell and Sons of Thetford, in Suffolk.

Near Redruth is **Gwennap Pit**, in which Wesley used to preach to huge concourses of repentant tin miners. One gathers that they had plenty to repent about, because pre-Wesley they were a boisterous lot. There are many other things of interest to be seen in this immediate locality. One is Saraah's Foundry, near Treleigh, east of Redruth. This has closed down now as a foundry, alas, but should immediately be restored before it is destroyed. The whole great foundry worked on the power provided by one enormous water wheel, which is still there and in good condition. The place is of the greatest archaeological interest, and there is nothing else like it anywhere in the country. It is not open to the public.

A much happier story can be told of the Tolgus Tin Company, on the Portreath Road from Redruth. This runs a large tin stream-ing works, in which tin-bearing beach sand and material from old mine dumps from which the tin was not efficiently extracted are subjected to a large number of complicated processes to extract the tin oxide, which is then sent to Liverpool or to Yorkshire to have the pure metal smelted out of it. A number of machines of great interest may be seen working. There is what is probably the oldest Cornish stamp mill in the world still working (driven by a water wheel), a calciner (no longer used but still complete) for the removal of arsenic (as described under Botallack, p. 164), such things as round frames ('boddles' or 'buddles'), bumper tables, kieves, heather brushes, dipper wheels and rag frames. All the latter devices are for separating the heavier oxide of tin from the lighter sand. The place can only keep going because it is a highly commercialized working museum, and is open to the public from Easter Monday to mid-October and you have to pay. There is a large shop and a slightly unfortunate catch-penny air about it all – which is a pity, but if it is necessary to keep such a place going is well worth it. There should, though, be two sorts of conducted parties through the works: those for people seriously interested who *really* want to know what it is all about, and those for crowds who are just out for an outing, and might just as well have gone anywhere else. But otherwise the whole enterprise is admirable. Saraah's Foundry should be worked in the same way.

Porthtowan is nowadays a holiday place only. **Chapel Porth** has a good (and popular) beach and two large car parks (where you pay, of course), and the Trevithic Society has started work to install a water-driven Cornish stamp mill here. A stamp mill was a device which pounded rock to dust by means of a series of iron stamps which were made to go up and down in a trough. The cliff path to **St Agnes Head** is delightful, through most brilliantly flowering heather if it be the right time of the year. St Agnes Beacon is worth climbing to, is a great viewpoint and has tumuli. **St Agnes** itself is a pleasant town, a little inland, and has two good coves: Trevaunance, and Trevellas Porth.

Trevaunance was the harbour of St Agnes, and also, surprisingly, a port for Truro, which is on an arm of the sea of its own. But Truro required a harbour on the north coast of Cornwall, so that trade could be carried on with Bristol Channel ports without the perilous rounding of Land's End. In 1632 one John Tonkin tried to build a harbour here – but it was washed away by the sea. In 1684 Hugh, another Tonkin, tried, but his work was destroyed by a gale in a few hours. In 1699 he tried again, to a design by Henry Winstanley, the great engineer who built the wooden lighthouse on the Eddystone. In 1705 Winstanley's work was swept away, but by 1710 another Tonkin, Thomas, had completed it again. In 1736 Thomas's work was completely destroyed and so was the fortune of the Tonkin family: it had all been dissipated by the sea.

In 1793 a company of adventurers obtained an act of Parliament to start another harbour works, and they were more or less successful. Schooners were built here, and trade was done with Newfoundland and the Mediterranean. Ships were loaded and unloaded by hoist from wooden stages on the high cliffs above. In the 1920s the two harbour arms were washed away, and now nothing remains but four little boats on a dangerous beach.

At St Agnes is the Cornish Seal Sanctuary, in which baby seals which are injured by the sea, or washed up on beaches and not discovered by their mothers, are kept, and healed, and fed, and, if they recover enough, put back into the sea. Nobody could fail to be delighted by the animals, although the ecological *rationale* of keeping even more seals alive in seas which are infested with them (a seal eats a stone of fish a day and our seas are getting denuded of fish) may be questioned. The seal has no natural enemies in British waters except a traditional one: man. If man stays his hand – what agent is going to control the number of seals? The answer, unfortunately, is starvation. But nothing could be more delightful than to watch their keepers feed and play with the seals: it is a perfect human–animal relationship and gives enjoyment to thousands of people. Unfortunately the latter don't put very much money in the collecting boxes provided for the purpose, and much-needed improvements cannot be done.

On the one side of **Trevellas** is Harmony Cot, where John Opie was born (really named Oppy), the son of a carpenter, in 1761. He died in 1807, having made his name as a painter. On the other side of Trevellas is the Cornish Gliding and Flying Club. On the coast here is a wolfram mine, which was operated until the Second World War.

And then we come to **Perranporth**. This has been developed as a large and very crowded holiday resort, for it is near the splendid beach of Perran which faces west, and is ideal for surfing. The sport of malibu boarding has swept this coast, and a car looks naked if it doesn't have a couple of these devices strapped to its roof. Perranporth was a port, and a railway connects it to a group of mines at Newlyn Downs.

Penhale Sands are supposed to cover the lost city of Longarrow or Langarrow. The legend is that this was a great city, stretching for four miles. The people kept slaves, but the free women began having it off with the slaves and so the place was destroyed by a storm and overwhelmed by the sand.

Overwhelmed by the sand too, eventually, was St Piran's church which, built in the 6th or 7th century, was dug out in 1865, and found to be in perfect condition having been preserved since it was buried in the 8th or 9th century. Many skeletons were found, including three martyrs, with their heads on their breasts. It was the only perfect Celtic church that had come down intact into the 19th century. But alas – the Victorians, it seems, were just as vandalistic as people of our own time: within three days all the carved stone-work of the place had vanished! What remains is now protected by a breeze-block edifice of really hideous aspect: surely if a prize were to be awarded for the most ugly building in Cornwall this would win it? The door is unfortunately generally kept locked. It is poignant to see people, who have walked over the sand dunes to get to the place, piously taking photographs of the breeze-block building in the fond belief that it is the Celtic one. The position of the place is romantic, surrounded by a small ocean of sand dunes, and – thank God – it cannot be reached by car. It is a strange experience to visit this ancient place while the British Army conducts a mock battle in the sand dunes to the east, while an officer with a very British voice describes the action on a loud-hailer to a party of cadets. Just to the east of St Piran's church is the foundation of another Celtic church, and a Cornish cross. It is supposed that this second church was built after the first had been overwhelmed by the sand. St Piran, whom these ruins honour, was an Irish monk of the 5th century whom St Patrick first made Bishop of Ossory and then sent as a missionary to Cornwall. He is supposed to have crossed the sea on a millstone, but however he crossed it he landed at Pendinas, near St Ives, and travelled east to this place where he set up his oratory. He is the patron saint of tin miners and also of Cornwall. He is supposed to have been very fond – nay, over fond it has been alleged – of his mead.

Cubert is a strange little village on the edge of higher, less sand-overwhelmed ground, and it has a church which has a strange stone spire and a most beautiful old carved chancel roof. **Crantock** has a collegiate church of great beauty and interest. Cairnech, whose name was latinized to Karentocus, came here in the 5th century from either Ireland or Wales and built a church near the port of Guellit, which Leland, writing a thousand years later, called Guerith Karantuac. This is now believed to have been the present port of **Gannel**. At least Gannel was once a port. It is known that it was one in the 12th century, and that until 1840 ships were still unloading coal, culm and lime as far up the estuary as Trevemper Bridge, and schooners as big as 600 tons (very big) were being built at **Tregunnel**.

Crantock is a pretty village. On the 13th of October 1835 the huer cried 'hevva' (meaning the man set to watch out for a pilchard shoal saw one and alerted the people) at the time when a funeral was in progress. All the mourners rushed away to their boats, leaving the parson to finish the ceremony as best he could alone. That night, when the boats were out surrounding the shoal, a storm sprang up and four men were drowned. The question that exercised men's minds after this disaster was – was leaving the funeral in so unseemly a manner to blame – or was it because it was the thirteenth? **Pentire Point East** has magnificent views.

Now **Newquay** is just one large and very popular and crowded seaside resort. It is not a new place though, and was for long a port of importance. A glance at the map of North Cornwall will show why. There are very few effective harbours from the south-westerlies that are available at low tide. Ships would always have been driven to use Newquay Bay as a port of refuge, but then, if the wind swung northerly, they would have been embayed in a terribly dangerous place. It was essential that there should be an artificial harbour for them to run to in the event of the wind veering. In 1440 Bishop Lacy of Exeter granted forty days' indulgence to people who helped to build the harbour. In 1586 it is known that the Arundell family left a legacy to improve the harbour. Early in the 19th century the place began to grow in importance as a pilchard harbour. The old Huer's House still stands overlooking the Gazzle. In 1838 the harbour was bought by J. T. Austen, the man who built Par Harbour, and he wrought improvements. By 1855 the place was absolutely booming – a big schooner port, with a hundred and fifty ships owned in the port (a high proportion of the inhabitants owned shares in ships). The railway came, and with it a big export of china clay. In 1870 the jetty inside the harbour was built, and connected by rail to the main line through a tunnel through the cliffs, the mouth of which can still be seen. But, alas, it all died away. In November 1922 the last schooner, the *Hobah*, sailed in with a freight of fertilizer, and sailed out again, and that was that. Newquay was given over to a small fishing fleet, and to holiday-makers in increasing thousands.

It is a very pleasant holiday town. It has 'every amenity'. It is surrounded on most sides by sandy beaches and lovely bays. The harbour, which dries out at low tide, still has enough lobster boats, and piles of lobster pots, in it to make it seem like a real harbour. There are some beautiful gigs used for racing by the fishermen at the Harbour Aquatic Sports which are held in July. The Trenance Gardens are lovely. Towan Head is grand, and its caves – the 'Tea caverns' for tea used to be smuggled from them – well worth visiting.

Porth, once a separate little harbour of its own which used to ship ore out and coal in and had a fishing fleet, is interesting for its Porth Island, with the great multivallate Iron Age fort at **Trevelgue Head**. This was excavated in 1939, to yield a fine Bronze Age stone battle axe (there was Bronze Age occupation too) and retorts for the smelting of iron ore. There is supposed to have been a Roman signal station here.

Little **Flory Island** is sometimes called Black Humphrey's Rock. Mr Humphrey was a great smuggler and wrecker, but principally the latter. He is said to have been the author of the lines:

> When the Wind is in the East
> I'll go to church as soon as Priest.
> When the Wind is in the West
> Pray for me among the Rest.

He was not going to waste a time of westerly wind on his knees when ships were likely to be wrecked along the coast.

At **St Columb** there used to be practised the game of hurling on Shrove Tuesday, and the Saturday next to one after it. The goals were two miles apart and anybody could play. A writer of 1650 described the protagonists as going home 'as from a pitched battaile, with bloody pates, bones broken and out of joint, and such bruises as serve to shorten their days.'

A pleasant village, which lies about three miles west of Newquay, is **Newlyn East**. Saint-knowers will be interested in the fact that that little-known lady St Newlyna gave her name to the place. In the south wall of the church, east of the main door, outside, a famous fig tree sprouts from quite high up in the wall. St Newlyna is supposed to have stuck her staff in the ground here after having landed at Holywell Bay from Ireland, and the staff blossomed into a tree and has grown here ever since. Certain it is that no local person will take so much as a leaf off this tree, for there is a curse on anybody who harms it that such person will die within the year and there are a surprising number of stories told about people who have done. One particular gentleman, determining to defy the curse, decided to take a leaf of it home to Australia with him. He was buried at sea.

Back at the coast again, the first half of beautiful **Watergate Bay** has splendid fallen rocks from the vertical cliffs on it. **Porth Rock** is spectacular, with a dizzy bridge from the mainland of Cornwall, the famous **Banqueting Hall** just north of the bridge – a natural cave two hundred yards long in which concerts are held, **Fern Cave** near **Zacry's Island**, which is draped with *Asplenium marinum* and many other splendours. The fine beach stretches for a couple of miles.

Mawgan Porth is at the mouth of the beautiful **Vale of Lanherne**, and there is a fine walk up to **St Mawgan**, which is beautiful, has a Carmelite nunnery, the fine home of the Arundell family (whose name came from the French *hirondelle*, for swallow), and a fine church. The latter has a memorial to nine men found in a boat, frozen to death, in Beacon Cove in 1846, but I have not seen it. **Bedruthan Steps** are well worth visiting. You can get down the cliffs here to see the fine rocks and visit some fantastic caves.

The coast is fine, with some small coves which provide rather dangerous bathing in fine weather (beware particularly low tide, when the swimmer is then exposed to the coastwise current which may carry him beyond the bay he is bathing from) until we get to **Trevose Head**. From this great greenstone promontory there is a splendid view and on a very clear day I once saw as far as St Ives. The little rocks off-shore are the Quies Rocks, with the Bull further in. The lighthouse on the head flashes three times at every minute. If you are sailing either way along the coast you want to give the Quies a good berth: they, and the Head itself, have killed many a good ship.

Harlyn Bay is a good bay to bathe from, and used to be a good place to be buried in, for near by about 150 grave cysts were dug up out of the sand after a man had started to dig foundations to build a house and discovered the first of them. The occupants of the cysts were short, with long heads, and probably of Celtic stock. They had been buried in the crouched position, heads to the north, faces to the east. Most of the interments have been dated early Iron Age, from 300 to 150 B.C. Pieces of white quartz were found with them (in Pembrokeshire too white quartz had a ritual significance), also red ochre, and iron pyrites which was used for striking sparks for making fires. A kitchen midden near by indicates that these people kept horses, oxen, sheep and pigs, and ate large quantities of limpets, mussels and whelks. They grew corn, for querns for grinding were found – both of the 'rubber' type still universally used by South Indian cooks for grinding curry-stuffs (a slightly U-shaped stone with a stone roller) and also rotary querns. There was tin ore, also weaving equipment, also spinning, and a large quantity of the shells of *Purpura lapidus* with which creature it is supposed they dyed their cloth. There were many implements made of slate. There were ornaments of bronze, black pottery: some of it highly polished, some incised with patterns. They had large storage jars for grain. Everything indicates a large community of pastoral and trading people (it is known that they traded with Ireland), peaceful, for only one weapon was found – a short knife, living on grain, meat and fish, and with a fairly advanced standard of living.

But what is interesting is that – before the Celts – several generations of Beaker Folk were buried at Harlyn round about 1900 B.C. It is strange that a burial ground should have been used for quite such a long time: from 1900 B.C. to 150 B.C. – 1750 years.

There is a small, but very rich, museum on the site, open in the summer, but in the winter the curator, Mrs Bellers (telephone St Merryn 335) is pleased to show people round. Besides many skulls (including those of Beaker Folk) are other bones and teeth galore, stone and bone implements by hundreds, and some graves outside preserved intact.

In the Iron Age Harlyn Bay must have been a port for the rich tin and copper country round St Austell on the south coast, and thus an important place of trade. With the little open boats of the time it was probably easier to launch off an open sandy beach (which they would only do in an off-shore wind anyway) than to cross the bar of an estuary.

Inland there is the ruined Celtic church of **St Constantine**, once overwhelmed by the sand, now overwhelmed by a golf course.

There were two Constantines, but one was King of Damnonia, which included Cornwall and Devon in about the 6th century. He is said to have been descended from Constantine the Great of the Eastern Roman Empire.

Trevone is a new seaside resort, with safe bathing.

Towards Stepper Point is the **Butter Hole**, a cave at the head of a steep-sided cove which is difficult to access except from a boat, and beyond it the **Pepper Hole**, a great chasm. On **Stepper Point** is the Daymark, a beacon to show sailors where they are, and a coastguard look-out. Padstow lifeboat station is just in the mouth of the Camel in **Hawker's Cove**. The same people who erected the Daymark, in 1830, the Padstow Harbour Association, also put two capstans inside Stepper Point, for warping ships into the river across the sand bars in contrary weather.

CHAPTER 17

Padstow to Widemouth

&

ST SAMSON is said to have landed at **Padstow** from South Wales,
with books and holy vessels. He found heathens dancing and
wrestling, and remonstrated with them, and then cut crosses on all
their holy stones. The pre-Christian holy stones of Cornwall were
carved as circles on tops of pillars. The Christians cut crosses on all
these whenever they found them, and wherever you go in Cornwall
you see these crosses cut on circles and nobody can possibly tell
how old they are.

St Petroc next came on the scene, a Brythonic Celt who had been
educated in Ireland, which was then the repository in these islands
of Christian civilization. Much is known about St Petroc, for there
are French, Welsh and Northumbrian chronicles which describe
his life. He sailed across the sea in a coracle, came to St Samson
who handed over his monastery to him, St Samson wishing to travel,
and St Petroc went on converting the Cornish and extending the
monastery, or religious community, at Padstow. It was probably
where Prideaux Place now is, although Padstow church of St
Petroc is on the site of the original 6th-century church. The community was destroyed by the Vikings in A.D. 981 according to the
Anglo-Saxon Chronicle. The present church is largely 15th century
and a very fine building. Note particularly the font and the pulpit,
but there is a great deal of interest in this church. A very good little
guide is on sale within – particularly informative about the stone of
which the church is built, some of which came from Caen, in
Normandy.

While on the subject of St Petroc, if the reader likes buildings
strange and different let him whatever he does go to **Little Petherick**
or, to give it its proper name, **St Petroc Minor of Nansfounteyn**.
There is something most beautiful and unusual about this little
place, and the guide book on sale within, although twenty new
pence, is worth every penny of it.

Padstow was early a harbour of importance. It sent two ships to
the Siege of Calais. But, unfortunately, somewhere along its history

a man shot a mermaid with an arrow (some stories have a gun):

> It is Long Tom Yeo of the town of Padstowe
> And he is a ne'er-do-weel,
> 'Ho Mates!' cries he, 'rejoice with me
> 'For I have shot a seal!'

Anyway it wasn't a seal, and the outraged mermaid put a curse upon the place and the harbour silted up. The aptly named Doom Bar formed across the mouth of the river, and Padstow, no longer a big-ship port, fell from prominence. Of course every shoal draught port around the British Isles is supposed to have 'silted up' and thus dwindled in importance, but the fact is that ships got bigger and deeper, and natural harbours that could formerly take the biggest ships that there were were incapable of accommodating the new ones. As ships got bigger trade went to the deeper draught ports. With the invention of power shoal draught ships became practical again.

In a northerly gale, and particularly with an ebb tide, the Doom Bar seems aptly named. This whole North Cornish and North Devon coast was a graveyard of sailing ships and Padstow was one of the few places along it into which an embayed ship might hope to run for refuge. Padstow men have always been great seafarers – ever since St Petroc sailed from Ireland in a coracle. The lifeboat station was established as early as 1825 and already by 1955 461 lives had been saved, and twenty-four silver and four bronze medals won by the crew. On the 6th of February 1867 the Padstow lifeboat *Albert Edward* went to the assistance of the *Georgiana* of Boston and five men were drowned out of her. In 1900 the new steam lifeboat capsized and all her crew of eleven lost their lives. On the 23rd of November 1944 the lifeboat *Princess Mary* was launched at half past three in the morning into a tremendous gale to go to the rescue of the Norwegian ship *Sjofna*. The lifeboat had to cruise twenty-eight miles along the coast, and then anchor and get a line aboard the *Sjofna* and the latter's crew were literally dragged through enormous seas and all were saved.

In 1381 there was a law suit in which a Padstow ship-owner claimed from a Plymouth one that the latter's ship had pirated the Padstow man's ship which was laden with cheese, beer, flour, beef, salt, hogs, fish, cloth, wooden vessels, linen, wool, and other items. By the end of the 17th century the port was shipping large quantities of ore to Bristol, much of it antimony and lead ore. In the 18th century it is known that cheese, wheat, barley, oats, fish and slates were going out. By 1850 Padstow was a big ship-building place: one yard launched 29 ships between 1858 and 1870. Padstow was an important schooner-owning port at this time. As schooners waned sailing trawlers waxed, and by 1900 many of these were owned in the harbour, and the Brixham Trawlers were coming round to trawl the approaches to the Bristol Channel and were using Padstow to land fish and as a port of refuge. In 1912 there were 151 fishing vessels registered in the port.

There is a terrible shortage of harbours on this North Cornish coast, some of the strongest tides in the world, complete exposure to the westerlies and south-westerlies, all the harbours except two dry out at low tide (which means you can't get into them) and the two that don't have ferocious sand bars. In the twenty-three year period after 1823, during which records, albeit very incomplete, were kept, it is known that 131 big ships and 12 small ones were wrecked on the forty miles from Land's End to Trevose Head and over two hundred men were lost. The Padstow men had to be good seamen to survive.

As for Padstow *now* as a port it still is one, and has a Harbour Master, but if you wish to see this gentleman you must make an appointment well in advance, for he is very busy: on occasions two coasters come in in a week with timber, cement and fertilizers. As for fishing, there is one full-time trawler and about ten full-time crabbers and lobster-men. The latter shoot from eighty to a hundred pots each, mostly of the Breton barrel-shape made from wooden hoops, as these seem to be better for taking crayfish for which there is a good price. Wire pots will not take crayfish, it is thought because the tide flowing through the wire makes it vibrate, but that is anybody's guess. The creel pot, that has been so successful in the rest of the world, has never taken on in Cornwall. The old traditional 'ink-well' pot, made of withies, is still used, and is fine for crabs but not so good for lobsters. The coast is dreadfully overfished, by skin divers as well as potters, and the time will soon be here when there will not be a living along it.

Down by the railway dock there is a long range of fish merchants' offices, now disused, which speak of Padstow's eminence as a fishing port in days gone by. There is also a huge fish market. One end of it is now used by a boat-builder, the rest of it by a merchant who buys shellfish, keeps them in big salt-water tanks, sends them to Southend Airport twice a week, and flies them to France. He even – in the cooler weather when these creatures don't 'go off' so quickly – buys spider crabs – for the French will eat 'anything that moves' according, that is, to English fishermen. Actually, the claws of spider crabs are delicious – as good as any lobster. They infest the seas around here, and it is a pity that the English do not emulate the French and eat what the good Lord has sent them.

There is one salmon-netting licence at Padstow: there used to be a fleet of salmon netters. There is an ancient ship called the *Westmead* that suction dredges sand from the banks just over the river and discharges it by grab in the railway dock. It is loaded into lorries and taken to farms to spread on the land, for it is rich in lime. A new little ship, the *Field* of Bideford, has been bought to replace the ageing *Westmead*. Padstow, in the winter, is a rollicking and rip-roaring place and one feels very much that it is an old seaport. In the summer like every other town along the Cornish coast it is just inundated with holidaymakers – all one feels is the need to get out of it. Prideaux Place is a huge and imposing mansion of about 1600, with paintings by Opie inside.

The railway hugs the south bank of the **River Camel**, and the best way to see the estuary is in a boat. **Wadebridge** is an interesting old town, crucified with traffic at the moment, but once you get off the terrible A 39 it is fairly peaceful: blissfully so in winter time. A bridge was built here in 1450, with 17 arches, and this prevented ships going further up and turned Wadebridge into an important place. Above Wadebridge, the Camel is in fact an absolutely beautiful river, and if I had the time I would canoe it. During the 19th century Wadebridge was a busy port. Granite was shipped out of it to build the Eddystone lighthouse and London's Blackfriar's Bridge; china clay went out, coal, nitrates, groceries, timber, iron rails, limestone and hardware all came in. There was an important export in iron ore at one time. The second railway in the world to employ steam as a propulsion was said to have been the one from Wadebridge to Wenford. It is interesting that Wadebridge, like other shoal draught ports, benefited from the Merchant Shipping Act of 1854, which made it more economical to operate shoal draught ships.

Rock, a large and rich yachting centre, with expensive hotels, a golf course to the north of it (mixed up with the site of a Roman settlement, for Roman sailors braved this coast of shipwrecks), **Trebetherick, Polzeath** and **Pentireglaze** are all one great residential and holiday area and you either like them or you don't. There is the chapel of St Enodoc here, until 1863 buried in drifted sand. For many generations a shepherd's family held land hereabouts for the annual rent of a Cornish pie containing limpets, raisins and

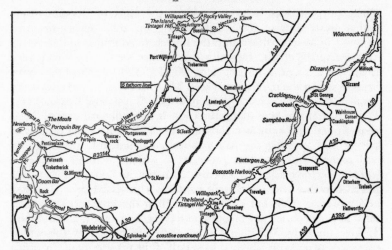

sweet herbs. In the 18th century when the church was discovered
under the sand a hole was cut in the roof down which the parson used
to climb to take services and thus qualify to collect tithes from the
nearby farmers and fishermen. **Pentire Point** with **Rumps Point**
on which is an Iron Age cliff fortress, is a great mass of greenstone,
from which are splendid views both ways along the coast, and it's
impressive to see the seas breaking on Newland Rock and the Mouls
during westerly gales. **Portquin Bay** is mostly National Trust
owned and has beautiful cliffs.

   Portquin is the ghost of a little fishing village: an almost non-
existent place, but I find it of great interest. The little scattering of
houses at the top of a long narrow fjord is now uninhabited, except-
ing in the summer, and there is only one permanent resident and
he lives in a caravan. The stone pillar that stands up so strangely
below high water mark in the harbour is not for tying boats up to,
but is there to mark the boundary between two estates at the point
at which it intersects the Mean High Water line. There is nothing
that I can see left to show that Portquin once imported granite from
Lundy Island, to build the local churches, but what is of great
interest is the 'pilchard palace', which is the long low building inside
the gate just inside the harbour. This belongs to Mr Collins, the
last remaining inhabitant, but he is willing to show it to the truly
interested. The end of the building nearest the sea was a dwelling
house. In the wall on the ground floor are a series of holes at a
regular height. They are as high as the top of a pilchard barrel.

Their purpose was to accommodate the ends of wooden levers which were used – with weights hung on their ends – to force presses ('followers') down into the barrels to compress the pilchards and squash the oil out. Upstairs (but beware the floor, which is very rickety) is a long row of fireplaces. Mr Collins thinks these may have been to warm the pilchard packers. My own belief is that they were connected with the curing process, although just how I cannot say. It is sad that nowhere along the coast has a 'pilchard palace' been re-equipped and kept as a museum, to show us how the process of salting and pressing the fish was *really* carried out, and smoking and sousing and the other processes to which pilchards were subjected. We have seen the Cornish Museum in Looe, which was a pilchard cellar and which still contains a pilchard press – a later and more sophisticated kind of press than the lever presses which must have been used at Portquin, and there is some equipment in the St Ives museum, but there is no complete record of the whole process: a process on which at least half of the prosperity of Cornwall once depended.

The big spar which hangs up in the roof of the Portquin pilchard palace is the main boom of the schooner *Madeleine*, which was wrecked in the harbour in 1911. A local farmer bought the wreck for twenty pounds and broke her up. There is still some of her planking in the pilchard shed, and Mr Collins has called his own boat after her. The pilchard palace was built in about 1600, but for a hundred years has served as a farm building. Now, apparently, nobody can find any use for it.

The 'castle' up at Doyden Point was built in 1830. It is now National Trust and let as flats to holidaymakers. The previous owner was Captain Connor, who was Governor of Parkhurst Prison on the Isle of White and the local grandee.

But the most interesting thing to me in Portquin is something that you might live there for a year and not notice, and that is a pair of ruined cottages against the cliff on the left just along the road that leads to Port Isaac. You could easily walk by them without seeing them, for they are almost covered in undergrowth. If you creep through this and get in the doors, however, you can see the walls, the big open fireplaces (*simnai fawr*), the cloam ovens built into the wall beside them for baking bread (a fire of faggots was lit inside it and then, when the oven was nearly red hot, the ashes were drawn and the bread put in to bake). The cottages are tiny, and as there are two fireplaces in one room, one imagines that two families lived in it: a practice, apparently, not unknown in Cornwall. The roofs are gone, but creepers and bushes form new complete roofs and make the little houses fairly dark. One imagines they may have been thatched for there are no roofing slates lying about.

The timber would, of course, have been used by other people for firewood. The inhabitant of one of the cottages must have been an ox farrier, for at the east end of that cottage is a stone pen that was used for 'crushing' an ox that was having its feet shod. Oxen were used for ploughing and pulling carts within the lives of very old people in Cornwall: as we have seen there is an ox cart in the Moss Museum at Nancekuke. An ox was shod with two little half-moon-shaped bits of iron on each foot. One can still watch them being shod in just such stone crushes as this one at Portquin in parts of France. At the other end of the little row of cottages are the pig styes. These cottages were occupied as late as 1905.

On **Doyden Head**, by the way, beyond the bogus castle, is Long Cross, which has inscribed on it: *Broegen hic jacet*. This is almost certainly a cross put up by Brechan, the Welsh prince who gave rise, in his issue, to a large brood of holy Celtic saints. I have never seen this cross myself, but gather only the shaft is left.

Roscarrock Manor is now a guest house, in the middle of a five-hundred-acre farm which, one gathers, is being worked by one elderly gentleman, so far has been taken the 'flight from the land'. This is a fine example of the heart and centre of a great working farm, with a complex of great stone buildings, marvellously built many hundreds of years ago and still potentially very useful. There was a monastic building (in fact the whole great group of buildings look as if they have had a monastic origin), a holy well, beggar's window, a monk's walk, and an enormous kitchen with great chimney, spit, and cloam oven. This farm and great building complex once did, and still could, provide a home and living for several scores of people. The Roscarrock family came here in the time of Richard I, and died out in 1673.

Port Isaac is a most attractive little place, and one of the many into which no motor cars should be allowed on any account. There should be a very large *free* car park at the top of the hill down to it – and a barrier further on.

But Port Isaac is a most beautiful little place, with narrow winding streets, a charming little harbour (if you are not trying to hang on in it in a boat in a northerly gale) and some splendid pubs. It is still a small fishing port, being in the middle of a short stretch of good lobster coast which has not yet been too ravaged by skin divers.

There is an organization called the Port Isaac Fishermen Limited, a co-operative, with about fifty members, with lobster storage pits down by the harbour, a cold store, an indoor lobster storage tank and a number of fish hawkers who come and buy fish to take them around the countryside to sell. There are about four full-time fishermen but many part-timers. The pattern of long-shore fishing seems to be altering to it being a part-time occupation for men who have some other profession or occupation ashore. This is probably a healthy development, although it means losing eventually that magnificent class of people: the full-time professional inshore fishermen.

A stone pier was built in Port Isaac about 1500, and there was a very large pilchard fishery here with four large cellars. Port Isaac is pronounced 'Portissik' by local men. *Issyk* was Cornish for lower, compare with the Welsh *isaf* which means the same thing. (Some people though say it meant 'corn port'.) Port Isaac harbour was built in the last century, and badly built. As usual the advice of local fishermen was not taken, and two jetties were built which do not provide anything like adequate shelter for vessels in the harbour. In a northerly quite large boats get swamped at their moorings. It is obvious that a breakwater should have been built from the west side of the harbour mouth much further towards the sea than the existing breakwaters. But most Port Isaac men haul their boats out of the water. There was a lifeboat from 1869 to 1933.

Portgaverne (pronounced port*gave*-en) is really part of Port Isaac. It has a large kippering kiln in it, still there to see although not used, pilchard cellar and lime kilns. Once the famous Delabole slates were shipped from here: handed up to beached ships from carts and carefully packed in the holds in straw. When the railway came and took the traffic the village lost £1500 a year.

If you take the main road inland from Port Isaac and turn right when it hits the B 3314 you will soon see, on your right, **Tresungers**, which is a fine group of farm buildings, with a medieval embattled gateway. Most of the existing buildings were put up in 1660. **St Endellion** has a fine church, **St Minver** has another. The Cornish Arms at **Pendoggett** serves fine food.

The coast path from Portgaverne to Port William is tough indeed, and has many ups and downs to it. **Port William** has a sandy beach, but you want to be careful when swimming from it. **Trebarwith**, half a mile inland, is one of those fine stone hamlets, or groups of farm buildings, that look like fortresses, and in fact probably were fortresses when Barbary pirates roved the Bristol Channel. Just

north is a fine watermill, with a slate-hung gantry. The hoist, which
hove the sacks of corn to be ground up to the gantry, was driven
from the water wheel like every other piece of machinery in the
mill.

National Trust land, and a good footpath, stretch north from
Port William, and we first come to **Tintagel** church, which is of
great antiquity and interest. It is a Norman church on a Celtic
foundation, dedicated to St Materiana. The north doorway is
thought to be Saxon, although the use of the word Saxon in Cornwall or Wales seems to me to be doubtful: perhaps it should be
Celtic Saxon-style? Certainly this is a very beautiful and unspoiled
building.

The path takes us on from here to what people insist on calling
'King Arthur's Castle'. Whether King Arthur in fact had anything
to do with this spot or not it is a very romantic place. The strangely
sited castle was in fact built after the Roman conquest, some six
hundred years before King Arthur, if there ever was a King Arthur,
rallied the Celts to resist the invading pagan English. King, if he
was a king, Arthur managed to keep the Germanic hordes at bay for
fifty years, but after he died, and the Brythonic Celts resumed their
normal state of complete disunity, the newcomers prevailed and
drove them into the Welsh and Cornish hills. All the Celtic leaders
were mobile, travelling freely between many dwellings, and there is
no reason why Tintagel should not have been one of Arthur's
fortresses. But the tradition that he lived and died here was fostered
by Geoffrey of Monmouth who wrote in about 1140, when the
present castle was being started. Geoffrey, like other writers of his
time, was pretty credulous, but there must have been some legend
or local tradition to have made him choose Tintagel for Arthur's
seat. Certainly he had the advantage over us of having lived nearer
the period about which he was writing, albeit still some seven
hundred years after it. His story, related in his *History of the Britons*,
was that Gorlois, the Duke of Cornwall, placed his wife Ygraine in
the impregnable fortress of Tintagel to save her from Uther the
King of the Britains who was invading his country. Uther, helped
by the magic of Merlin, disguised himself as Gorlois and got admitted into the castle. He seduced Ygraine and from this liaison
Arthur was born. This might be held as an allegory of the Iron Age
Celts coming into Britain and outwitting, conquering, and then
intermarrying with the former Bronze Age inhabitants. That does
not accord though with the popular theory of the present time that
Arthur lived in the 5th century and led the Britons, deserted by their

Roman masters, against the invading hordes of Anglo-Saxons from the East. There were one or two other references to Tintagel in Arthurian romances, mostly the French ones, and then Tennyson seized on the place and in the 19th century there was a great upsurge of interest in it. So much so that in 1852 the castle ruins were repaired, and some of them built up again, and a large building called King Arthur's Hall was built in Tintagel (which I have to confess I have not been in), which has seventy-three windows and is full of pictures and maps and other objects dealing with the Arthurian romances.

The castle is now in the care of the Ministry of Works and is visited by countless tourists: in fact the never-ending procession, in the summer, winding down the steep narrow lane from the village, and then up the steep stone steps to the Island, reminds me of the procession of pilgrims climbing up Adam's Peak in Ceylon. Incidentally the present practice of carrying passengers down that steep, dusty and narrow lane in a Land-Rover is dangerous, dirty (it smothers everybody with dust), inconvenient, irreverent and downright rude. For many people the visit to Tintagel Castle is in the nature of a pilgrimage, and their peace should not be disturbed.

The castle was in fact begun in the 12th century, probably by Reginald of Mortain, Earl of Cornwall, whose father had held the castle at Bossiney, but who probably decided to build a castle on this more defensible spot. After this various nobles enlarged and improved the castle, until it fell into the hands of the Duchy of Cornwall, and in the 14th century was used as a state prison, and Leland, about 1640, could say that it was a deserted ruin. One does not hear that it ever suffered any great assaults or sieges. It is a little difficult, on cursory inspection at least, to figure out the military *rationale* of the fortifications at all. There was a Lower Ward and an Upper Ward on the 'mainland', which were once connected by a narrow neck of land to an Inner Ward and the Great Hall on the 'Island', which is not, and never has been, an island at all. The neck of land has crumbled away, with one end of the Great Hall, and a subsequent bridge connecting the two parts of the Castle has fallen too, and now you have to walk right down to near sea level and up again to get to the Island. But certainly a superficial examination of the ruins seems to indicate that the defensive advantages of a superb natural site were largely thrown away. The ruins should be much more fully sign-posted by the Ministry of Works.

Of far more interest to me than the castle are the ruins of the

Celtic monastery that existed before the Normans ever crossed the English Channel. Outside of Ireland these are probably the most complete remains of a Celtic religious foundation that there are. The foundations of many tiny cells can be seen, sited more or less higgledy piggledy and at random, with few and small public or common buildings (a small chapel, a well, a walled garden and not much else), and which accord well with such literary descriptions of the homes of the early Celtic saints as have come down to us. We can stand among these humble stone works and imagine simple and primitive but devout men living their lives of meditation and great austerity on this grandly beautiful site. There is a booklet on sale at the Ministry of Public Buildings and Works hut at the entrance to the site, which at least tries to unravel a building history which started perhaps in the 4th century when an Iron Age farmstead was built, and went on for several hundred years, although by th_ time of the Domesday Survey the place was deserted. The various stages of building, which were done as the centuries passed, showed a progressive deterioration of building techniques, as if the first fervour of the new religion had not lasted. St Juliot, the Welsh missionary who arrived in Cornwall about A.D. 500, and who was one of the many saintly descendants of King Brychan, is said to have founded the monastery.

As for Tintagel village, it is old and was no doubt picturesque once. It is very hard even to see it in the summer time for tourists, and of course it is absolutely infested with *piskies*. It was once a harbour, albeit one of the most inconvenient and perilous sort. From 1700 onwards slate was lowered down into beached ships from the vertical cliffs above. In 1910 there still existed a crazy wooden staging from which ships, far below, had been loaded.

Bossiney is a fantastically beautiful and romantic spot, or at least the coast near it is, with **Willapark**, an Iron-Age-Fortified headland rather like Tintagel Island in conformation, Bossiney Haven which is truly awe-inspiring. The place once sent two members to Parliament, and one of these used to be Sir Francis Drake. Beyond is the **Rocky Valley**, with a wooded gorge going up to **St Nectan's Kieve** and a pleasant waterfall. Wilkie Collins describes walking up to here and meeting two strange ladies who lived in seclusion there. **Trevalga** is a grey stone huddle of fine dwellings.

And so we come to **Boscastle**, which is a most beautiful village, and an ancient port. The tiny harbour, which looks well protected from the seas, must have in fact been a fiendish place to sail into. But many a captain did, for at one time it was a very busy little port.

In the middle of the 19th century there were warehouses, workshops, shipyards and timber-yards, and slate and china clay were shipped in some quantities. As early as 1547 it is known that there was a pier, and corn, slate, and oak bark were being shipped out. Now it lives almost entirely by tourism. Boscastle church was rebuilt in 1868, but it has a very old Celtic cross. It is dedicated to St Symphorian, who converted the natives of Autun in Belgium, from the worship of Berecynthia, or Cybele, the Great Mother, to the Christian religion. In doing so however he was martyred in A.D. 282.

There is magnificent walking, and magnificent coastline, right past Crackington Haven. **Pentargon Bay** is superb, with a waterfall, and in it, on the 7th of April 1899, the French schooner *Gazelle* came to grief, and her skipper is buried here. There was a very gallant rescue from the shore of her only two survivors. Fantastically folded cliff scenery here. **Trevigue** is one of the many absolutely superb farmhouses along this rugged coast. **Samphire Rock**, islanded at high tide, reminds us of what used to be an industry on the North Cornish coast. Shakespeare mentions it in *King Lear* when he has Lear speak of the Samphire gatherer carrying on his 'awful trade'. Certainly people fell to their deaths looking for the stuff. The 'Golden Samphire' (*Inula crithmoiaes*) that grows on such dizzy cliffs is not to be confused with Glasswort (*Salicornia stricta*), the samphire of the saltings, which is collected in large quantities in such places as the Wash, and eaten pickled or boiled.

Tremoutha Haven is interesting for what might have been but was not. In 1836 it was proposed to build a 'haven of refuge' here to be called the Duke of Cornwall's Harbour, and a whole new town to be called Victoria, and a railway from it to Launceston. Sites were marked out for three hundred houses. But the whole thing fell through and there is no sign of harbour, railway or houses. **Crackington Haven**, which would have been protected by the great breakwater that was planned, is now just a bathing and surfing beach, rather dangerous in rough weather, with two small hotels and a flock of the most voracious tame ducks. There was a trade into it once of coal and limestone. There is a graveyard here in which sailors from the many wrecks that this coast claimed were buried, because at one time it was not lawful to bury them in consecrated ground. After all – who knew? – they might have been heathens. Fine photographs of surf riders in one of the pubs.

A footpath climbs steeply beyond Crackington and you can cut inland to **St Gennys**, which is peaceful and beautiful, with a working farmhouse and – rarer still – a working village school.

Why the latter has not been swept away in the drive to cram all children into human sausage factories is hard to say. The little church is in a most beautiful setting.

There are splendid foundered cliffs at **Dizzard Point**. The rocks around **Millook** show most spectacular folding, and there are great landslips of the cliffs here. We are in the Millstone Grit and Culm Measures country here, having progressed east of the Cornish Killas. The coast is less indented but more folded and spectacular. Much of it is weirdly contorted sandstone. **Widemouth** (pronounced Widmouth) **Sands** are just sands, and very crowded in the summer time.

CHAPTER 18

Bude to Westward Ho!

❧

Bude is now a fine open breezy place, with wide green open spaces
and a lovely long beach – long that is from its shoreward end to the
sea – narrow long-shore-ways. The waterfront is given a fascination
by the big lock gates, all kept in good order although short-sighted
men have built low fixed bridges over the Bude Canal so that, quite
wantonly, it has been destroyed. A few yachts winter in the small
stretch that remains available.

The Act empowering the company to build this canal was in
1819. Once this was one of the most interesting canals in the country,
winding up, in places by means of inclined planes, to the Tamar,
down which boats or barges go to Launceston. Great quantities of
lime-rich sand for the farms, and coal, went in, corn and slate came
out to be shipped away and there was a big trade in general merchandise. Instead of being floated up locks to a higher level the boats
were hauled up inclined planes on rails, the power being provided
by big tanks which were filled with water so that they dropped down
great shafts (one 220 feet deep) hauling the barges up by chains.
At the bottom the water was run out of the tanks and down-going
boats would haul them up again. The canal cost £130,000, but
was closed in 1891.

Bude was never a good harbour, but it is the only break in twenty-
five miles of high cliffs, and the only place where a harbour could
possibly be. Bude had a breakwater in the 18th century. This was
completely destroyed in a gale in March 1828 and not rebuilt until
1840. It was always a difficult harbour to get into with a westerly
wind, and of course is very tidal: if you seek its refuge at anything
other than fairly high tide you will be disappointed: if you can get
in leave the beacons to starboard. Being on such a very dangerous
piece of coast it early came in for a lifeboat. King William IV paid
Wade of Sunderland £100 to build one – the *King William IV* –
but she capsized on her trial run in 1844 and was not a success.

In the modern folly 'castle' near the canal mouth lived Golds-
worthy Gurney, who invented a new light, called the 'Bude Light',
for lighthouses. The 'castle' is now used for council offices. Bude still

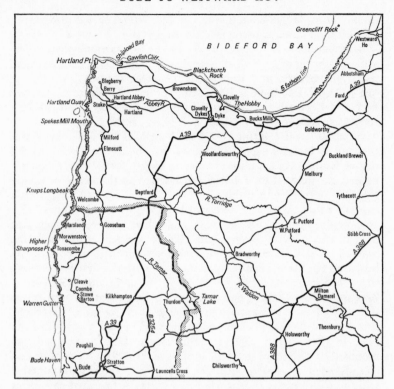

has a faint smack about it of an old seaport. Once there were shipping agents, brokers, ship owners, merchants and banks. Now there are hotels, boarding houses, and bed and breakfast places. It is interesting though, and not a vulgar place. The strange 'whale rock' south of the harbour is an eroded upfold of sandstone.

Coombe Valley is superbly beautiful, and has a 'nature trail' in it, which means you are allowed to walk through it if you pay somebody. **Stowe Barton** looks to me as if it were once a fortified farmstead. Cars can get down, alas, to **Duckpool**, where is bathing. What Cornwall cries out for is more and more places on the coast where cars are not allowed – and what is more important – cannot get.

Cleave Camp is a huge place with weird radar bowls, one apparently looking straight up at the sky. This is all part of America's early warning system. **Tonacombe** is a private house, but approachable by several footpaths, and a very beautiful Elizabethan manor

203

house. There is a cross of about A.D. 250 here. There is also said to be a strange lantern, made from broken glasses. I have not seen it.

Morwenstow is a place of pilgrimage for eccentric-lovers. The great flowering of English clerical eccentricity was, of course, in the mid-19th century, and Robert Stephen Hawker was born on the 3rd of December 1803 at Plymouth, the son of a doctor. As a boy he dressed himself up in seaweed (and nothing else) and sat on a rock at Bude combing his long hair. The locals thought he was a 'merrymaid' and a farmer tried to shoot him but fortunately was prevented. Hawker went to Oxford, but before he could get his degree heard that his father could no longer finance his scholastic career. He jumped on a horse and hurried to the home of a lady twice his age (he was twenty, she was forty) who had long been a close friend of the family and who had 'taught him his letters'. He proposed to her, married her and, as she had plenty of money, was able to carry on at Oxford and take his degree. Apparently the marriage was an idyllic one and Hawker was a most considerate husband. He came, eventually, to the living of Morwenstow (called, then, Moorwinstow, but he changed its name to Morwenstow because he knew that it had originally been named because it was the *stow* of St Morwenna), and found it a parish of wreckers, smugglers and – worst of all – dissenters. He ruled his parish from 1834 to 1875, firmly and eccentrically. He built a vicarage surmounted by chimneys shaped like the towers of the churches he had already been associated with. He built a school and maintained it with his own slender means. He loved animals, tolerated cats in his church, allowed jackdaws to nest in his chimneys, and once moved some there in fact, from a tree in which they were nesting, to make room for rooks for he wished to establish a rookery. Having removed the jackdaws he publicly prayed for rooks – and the rooks came! He had a tame Black Berkshire pig named Gyp, who was so well behaved that he was, we are told, allowed into ladies' boudoirs. If he (Hawker) went into a cottage, and saw a child whom he knew had not been baptized, he would sniff the air and say: 'I smell brimstone!' When he did baptize the infant he would pinch it to make it squeal and thus let the Devil out. Out of doors he wore a long-tailed claret-coloured coat with a yellow poncho over it, a blue fisherman's jersey with a cross on one side to mark the spot where Jesus was speared by the soldier, long sea boots and a brimless beaver hat. He loathed the contemporary state of the Church of England, and favoured a return not so much to Rome as to the Celtic Church, or to its predecessor the Church of Constantinople. When a Church dignitary asked him, very seriously, 'what are your views, Mr Hawker?' he waved his hand to the great prospects along the Cornish coast and said, '*That*. And *that*!'

He was though, besides being eccentric, a humane man and, within the limitations of his time, a poet. He published 'Song of the Western Men', 'Quest of the Angreal', 'Cornish Ballads' and much else. He was diligent in trying to rescue shipwrecked men, of which there were many for Hartland Bay was without doubt the most terrible place for shipwrecks in England. In Bideford Bay at least you've got a sporting chance of flying over Bideford Bar in a north-wester – a sailing ship embayed in Hartland Bay in a gale has no hope whatever. She will harbour herself on jagged rock at the foot of vertical rock cliffs.

> From Hartland Point to Padstow Light
> Is a watery grave, by day or night.

Hawker buried more than forty shipwrecked mariners in Morwenstow churchyard. The figurehead of the *Caledonia* is still there to see – standing up white and sepulchral if you visit the graveyard by moonlight. She stands over the graves of the captain and crew, and Hawker wrote:

> We laid them in their lowly rest
> The strangers of a distant shore,
> We smoothed the green turf on their breast
> 'Mid baffled ocean's angry roar!
> And there, the relique of the storm
> We fixed fair Scotland's figured form.

After a long life his first wife died, and was buried at Morwenstow, and he, at sixty, married a girl of twenty: a Belgian Roman Catholic. This marriage, too, was said to have been happy. When he died he was, in his last hours, received into the Roman Catholic Church.

Morwenstow church is very beautiful (marvellous Saxon font but very much else to see, and a good guide within), its site is perfect, there is a holy well in the vicarage garden, but the one half way down the cliff is now dry. You can easily clamber down the cliff to the small beaches below.

Marsland is an absolutely astonishingly beautiful Tudor farm-house, not open to the public and unknown. It is not many yards from the Devon–Cornwall border. Just over this is the Old Smithy Inn, very picturesque, with good bar food and meals and rooms to let. Caleb Wakely was the last blacksmith here before it became an inn and he used to pull teeth as well as shoe horses. Looking down at the beach here at low tide one sees fantastic parallel ridges of rock running out to sea. The strike of the rock along this coast is east to west (the rock dips down to the north) so we have this effect of parallel ridges of rock running out to sea at right angles to the beach. This made a terrible reception for stranded ships. They were caught by these claws of rocks which reach out to sea and held clear of all hope of rescue from land.

Welcombe is a tiny village with an absolutely superb farmstead: but so many of these huge North Devon farmhouses, and their attendant buildings, are delightful to look upon and must be delightful to farm from. The farms in this corner of Devon are large, and were until recently at least all owned by Hartland Abbey Estate, and this having for long been a rich estate they are well built and beautiful. The church is interesting and has some Saxon work in its screen: perhaps the oldest screen in the country. Another great farm group is three miles further north: **Milford**. The tractor shed of this was a medieval chapel. Below the cliffs here the *Green Ranger* was wrecked: the last of the endless series of wrecks along this coast. She has been broken up and the steel from her salvaged by winch from the cliff top.

Speke's Mill Mouth has a famous waterfall, or rather series of waterfalls. Most of the streams along this coast end in waterfalls. The valley above is a nature reserve and there are ravens in it.

Hartland Quay is a very special place. There is here one of the most superbly *sited* hotels on the coast of Britain. It is a measure of the extreme difficulty of constructing a harbour anywhere along this coast, and of the great incentives that operated on our forefathers to build as many harbours as they could (land transport being so expensive) that a quay was ever built at Hartland at all. But built one was, and that by the monks of Hartland Abbey five centuries ago, although it was improved under an Act of Parliament dated 7th December 1566: a bill sponsored by Sir Walter Raleigh, Sir Francis Drake and Sir John Hawkins. There was a solid little harbour right up to 1887, when a gale damaged it, and another gale of 1896 took it away completely. Only a stump remains. A steep road has been cut down the cliff-side – now to take motorists to the hotel – before to carry cargoes up and down from and to the harbour. There are photographs, and several paintings, of the harbour in full swing, with schooners in it. Coal, lime, and general merchandise came in – and in 1616 lead for the roof of Stoke Church – and corn and malt went out, but it must have taken an intrepid mariner to have sailed his vessel into that perilous hole in the rocks.

The hotel was established in the Harbour Master's house and other harbour buildings, and it has charm. Inside the bar are a great many photographs of wrecks, and a map with paper stars to show some of the more recent ones. Between 1857 and 1908 forty-eight ships were wrecked on the few miles of coast of Hartland and Welcombe parishes. Only one ship that has struck this coast ever got off it again intact, and that was the Greek steamer *Katina*, which was refloated in 1913. There are many tales of 'wrecking' activities along this coast: Rev. Hawker of Morwenstow was responsible for many of them, with his tales of 'Cruel Coppinger' and others, and the tying of lamps on to the tails of asses, which seems to me – as I have said – a bit of an ass's tale itself. Of course, when a ship did come to shore the locals would have tried to have snatched what they could from the clutches of Her Majesty's Coastguard – who wouldn't? But I doubt very much if many countrymen – let alone seamen – ever consciously tried to lure a ship to her doom, and in any case, if they had tried, I doubt very much if they would have succeeded. I can just believe, though, the story that a man along this coast who was being given a lesson on first aid to the drowning, and on being asked 'What is the first thing you do if you find an apparently drowned man?' answered: 'Search his pockets!'

There is a good swimming pool at Hartland Quay Hotel, and it is best to use it in all but the calmest weather because the sea bathing here is tricky in the extreme. And I can think of nowhere better on the coast of England than Hartland Quay to go and watch the terrible fury of a westerly gale. The waves that thunder on these cruel rocks may have travelled unimpeded from America.

Blackpool Bay is where the Hartland Abbey Stream falls into the sea. At low tide here are wonderful rock pools, and at half tide a pleasant little beach. The contortions of the rock strata here are interesting to see. The little tower up on the headland was in the 17th century a look-out for Barbary pirates, but the squire of the Abbey, one Paul Orchard, built a 'folly' tower there in the 18th century, and there it still stands. **Blegberry Farm** is a splendid example of a fortified farmhouse, and much of its fortifications still remain. In the 16th and early 17th centuries and earlier galleys from the North African coast used to sail into the Bristol Channel, searching for slaves and plunder, and hence most of the lonely farmhouses near the coast were fortified and the inhabitants armed against their incursion. There are two little huts near this farm on the seaward side. One has 1657 W.A. on it. The other 1950 T.B. and contains an electric water pump. What did the older one contain? I confess I do not know. You can clamber down to the shore from here, to Berry Beach, but it's pretty steep.

The countryside around these parts, on a breezy summer day, is one of large rolling fields of waving barley, chequered by the field hedges, with occasionally a glimpse of the four corner pinnacles of the great tower of Stoke Church.

Hartland Point, with its lighthouse and coastguard station, is an exhilarating place on which to stand, with splendid coastal views both ways, and the sight of the fierce overfall in the sea a mile or two off the point. This is caused by the tidal current surging around this prominent point. If you get caught in a boat off Hartland Point in a fresh south-wester, and a strong ebb tide in the Bristol Channel, you will know all about it. It is sad that the English are sinking to the undignified expedient of collecting money from people who wish to get to their coast, as they do here at Hartland.

As for Hartland Church, or **Stoke Church** as it is called on the map, it is one of the most splendid buildings in Devon. It is fantastic, really, that a scattered agricultural parish has managed to rear up this cathedral-like building. Here was no great wool industry, such as paid for the building of the beautiful 15th-century churches of Suffolk, no great seaport (Hartland Quay was but a perilous little hole in the rocks into which a small ship might bolt in fine weather to load, or unload, and get out of it again before the wind swung westerly), no mines of importance, or manufactures. Here even could have been none but the most rudimentary fishing industry. And it is not even in the centre of an agricultural district, but right on the edge of one, in a corner in fact: its surrounding country to the west and to the north is the salt sea. It is and always has been in a situation remote from metropolitan England: Hartland people boast that their parish is the one furthest from the railway in all England, and that this is so is proved by the fact that the Institute of Geological Science chose Hartland for the establishment of one of their three Magnetic Observatories, for proximity to a railway would interfere with their delicate observations into the magnetic field of the earth. And yet here was found, around the middle of the 14th century, the effort and the resources to build this splendid church, which has been rightly called 'the Cathedral of North Devon'.

The explanation may be that it was the church of the abbey of Austin Canons which was set up half a mile away from here in about 1170, and which itself succeeded a college of secular canons

Above, Bedruthan Steps; *below*, Boscastle.

CLOVELLY: *Above*, the harbour; *right*, the main street.

which had been established by Gytha, the mother of King Harold of England, as a thanksoffering to St Nectan for the preservation of her son (although some say husband) from shipwreck. It is known, of course, that Harold, before he became king, was shipwrecked on the coast of Normandy, and entertained by the man who was eventually to kill him: William the Bastard, but then his father may have been shipwrecked too. But the church was built on the Celtic shrine of St Nectan, and in the church the saint's bones were preserved up to the Dissolution and it seems to me possible that much of the money needed to build this great church came from pilgrims to the shrine of St Nectan, who was a great Brythonic (Welsh) saint, who came across the sea to Cornwall with his sister Morwenna, the latter to settle at Morwenstow and the former at Stoke. After St Nectan was beheaded by his enemies he carried his head under his arm from his place of martyrdom to his cell at Stoke, and wherever a drop of blood fell a foxglove grew up, and hence children still bring foxgloves to Stoke church on St Nectan's Day which is 17th June. The cult of St Nectan in the Middle Ages was fairly widespread, and many pilgrims must have come to this spot. You can buy a translation of the 12th-century *Life of St Nectan* in the church. It is sad that the arrogant Victorians pulled the 14th-century windows out of the building and replaced them with 'perpendicular' ones, but otherwise the church is much of a period. There is a 'Pope's Room' over the North porch, where a priest used to live, and where are now several relics; and one of the finest late Norman fonts in existence; and most of all, a most wonderful screen. The great oak beam over the screen, which had to be put in to tie the church together when a heavier roof was put on, is a beam from H.M.S. *Revenge*, one of the last wooden ships of the line. The vaulted roofs, like inverted ships, inspired Hawker of Morwenstow to write the lines:

> Enter! the arching roofs expand
>   Like vessels on the shore;
> Inverted, where the fisher band
>   Might tread their planks no more;
>
> But reared on high in that stern form,
>   Lest faithless hearts forget,
> The men that braved the ancient storm,
>   And hauled the early net.

The present Hartland Abbey was built about 1779. It is a large and very grand building but not open to the public.

As for **Hartland** itself, it is a fine example of a largish farming village, with some good pubs, the St John's chapel of ease which is the old town hall converted into a church about 1837, has a Nativity painted by Girolamo Romanino, and a lovely little Madonna on the left of the altar. The place has impressive box pews.

Back to the coast again, just east of the Point is **Shipload Bay**, where few ships have loaded, I suspect, but where a steep and high path winds its way down to the shore where is a splendid beach which provides most excellent bathing. Bryan and Rita Burn live at Gawlish Cottage, just inland from Gawlish Cliff, and make very nice patchwork slops and smocks and other garments, also bedspreads and other things, which they sell. If you go to **Brownsham** you will find, near one of the so numerous magnificent complexes of farm buildings about here, a bridle path leading down through a gorgeous wooded valley to the sea near **Blackchurch Rock**, at **Mouth Mill** where is a beach and a lime kiln, climbing up to the heights of **Gallantry Bower** the other side and eventually getting to Clovelly. It is to be noticed that on rounding Hartland Point the whole character of the shore has changed. Where before the strike of the rock strata was at right angles to the coast here it is parallel – the jagged teeth running out into the sea are now replaced by serried ridges of rock running along it.

Clovelly is a welcome place to come to if you have just rounded Hartland Point in a small boat in a fresh westerly wind. The coast here faces north-east and the harbour itself east and so, even if the tide is out and you cannot get into the harbour, at least you can lie outside with a tolerable chance of not dragging your anchor while waiting for enough water to get behind the breakwater. In a north-easter the situation is not so pleasant, and most people would run on and around Hartland.

Clovelly is a little place of extreme picturesqueness, which is its undoing in the summer time because it is absolutely thronged with visitors. What saves it from total destruction is the fact that motor cars just cannot, at any price, get down its main street, which is a three-in-one slope and anyway steps. Donkeys can, and still do in a sort of token manner, but furniture which has to be taken down to the houses is lowered down on sleds. The internal combustion engine today is not to be denied, however, *anywhere*, from the Kalahari Desert to the South Pole, and a track has been hacked, coming down to the shore just behind the Red Lion, down which horseless carriages can be got. Indeed, the beer for the Red Lion comes this way. The little harbour is charming, still used by fishing boats which can take the ground in it, and still are caught here many herrings. Prince, in his *Worthies of Devon* of 1810, says that such abundance of 'that very good fish' is taken here that they are often sold at two shillings a *meas* – there were 3 herring to a *cast* and 104 *casts* (thus 612 fish) to a *meas* – and that above four hundred horses were used to carry the catch up above, to the value of £1500 a season. Also, here were taken 'the best cod in the world'. Now, in the summer, some soles are caught in beam trawls, visitors are taken angling, and the herring concern the fishermen in the autumn and winter.

At Clovelly is based the new 'cruising lifeboat' of the R.N.L.I.: the 70 foot long 'W.O.1'. She lies out at moorings in the bay, or cruises the seas, and runs for the shelter of Lundy Island when the weather gets too bad for her to lie off Clovelly. She has a full-time crew, some of them always aboard, she is always ready to steam off at 11.14 knots either way along the coast, and has a cruising range of 860 nautical miles. She is considered a better way of providing a lifeboat service for this terrible harbourless graveyard of ships than small local boats kept out of the water and manned by volunteers. She can keep the seas in any weather at all. The old shore-based Clovelly lifeboat did marvellous service from 1870, when the station was established, to 1969, when the station was closed (except for an inshore rescue craft) and the present cruising lifeboat substituted. Over three hundred people were saved from the sea by the shore-based lifeboats here.

Clovelly was once a much more important fishing harbour than it is now. A measure of this is that in one night, that of 4th of October 1821, twenty-four Clovelly boats were lost while out herring driving and thirty-one men were drowned, and on 28th October 1838 another twenty-one men were drowned within sight of their houses. Two disasters that must have been absolutely devastating to a tiny community such as this.

Clovelly has been much painted by artists: Turner had a go at it, as did Rex Whistler, who put it on pottery, F. W. Sturge, L. R. O'Brien and Hook. Charles Dickens described it beautifully, through the words of his Captain Forgan, calling it 'Steepways'. in *Christmas Stories*. Charles Kingsley's father, also Charles Kingsley, came here as curate in 1831 and left as vicar in 1836, and was said by the fishermen to be: 'a man who feared no danger, and could steer a boat, raise and lower a sail, shoot a herring net and haul a seine as one of themselves.' Kingsley of course used Clovelly and Clovelly men freely in *Westward Ho!* Kingsley was eleven when he came with his father to Clovelly

Clovelly is part of a large estate, and thus safe from despoliation by people of no taste. Recently an attempt is being made to prevent too many people from crowding down into the little one-street village: the car parking fees up aloft are being steeply raised. The pressure of populace was becoming completely unendurable. The winter is the only time to see Clovelly. There is a pleasant drive, called the Hobby Drive, through the woods of that name that clothe the steep north-facing hillside east of the village, and for this you now have to pay *twenty-five pence*. This steep charge has been rendered necessary by the vast number of motorists wishing to use it.

Clovelly Dyke, at the hamlet of **Dyke** up top, is a grand Iron Age hill fort: a concentric multiple enclosure of a cattle-keeping people. **Buck's Mills** is a little beach approached by a steep and narrow lane through woods down which motors crowd in the summer time. It has two ranges of lime kilns on the shore: one a most elaborate and splendid one: a veritable castle among lime kilns and worthy of study. The local young men go herring fishing in the autumn: old men tell of sixteen full-time fishing boats in this tiny place. **Woolfardisworthy,** inland, is pronounced Woolsery.

A shelterless coast takes us to **Westward Ho!,** which is a great big seaside resort with a great sandy beach to the northward. It has everything, I suppose, that a seaside resort should have. Modern holidaymakers warm their bones in the sun here over the bones of *Bos longifrons*, goat, swine, roebuck, the shells of oysters and cockles and winkles, all brought in by ancient man for his food, some of the bones split open for their marrow, for all such have been found here under the sand of the beach at low water. Pottery with a vandyked pattern incised on it has also been found, and a millstone grit pestle, for pounding grain or grass seeds in a mortar. These finds were all thought to be Neolithic.

CHAPTER 19

Bideford Bar to Lynmouth

꙳

Bideford Bar, the sand bar that occludes the mouth of the combined Rivers Taw and Torridge, is one of the most dangerous around the coast. Although it never actually dries out, even at low spring tides, waves break on it in any sort of westerly weather and it has claimed a great many lives and a great many ships. An hour before high water is the best time to get over it, but many a ship has not been able to wait for high tide and Appledore lifeboat has had to run its gauntlet hundreds of times at high water or low. On the north bank, nearly a couple of miles upstream from the Bar itself, is a big leading mark and behind it a lighthouse, and these show the way through the deepest water. It was this bar and this lighthouse that Kingsley was thinking of when he wrote:

> Three wives sat up in the lighthouse tow'r,
> And they trim'd the lamps as the sun went down,
> They look'd at the squall and they looked at the show'r,
> And the night-rack came rolling up ragged and brown.
> But men must work, and women must weep,
> Though storms be sudden and waters deep,
> And the harbour bar be moaning.

It is not for nothing that the sailors of the Taw and Torridge were known, to themselves as well as to other people, as 'Bar Men'. Their lives were governed, and all too often ended, by that terrible sand bar. Brian Waters in his book *The Bristol Channel* states that in the 1920s sixty-three ships came in over the Bar on one tide. This is a measure of the scale of the coasting traffic in the Bristol Channel up to recent years. Now you may see the venerable motor vessel *Despatch* lumbering in with 150 tons of coal from South Wales, for her owner-skipper Captain Trevor Davey manages to keep her trading despite all the motor lorries which infest the roads.

Of the towns of the estuaries of the Taw and Torridge **Bideford** was the most important in years gone by. Five ships were sent against the Armada from the combined ports. Sir Richard Grenville,

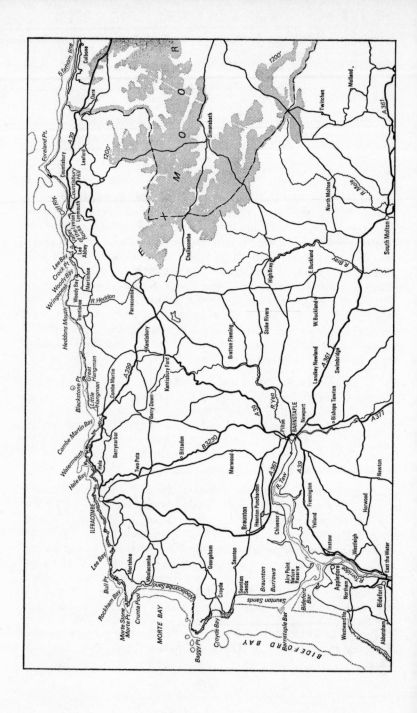

who died in battle after having fought his lone ship the *Revenge* for fifteen hours against fifteen Spanish ships, was a Bideford man and voyaged to Carolina and Virginia in a not altogether successful effort to plant colonies. But Bideford benefited when colonies were successfully established in the reign of James I, for Bideford played a big part in their opening up. She became the first English port to import tobacco on a large scale. Besides this a third of Bideford's ships were engaged in the Newfoundland trade, and Huguenot weavers came and established an important textile industry using merino wool imported from Spain by Bideford ships. In the mid-18th century, however, the tobacco trade left Bideford for Bristol, the French had by then already muscled in seriously on the Newfoundland trade, and French ships privateering in what their crews called the 'Golden Bay' (Bideford Bay) had done great damage to Bideford shipping. The wool industry, too, went to places with greater natural advantages: i.e. more hydraulic power. And, of course, like all shoal draught ports, Bideford fell out of the big-time race as ships became larger and keels became deeper. The efficiency of a sailing ship is directly related to the depth of her main frame and her keel. This rule does not apply to power vessels, and there is no reason why shoal draught ports such as Bideford should not one day come into their own again. The North Europeans are building shoal draught ships as fast as they can, and now that Britain has become a member of the European Economic Community she will have to do likewise to play her full part. A ship that can load a cargo in, say, Frankfurt, can perfectly easily unload it in Bideford: she doesn't *need* a large (and therefore expensive) harbour to unload in.

As for Bideford now, it is still a port, with some ball clay ships occasionally coming in to load at the quay, the afore-mentioned M.V. *Despatch*, and some occasional ships of up to a thousand tons and drawing ten feet, but perhaps the average is about 700. Fertilizer, timber, house coal and salt for the roads all come in: ball clay goes out.

There are three hard-working old trawlers at Bideford: the biggest, the *Margaret*, habitually fishes over on the Welsh coast. One trawler supplies a local shop and here you can buy that rare commodity – fresh fish. The rest of the fish is sold through the Brixham Fishermen's Co-operative. Bideford still has some remnant of the charm of an old sailing ship port. The Grenvilles made Bideford. Kingsley romanticized it. There are Armada cannon in Victoria Park.

Appledore has even more of this tar and timber charm, and still builds tar and timber ships: the yard of Messrs Hinks being the last yard in England capable of building large vessels in the traditional manner of wood. A visit to their yard is fascinating, for we see large pieces of timber being slung up into position by wooden cranes worked by man-power, and men using adzes and caulking hammers and serving mallets, and can imagine ourselves back a hundred years in time. In fact this is a highly efficient yard, turning out the largest wooden fishing vessels at present being built anywhere and competing very well with steel or other material. Hinks can only survive this competition because of the fact that it is very much a family concern, most of the shipwrights or other craftsmen are either relations or old employees and have strong loyalty, there are no 'demarcation disputes', everybody knows his skilled job and they all work marvellously as a team. For the devotee of that ancient sport – *watching men work* – I can think of no better place. When historical replicas have to be built, such as the *Nonsuch*, which was the replica of the ship which crossed the Atlantic to found the Hudson's Bay Company, or the *Hispaniola* which was used in filming *Treasure Island*, they are generally built in Hinks's yard at Appledore.

Another Appledore yard, however, Appledore Shipyard, has moved right into the 20th century, and is equipped with the latest plant for turning out steel ships.

The 'Bar' pilots operate from Appledore, and there is a very active lifeboat station. The sand barges that normally unload at Barnstaple unload here at neap tides. There are salmon netters in the Taw and Torridge, but here, as elsewhere, salmon are getting very scarce. Pollution and disease have much to do with it.

Back at Bideford you cross the Torridge by a great and fine bridge of twenty-four arches. **Instow** has an early Victorian unity and charm. There is an old sand barge loaded with scrap on the foreshore, and the Army's Amphibious Experimental Establishment. The south bank of the Taw is cut off from the rest of the world by the railway, and is lonely and desolate in the same way as the Lower Thames or the Hooghly. Michael Leach, one of the sons of that great pottery innovator (or at least rediscoverer of ancient art) Bernard, keeps his pottery at **Yelland**. Tankers unload at **Fremington**, as do colliers now but they won't for long. The road between Instow and Barnstaple is a beastly piece of ribbon development. There is a bungalow (one of hundreds) which delights in the name of 'I-Won-Der' and this sets the tone of the place.

Barnstaple is approached from the south by the Long Bridge, which was there in 1303, was widened in 1796 and again in 1963. The north face is old. The sand suckers *William Woolaway* (400 tons) and *Pen Taw* (60 tons) discharge their sand at the quay at Appledore and it is used straight away by builders who don't seem to worry about the salt in it. It is dredged up from the Bristol Channel off Porthcawl. The sand bargemen in the Torridge and Taw have always been a race apart. In former days they beached their vessels on the sand and loaded the sand with shovels. Two men would take four hours to load twenty tons. This is said to have engendered a thirst. Even now there are some small barges which load sand from the north bank of the Taw, but they load it with mechanical elevators.

Barnstaple has celebrated its millennium as a borough, and claims, along with many other towns, to be the oldest borough in England. In A.D. 878 the Danish marauder Hubba sailed into the Taw, from Milford Haven, and he and his 1200 fellow pirates were quite rightly killed at Cynuits Castle by the men of King Alfred. When Charles II was still a prince, and only fifteen, he was sent to hide at Barnstaple from the Roundheads. Shakespeare almost certainly played here. John Gay was born here in 1685, and went to the grammar school, and was apprentice to a draper until he turned poet. His *Beggar's Opera* ran for three very successful months in London and is still very popular. The burghers of Barnstaple seem to have had very little respect for what was of interest and beauty in their town and very little remains of what must have been a fine old seaport. When John Gay's own (very beautiful) chair was offered to the Borough some time back, for fifty pounds, the councillors could not find it in their hearts to spare the money and it went elsewhere. But Queen Anne's Walk remains, with a large statue of that monarch on its roof and an old people's resthouse inside, and the Tome Stone in front of it, which is a stone similar in shape to the 'Nails' of Bristol – that is mushroom-shaped. When merchants paid each other they had to do it in front of witnesses by throwing the cash down on the Tome Stone (in Bristol they 'paid on the nail'). Butchers' Row is very fine – an elegant and workmanlike row of shops in which Barnstaple's butchers have to keep their prices down to compete with each other, and there is a nice market building opposite, with the old Guildhall at one end of it, built after 1827 when an even older one was pulled down, within it portraits of citizens by Thomas Hudson (who is said to have been assisted by Sir Joshua Reynolds), and there is the

Pentecost-Dodderidge Parlour here with some very good 17th-century oak panelling, and here is kept the fine collection of plate and seals of Barnstaple. The Guildhall seems a bit empty and deserted nowadays, because some kind of *folie de grandeur* seems to have seized the Borough Council and inspired them to build a simply enormous skyscraper of a civic centre down on the river bank. It would be interesting to know what on earth they do in it.

The waterfront of Barnstaple, upstream of the bridge and beyond the Imperial Hotel, is fine and has an air of civility.

On the Lynton Road is **Arlington Court**, open as a museum and garden, once owned by the Chichester family, from which sprang the circumnavigating Sir Francis.

Braunton is, surprisingly, also a seaport. The long, tidal Braunton Pill goes up to it and ships used to use this. **Chivenor** is given over to a big R.A.F. training camp. **Heanton Punchardon** has a fine church with a marvellous chime of bells. **Heanton Court**, although castellated, is not as old as it looks. It has a kestrel nesting high up (out of small-boy-reach) in its masonry. It is an hotel.

Braunton Great Field is a very interesting survival from open field days. It is a field of 365 acres, of the best soil in the neighbourhood, and farmed by a multiplicity of cultivators on the ancient strip system.

Braunton Burrows is an area of from three to four square miles of static sand and dunes. Much of it is a nature reserve and the whole area is of great interest to naturalists. **Saunton Sands**, between it and the sea, are vast: enough sand here to keep seven maids with the appropriate number of brooms sweeping for a very long time indeed. At **Saunton** are hotels and boarding houses the visitors to which take full advantage of these marvellous sands. From here on to Morte Point are apparently unlimited and very good bathing and surfing beaches: perhaps the best surfing beaches in England. **Croyde Bay** and **Woolacombe Sands** are splendid, and as safe as any beach exposed to the full force of the Atlantic rollers can be expected to be. The sight of the ranks of creamers marching in one after the other to hurl themselves on the sands of Morte Bay is spectacular, and this short piece of coast between the Torridge and Bull Point can vie with any other around the British Isles for the number of ships that it has claimed. There are all the usual silly stories about 'wreckers' luring ships ashore. In fact, the files of the *North Devon Journal* of the 19th century are full of accounts of shipwrecks here, and very often of gallant attempts, often successful, to get the crews off, and also of kindness and hospitality shown to survivors ashore. One wreck must have caused a great deal of excitement. A ship loaded with live pigs was wrecked in, of all places, Grunta Bay. The pigs were quickly rounded up, and in due course eaten, except one wily animal who escaped and lived on seaweed for about a year, near a large rock pool here which is still called Pig's Pool after him.

Woolacombe is a quickly growing place of many hotels and boarding houses. An attempt was made to establish a lifeboat here, where one was so sorely needed, in 1872, and manned by Ilfracombe men, there being no fishing community at Mortehoe. The boat had to be hauled into the sea by horses, but it was found impossible to launch her in the sort of weather in which she was needed and in 1900 the station was abandoned. At **Mortehoe** church is the tomb of William de Tracey, one of Thomas à Becket's murderers. **Barricane Bay** is rich in sea-shells – unusual for this coast.

Morte Point is a dangerous place if ever there was one, with the Morte Stone standing off it and a lot of half-tide rocks which sometimes show their fangs and sometimes do not. There is a bad tide race off it. There is a legend that anybody who is the master of his wife may remove the Morte Stone. So far nobody has done so. A footpath goes round Morte Point, and you can climb up to the coastguard look-out where is a fine view. The slate cliffs here have been fiercely eroded. There is a little gut into the cliffs on the west side of **Rockham Bay** where is a beach, or rock slide, up which a few small local boats are hauled by a windlass. Further east there is a rock-studded beach with a path down the cliff to it and steps. There is good bathing here with an off-shore wind. I have beached a boat here and lain out a westerly gale, and been very glad to get off again.

Bull Point has a large and important lighthouse, of 320,000 candlepower. There is a road to it and a footpath coastwise. These cliffs, and the rolling hills behind them, are extremely beautiful. Herring gulls and fulmar breed on the cliffs. **Lee Bay** has hotels, a superb wooded valley cutting up into the hills, a beach on which boats can land, and do land for there is much 'pleasure' traffic from Ilfracombe to here in fine weather, and a café in a beautiful and very ancient watermill right down at the sea's brink. There is a fine footpath to Ilfracombe.

Ilfracombe is a pretty good harbour to get into, except at low tide and a northerly gale. The harbour dries out, but the Pleasure Steamer Pier sticks out, by the grace of God, some small distance to the eastward of the low water mark in the harbour, providing some modicum of protection for a shoal draught boat at anchor under its lee in a northerly. From any other wind the harbour is well sheltered, even the anchorage outside. The inner harbour, when you can eventually get into it, provides perfect shelter. Owing to the paucity of harbours on the south shore of the Bristol Channel, however, it is crowded in summer – in winter there is bags of room. It is a most beautiful harbour, with great beetling cliffs about it and that part of Ilfracombe next to the harbour is old and attractive, but most of the town is just like any other large seaside resort. From time to time a passenger packet comes in from Swansea or Barry and discharges an invading army from Wales, and the pubs of Ilfracombe ring with the Bread of Heaven and are the better for it.

The only possible harbour for ships of any size (i.e. too big to be dragged up a beach easily) on the North Devon coast, with the exception of the Taw and Torridge with their awful bar, Ilfracombe (called variously Alfreincombe, Ilfordcombe) was early of some importance. By 1208 it was important enough to be the rendezvous for ships and men for an invasion of Ireland by King John: Henry III also used it for the same purpose. The place was proclaimed a port by Henry III, was granted a market and fair in 1278 (by Edward I). In 1346 the port sent either six or eight ships and ninety-six men to the Siege of Calais: a big offering. Later Ilfracombe flourished, not so much as a cargo landing or shipping port for its trade was always small and local, but as a ship-owning port. By about the end of the 18th century there were sixty vessels of a total tonnage of 2615 owned in the port. Like most small schooner-owning ports (compare Arklow in Ireland where, fifty years ago, every person in the town was directly connected with the schooner fleet) most ships were owned by a multiplicity of people, each one holding a number of the sixty-four shares into which the ownership of a vessel was always divided. Thus the brigantine *Diana*, built at Ilfracombe in 1785, was owned by: two mariners, a shipwright, a ropemaker, a clerk, two gentlemen and a doctor. She was engaged in the Mediterranean trade and seldom if ever returned to her birthplace: after all, what had Ilfracombe to import or to export? Backed by the moors, very remote by land, not near a big mining district, she had very little to send away and only the modest requirements of her own small population to import anything for. For the latter there was a small fleet of sloops or ketches running to Bristol or to South Wales, and, as time went on, more and more cross-Channel packets, such as the sloop *Dispatch*, 58 tons, which in 1800 was carrying passengers, carriages and horses, sailing from Ilfracombe towards Swansea every Monday and Thursday and from Swansea towards Ilfracombe every Tuesday and Saturday, and this cut off two hundred miles of land travel for those wishing to go from the West Country to West Wales, or to catch the Irish packets from Milford Haven. Steamers were introduced early in the 19th century and from then on Ilfracombe began rapidly to expand. There were regular services between Bristol, Ilfracombe, Barry, Swansea, Hayle, and even sometimes the Bristol–Irish packets put in. Ilfracombe as a resort was built up by the steam packets, as Tenby on the other side of the Channel was. The railway came in 1874 and shattered the big complex of steamer routes, but after that Ilfracombe grew more rapidly than ever, and changed its character from a seaport town to a modern holiday resort which it now is.

A great spectacle in Ilfracombe, to be seen far more often during the gales of winter than in the halcyon days of summer, is the launching of the lifeboat. She is hauled, high up on her carriage with her crew perched up on her high above the heads of the watchers in the street, by a small tractor, from her shed under Lantern Hill to where she is launched from a ramp in the south-west corner of the harbour. There is just room for her to squeeze through the narrow streets, all traffic has to be halted and the process takes about ten minutes, but then as it takes about ten minutes for the crew to assemble anyway after the maroon has gone off no time is wasted. If you ask any local man the reason for this apparently cumbersome procedure he will probably say: 'If you can see a better way of doing it say so!' Well I can't. The Ilfracombe lifeboat has a wonderful record of service. During one period of twenty-four hours during which I lay in Ilfracombe Harbour in a small boat I saw her called out four times, and for thirty-six hours the crew never got their seaboots off, for every time they had performed the laborious job of getting her back in her shed again the maroon went off immediately and they had to launch her again. There is much of interest in the Lifeboat House, which is well worth visiting.

Also worth seeing is the little Chapel of St Nicholas on **Lantern Hill**. This is basically a 13th-century building, was a cell for some holy man who maintained a light, was dissolved as a chapel at the Dissolution, used until nearly the end of the 19th century as the dwelling house of a light keeper, then deserted, and recently restored by the Rotarians as a chapel, is open to the public, and used for occasional services. The light is still kept burning and is useful when approaching Ilfracombe from across the Channel.

The other place of great interest is the little museum. This is stuffed with objects of maritime interest, including a great collection of early photographs and paintings, many models, and quite an important little archive. It is run by volunteers who are most helpful to the enquirer. I would advise anybody going to Ilfracombe to visit it, if he visits nothing else. The little steamers of the White Funnel Fleet operate services all summer to Lundy, Swansea, Porthcawl, Minehead, Lynmouth and Clovelly, and occasionally to Weston, Cardiff and Penarth.

Hele Bay, much built up, has a small bathing beach in this coast of few bathing beaches. There is the trace of a lime kiln at the top of it, showing that lime and culm were once shipped in here. The practice, of course, was to sail in at high tide, beach and chuck the stuff overboard, and sail off at the next high tide. Men would come down with horses and carts at low tide and cart the stuff away at their leisure to be burnt in the kiln and then spread on the land.

Watermouth is one of the most beautiful inlets on the coast, now highly commercialized with many yachts, caravans, ice cream and all the rest of it. In all but north-westerly weather it is a fine shelter, and even in a north-westerly if you can wait for enough water you can creep up behind the small breakwater which has been built half across the harbour. There are many fixed moorings for yachts in the summer, and a small fleet of pleasure craft. The owners do some lobster potting. The 'castle' is a Victorian folly, large and grand and in beautiful grounds. Watermouth was the port for **Berrynarbor**, just inland. The church here is interesting. The squire's pew has a fireplace, a mantelpiece and fire irons, there is a 13th-century chancel and a leaning arcade of the 15th century. John Jewel was born at Berrynarbor. He fled the country during Mary Stuart's time thus saving his neck, returned when Elizabeth came to the throne and was made Bishop of Salisbury, where he wrote 'The Apology for the English Church' which had to be chained beside the chained Bibles in every church in the land. Down on the shore, east of Watermouth, are two fine caves at Smallmouth and Briery. They were praised by Gosse in *Ramblings of a Naturalist*.

Combe Martin has been called one of the ugliest villages in Devon, and who am I to argue?: it strings out for miles on either side of a busy motor road in the bottom of a narrow valley – an absolutely classic example of ribbon development. The valley in which it lies, however, is famous for strawberries and other market garden produce, which is mostly sold in Ilfracombe market, although it used to be shipped to South Wales in fast cutters. Cargoes of coal were landed on the beach here as late as 1930 and in the past lead ore was shipped out. For Combe Martin is, in fact, a mining village, although no mining is done there now. Up near Stony Corner you can still see the abandoned mine workings, and mine workings run under the village. In the 13th century it is known that miners were brought in to here from Wales and Derbyshire, and in the 16th century German miners were brought in. Silver and lead were extracted, and two tankards still used by the Corporation of the City of London were made in 1731 from silver melted down from a big tankard presented in 1593 from these mines. Astonishingly Combe Martin was once a ship-building port. Between 1837 and 1843 a man named John Dovell built at least eight ships on the beach, the biggest being the *Combmartin*, of 94 tons.

The name Combe Martin, incidentally, comes from the family of Martin de Turribus, a non-Norman adventurer who came with William the Conqueror, was allotted this part of England as his spoils but, dissatisfied with it, almost immediately sailed for Cemais, in North Pembrokeshire, which he conquered and there made his chief domain. A William Martin, the seventh Lord of Cemais, was drowned in the moat of Barnstaple Castle. He was riding back from a stag hunt and thought the drawbridge was down but unfortunately for him it was up. There are caves down in Combe Martin Bay, and shining rock of schists and quartz.

From here, if we are by land, we climb up into Exmoor proper. If we are afloat we embark on the long, practically harbourless, almost vertical, and extremely impressive Exmoor cliffs. Perhaps this is one of the most dramatic coasts to sail along in England: in many places the cliffs tower over us to peaks of over a thousand feet. Nesting along these cliffs we have razorbills, guillemots, fulmars, cormorants, herring gulls, jackdaws, ravens and great and lesser black-backed gulls.

The cliffs themselves at first are of a grit and have been called the Hangman Beds, but the whole shore to the east of us is made of Devonian rock which has a southerly dip, thus the oldest rocks are to the north and the rocks get progressively later as one goes inland. These rocks were formed at the bottom of a shallow sea some 350 million years ago, a sea which lay to the south of the Old Red Sandstone Continent which covered the midlands of England and which has been named the Devonian sea. We find here, and can easily identify in these naked cliffs, sandstones, clays, and conglomerates which have often been transformed to grits, shales, slates and flagstones by heat and pressure. It is generally believed that a great east–west fault in these rocks made this impressive shoreline.

Trentishoe has a tiny little isolated church. There is a 'neck' of corn carved on the wood of the musicians' gallery. The custom of 'carrying the neck' was only recently abandoned in Devon. A young man ran with the first sheaf of corn to be cut to the barn while the other farm people tried to throw water on it. If they succeeded – it would be a wet harvest, if not it would be a dry. In the musicians' gallery is a hole made especially for the bow of the double bass. Just by the door outside is the grave of 'My lovely little Tommy' with an epitaph which should wring a tear from the most unsentimental eye.

Heddon's Mouth, at the foot of a superbly beautiful combe – a violent gash in the mountainside, with woodland clinging to its almost vertical sides and water cascading down the stream in its bottom – was, amazingly enough, once a port. At least there is a lime kiln here, so vessels must have come in to unload in this fantastic spot. This was also a great smuggling place (as were Watermouth and Combe Martin – and in fact every little hole and cranny along this coast). In 1801 the sloop *Hope* landed ninety-six ankers of spirits here and headed towards Watermouth to unload the rest. Alas – she struck a rock on the way and went down with all hands and the rest of her cargo. In 1827 the revenue men found £1180 worth of brandy buried under the floors of the stables of a man named John Hoyle. Hoyle escaped out of a window and fortunately was not captured, but the spirits had to be moved to Barnstaple for safety because feeling ran so high among the crowd in Ilfracombe, who were on the side of Hoyle and, quite rightly, could not bear to see all this good liquor go to waste.

In about A.D. 50 when Caractacus was leading the Silures tribe of South Wales against the Romans, a fort was built at **Martinhoe** by the Romans guarding this coast. This was well defended with double ramparts and ditches, with an outer line of defence about seventy feet out from the main line, and enough accommodation inside for a century (eighty men). Traces of their field ovens have been found, and of a forge for their armourers, and also of their signal fires that could be seen far across the Severn Sea: as far as Wales on a clear day. They must have felt that they were in a terribly remote and isolated spot. They were probably withdrawn about A.D. 75 after Caractacus had been defeated.

From here follows a most dramatic stretch of coast, where the

ILFRACOMBE: *Above*, the harbour; *below*, Torrs Walks.

Above, the Torridge Estuary, looking to Instow from Appledore; *below*, the River Parrett at Combwich.

cliffs have foundered into the sea to form a confused mass of country rather like the Lyme Regis Undercliff. **Woody Bay** is most splendid, and woody indeed it is, for trees have established themselves well on these slipping mountains. **Crock Pits** is so named because it was once quarried for clay, allegedly by Dutchmen, although why these people should have come so far for clay when their country is made of it is hard to see. In 1800 nine acres of land here slipped incontinently into the sea one Sunday morning while their owner was at church. Near Martinhoe we pass over from the Hangman Grits to the Lynton Slates. At **Wringapeak** by the way is a sheer 500 foot drop into the sea so don't get shipwrecked here. There were lime kilns at both Woody Bay and **Lee Bay**, amazing though it may seem that any farmer would want to haul lime up those slopes. Lee Bay is interesting for its rocks, highly schistosed by heat and pressure, full of quartz and mica, and much split and sundered. Further east we find (in Wringacliff Bay) dark slatey shales and slates with quartz veins, dipping inland to the south like the other rocks along this coast.

Lee Abbey is a very large country house built in 1841 by Charles Bailey on the site of Ley Manor (which features in *Lorna Doone*) enlarged, disastrously from an aesthetic point of view, in the horrid 1920s and used as an hotel, and used as a boys' school during the Second World War. In 1945 it and the 260-acre estate were bought by a group of Anglicans who turned it into an Anglican centre which it still is. There are about seventy people in the community, but always a much higher population there, for anybody can stay if there is room, for fourteen guineas a week. Guests have the run of the large and extremely beautiful estate, can bathe from Lee Bay which provides very good bathing, and there are many activities into which they can join. The community members run a small home farm, providing milk and vegetables for the population. About 4000 people stay at the place every year. The atmosphere is relaxed, informal, but strongly evangelistic. The estate is a naturalists' paradise. There is a great variety of bird life, delightful green fields alternate with the wildest of woods, foxes, badgers and red deer abound.

The **Valley of Rocks** is what it says it is, a little miniature alpine valley complete with wild goats. Very beautiful, Coleridge loved it, brought the Wordsworths to see it, and wrote the *Rime of the Ancient Mariner* to pay for the excursion.

Lynton and **Lynmouth** are indivisible, although one clings high up on a steep hillside and the other is down in a steep-sided valley.

They are joined by a motor road of dizzy steepness, but also by the Lynton Lift Railway, a splendid affair built in 1890 at a cost of £8000, with a nine hundred foot long track which has a gradient of one-in-one-and-three-quarters rising to a height of 450 feet. When it was built it was the steepest graded railway in the world. It is worked by the simple and sensible process of filling a tank under the car which is at the top of the track with three tons of water, so that it thereby descends pulling the car which had been at the bottom up by a rope over a pulley. When the car with the water in it gets to the bottom the water is allowed to run out of it, while the other car, at the top, is filled. It works extremely well and there has never been an accident. While on the subject of Lynton railways there is the sad story of the spectacular two-foot gauge railway that, opened in 1898, connected Lynton to Barnstaple. Such was the terrain through which this had to pass that the twenty miles of narrow track cost £127,000 to build. With almost unbelievable blindness and stupidity the line was abandoned in 1936. If it were running now it would be a gold mine, for the track goes through some of the most superb scenery in England. The Exmoor Museum in Lynton is well worth a visit.

Lynmouth was never much of a harbour, although there was a small fishing community there which got pretty much wiped out in the great tidal surge of 1607. Several small trading craft were built there in the 18th century, probably for the local trade, for Lynton, Lynmouth and Countisbury were terribly cut off from the rest of humanity by land. There was an export trade in oak bark which went to tanneries: some of it to Ireland. But herring brought prosperity to the place about the beginning of the 19th century, when a jetty or pier was built, since taken away by the sea.

Lynmouth had a lifeboat from 1869 to 1944, and one of her services, to the steamer *Forest Hall*, is a quite astonishing epic, and an example of the extraordinary – landlubbers might think almost excessive – pains that seafarers will go to to help their colleagues in trouble at sea.

In the afternoon of 12th January 1899 a telegraph message was received in Lynmouth from Porlock, saying that the *Forest Hall* was showing distress signals in Porlock Bay. Before a reply could be sent the wires had been blown down by the growing northerly gale and Lynmouth was cut off. The coxswain of the lifeboat, Jack Crocombe, deciding that in that gale it would be impossible either to sail or to row as far as Porlock, ordered that the boat should be transported overland. Horses were got and these, and a small army of human helpers, managed to drag the boat on her carriage up the one-in-four slope of Countisbury Hill to the top of Exmoor, a thousand feet up, in spite of the fact that a wheel came off, the gale had blown up with drenching rain and was increasing all the time so that by the time they had reached the top it was officially recorded as Force Ten. The boat carriage was too wide to negotiate the lanes and gates, and a great amount of work had to be done tearing stone walls down – including the garden wall of one old lady who asked them just what they were doing in her garden at five o'clock in the morning, which it by then was. At one stage they had to take the boat off her carriage and slide her on skids for two miles, sending the carriage round by road to join them further on. Porlock Hill is supposed to be one of the steepest and worst bits of road in the British Isles, and the boat had to be lowered down this. It was seven in the morning before the procession reached Porlock and by then the gale was such that great damage was being done to buildings and property all over the country. The *Forest Hall* was still lying to her anchors, with her rudder out of action. She was dragging and would not have had long to drag before she would have been on the rocks. The boat was launched, a tug which had been standing by steamed nearer and the lifeboatmen managed to get a line from her aboard the steamer – and put a crew aboard the latter. One tug proved incapable of towing the ship against the gale but another arrived and ship and lifeboat were towed across the Bristol Channel to Barry. For this service each member of the crew received five pounds.

No account of Lynmouth can ignore the flood of the night of Friday 15th August 1952. After weeks of August rain nine inches of rain fell in that one night. This proved altogether too much for the already sodden soil and subsoil of Exmoor to absorb and down it all came to carry a great part of Lynmouth with it into the sea. Quite early in the proceedings the electricity station upstream was overwhelmed and so the village was plunged into darkness. It was dark when a ten-foot wall of water hit the village, carrying boulders as large as small houses and big tree trunks with it. All that part of the village that had been built since most of the place was washed away by the 1607 tidal surge was again washed away – houses, cars, people and trees being carried right out to sea. Thirty-four people lost their lives. The place has since been rebuilt and is now a popular, and very crowded, holiday resort.

One house carried away was the one in which Shelley spent his honeymoon with his sixteen-year-old bride Harriet *née* Westbrook. Here Shelley wrote 'Queen Mab'.

At **Brendon** is a splendid inn, the Stag Hounes, and a most beautiful pack-horse bridge. At **Old Barrow,** hard by **County Gate** from which runs a nature trail – right on the Devon–Somerset frontier – is another Roman fortlet like the one at Martinhoe. It was excavated in 1963, and is considered to have been of about exactly the same date and for the same purpose as Martinhoe.

CHAPTER 20

County Gate to Portishead

✌

THERE used to be a coast walk from County Gate to Porlock, but some of it has fallen down the cliff and you have to be pretty nimble to bypass this. But these Culbone Woods, and the whole estate of Lord Lytton (or such of it as he hasn't sold off to the tenants) is one of the most grandly romantic, nay Gothic, stretches of coast in the British Isles. Here are eight miles of very steep north-facing slopes, deeply scored by small streams, heavily wooded, finishing below for the most part at the cliff's edge, although here and there there are, if you can find them, precipitous ways down to the tumbled rocks below. In these woods are red deer and every kind of bird and beast that you could possibly expect to find in such places, except, as far as I know, pine marten. And if any local naturalist had seen one of those he wouldn't tell you or me about it. In these woods are curious buildings, if you can find them: a large rambling and decaying Italianate mansion, built hard up against a rock cliff and almost covered in with neglected shrubbery and full of bats, and – most curious and beautiful – Culbone church.

Culbone is a hamlet of two houses and a minuscule church, lost in the heart of a heavily wooded glen. The church is largely 12th-century, and has a Celtic cross standing by it, but the strangest thing about it, to me, is the tiny window in the north wall of the chanced which has two lights but which is carved out of a single piece of stone and which has what looks like a mithraic bull's head carveb on it. This church is very old, this window is generally said ol, experts to be 'Saxon'. But there were Roman forts hard by. Why knows if this could or could not have been a piece of stone taken from one of them?

Just by the church is the pottery of Waistel and Joan Cooper. Waistel is a Scotsman and Joan comes from California, and together they produce pots and ceramic sculpture of great style and individuality of very hard and high quality stoneware. The Coopers are potters of international stature. You *can* get to them by motor car, if you are very good at map reading and don't mind driving over extremely rough tracks, but by far the best way is walk along the lovely footpath from Porlock, and if you buy any pots the Coopers will deliver them for you to wherever you are staying. Coleridge wrote 'Kubla Khan' in a farmhouse in Culbone. We may wish that the 'person from Porlock' who interrupted him had got lost first in that labyrinthine wood.

Porlock is a mile from the sea, but its name means 'enclosed harbour'. It is probable that the marshes that separate it from the sea are a recent accretion. The church of St Dubricius is beautiful and interesting, with a most superb alabaster monument to John, 4th Lord Harington and his wife Elizabeth Courtenay. This latter alone is well worth going to see. Dubricius was one of the legion of Welsh saints who fanned out from South Wales in the 6th century: that golden age of saints and legends of King Arthur. St Dubricius is supposed to have married King Arthur to Guinevere. Whether this is so or not it is fairly certain that he retired at last from the world to Bardsey Island, in North Wales, and that when he died his remains were translated to Llandaff Cathedral. It is generally thought that he did live for some time in Porlock. There is a pre-Norman cross stuck on the west wall of the south aisle – very old indeed.

There is a highly dedicated spinner and weaver in Porlock: Miss Sophia Evans (telephone Porlock 319). She sells excellent and individual cloths made by her from the raw wool of local sheep.

Porlock Weir is the present port of Porlock and is an idiosyncratic little place. It was a herring port up to the 18th century when many of the fish were cured as red herrings. Up until 1910 there was an oyster fishery here, oysters being dredged out at sea at about the ten-fathom mark and kept in 'perches' or beds near the beach until they were needed. Porlock was also a schooner port. The last two Porlock ships were the schooners *Periton* and *Flying Foam* and the ketch *Bertie*. The *Periton* was built at Minehead in 1887 from oak from Periton Wood. She was run down and sunk by a steamer off the Smalls when she was sailing towards Ireland. The *Flying Foam* was torpedoed in the English Channel by a German U-boat in the First World War, and the *Bertie* was eventually cut in half by a steamer north of Lundy.

The Lee family of Porlock were schooner skippers and owners. They originally came from Combe Martin, in their own ship the ketch *Mistletoe*, and have been here ever since. The Harbour Master is a Lee, a close relation of Harbour Master Lee of Watchet. The Lees are pretty well known up and down the Bristol Channel and the Severn Sea. The funny little dock at Porlock Weir is sometimes

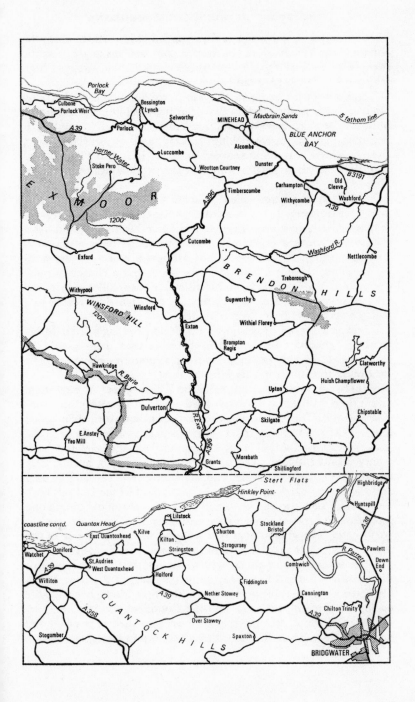

closed by a lock gate, which is then opened at low tide to scour the channel out. As you sail in you keep broom beacons to port and the stick beacons to starboard, and there is 16 feet of water at high spring tides. The bridge can be moved to admit a mast.

The marshes to the north of Porlock are famous barley-growing land, and it is strange to find this dead flat level among the mighty hills of Exmoor. **Bossington**, lush and beautifully situated, is becoming an expensive-looking holiday and residential village. **Lynch**, joined to it, has a simple but rather beautiful 16th-century chapel – built about mid-century but the window tracery has been renewed.

Selworthy has been called by some people the most beautiful village in England. It lies in a little combe cut into the south slope of Selworthy Beacon which is over a thousand feet steep, and has a grand view south over Porlock Vale towards the hills of Exmoor. The little group of farmhouses and cottages are of a picture post-card quality, there is a beautiful tithe barn, and a church of quite exceptional loveliness. The south aisle has been called one of the greatest treasures of English architecture, but I leave the reader to it and the very good little church guide.

There is a 'scenic drive' now for horseless carriages from Minehead to Selworthy Beacon. It is desirable that there should be *fewer* places to which the motor car can penetrate – not more. The car-bound tourist necessarily kills the thing he loves.

Minehead comes, in name, from the Welsh *mynydd*, or mountain, and indeed Minehead is shoved hard up against a steep and considerable hill. The earliest mention of the harbour is in 1380, when harbour dues were being collected for its maintenance. Early in the 15th century the Luttrell family, to whom the place belonged, built a jetty. Minehead had a charter granted to it in 1558, but the jetty fell to pieces, trade fell away, and the charter was revoked in 1604 and the place was given back to the Luttrells. George Luttrell built the existing pier – to the westward of the former one – completing it in 1616 at a cost of about £5000 and it soon became a prosperous port again. The great stones which lie on the seaward side of the pier, and which break the force of the waves, were floated into that position by being buoyed up with casks, in 1682, and about this time another Luttrell had a big extension built to the pier. Minehead was a considerable port at about this time, doing considerable trade with Ireland, and also with the Continent. In 1701 the port owned thirty ships, and there was a busy ship-yard near where the present lifeboat house is. The last trading ship to be registered here was the little sloop *Harriet*, built in 1805 and lost in 1852 when she was unloading limestone on the beach. This was the fate of so many Severn Sea traders. They used to have to load or unload on exposed beaches. They would beach themselves at high tide, load or unload, and get off at the following high tide. But if an on-shore gale blew up in the meantime? They could never warp themselves off the lee shore which they were then on and the incoming breakers would smash them to pieces. Other ships, registered elsewhere, were owned in the port and in 1894 there were still ten ships. The last Minehead trader, the *Emma Louise*, was sold in 1953, and coal was still coming into the port until 1958. Now there are a few part-time fishing boats, and 'pleasurers', occasional visits from White Funnel Line 'steamers' at high tide (the pier that this firm built before the war so that they could disembark passengers at low tide was wantonly destroyed during the Second World War in the ludicrous and panicky craze that destroyed so many of our piers), and a few yachts that come and go as the spirit takes them. It is a nasty harbour to be in when a westerly gale blows. As the tide comes in and lifts you off the hard sand you can get quite a bad bashing. And the same thing when it sets you down again. It pays to choose the softer ground to moor over. But in the summer it is generally all right. The long association of the Luttrell family with the harbour ended in 1951, when a Luttrell sold it to the Urban District Council for two pounds, glad, perhaps, to get rid of it. It is sad that it should so have dwindled, for Defoe, writing in 1716, called it 'the best port and safest harbour on this side of all these counties. No ship is so big but that it may come in, and no weather so bad but the ships are safe when they are in.' He compared its trade, with Ireland, Virginia and the West Indies, with that of Bristol! The imports then were mostly linen cloth, bay yarn, hides and skins, butter, tallow, pork and bacon, and the exports, much smaller, were oak bark for tanning, grain, and salt herrings.

Haematite, or soft red iron ore, was once mined at **Wootton Courtney** and shipped out of Minehead.

The Pier Hotel is a great centre of life here – you can moor your boat within a very few yards of it. 'Rough cider' or 'scrumpy' is served to locals only, but visiting mariners sometimes get dispensation. In summer it is usually pretty crowded with campers from Butlins. There is a chapel which adjoins the pub, and which is the only chapel in England on licensed premises, and in which the Holy Eucharist is offered every Friday morning at eight o'clock on behalf of sailors. The building was once a salt store belonging to a sailor named Robert Quirck. In 1630 he was returning from a voyage to the Mediterranean with salt herring when he was caught in a storm which threatened to overwhelm him. He vowed that if he got home safely he would build alms houses for the poor and give his salt store to them as well. The alms houses are still there to see, on the Parade, and there is a brass plate over the door of one of them with Quirck's dedication in which he says, amongst the rest: 'and curssed bee that man that shall convert it to any other vse than for the vse of the Poore, 1630.' There is a delineation of a ship then and the words: 'God's Providence is my Inheritance. R.E.Q.' It is said that the roof timber from the little chapel on the pub was from Quirck's ship, which he broke up on his safe return and used for the purpose, and the bell outside is his ship's bell.

I have searched for the 'submarine forest' that is said, by my Ordnance map, to lie out near the low tide mark at Minehead, but all I have got is wet feet. People still put 'set lines' out for fish here. They peg lines of baited hooks out at low water, wait until the tide has come and gone, and go and take the fish off them.

Along the Strand is an *enormous* Butlins Camp, with every delight, including a cable railway that carries you high over sand dunes and marshes.

Dunster needs a book all to itself. There is so much to see here, and so much to learn, that a writer on the coast is tempted to claim that this is inland. But it *had* its own port, in the Middle Ages, and it is only a mile from the sea. The village itself is quite beautiful (although overrun with tourists in the summer and furnished with 'souvenir shops' of the least attractive kind). The pigeon house with its wonderful revolving ladder is my favourite building there, but the church and castle are worth seeing too. The castle is colossal (but much of it 19th-century – by Salvin), and has had additions made to it ever since it was bought from the Mohuns by the Luttrells in 1376. The Luttrells have owned it ever since. Whatever happens don't miss the dining-room ceiling. The church is magnificent, having been a priory church of the Benedictine house here which was a cell – but an important one – of Bath. There is a great deal in the church to see. There is a fine 16th-century barn, still used as a workshop by the estate. Were the tourists in smaller numbers, and the knick-knack shops more discriminating, and *fewer*, Dunster would be one of the most delightful villages in all England. You need at least a whole day to see it properly: better still a week. If you can find it go to Bat's Castle, an Iron Age fortress with a splendid view.

Blue Anchor Bay is so called because if a ship lets go an anchor here it is caked with thick blue clay when it comes up. There is a pub called Blue Anchor here and an enormous caravan park. It is a very popular place. **Cleeve Abbey**, inland, is said to be well worth a visit. I haven't been there.

Watchet is a living refutation of the dismal doctrine that all small shipping is finished and all small ports should be filled in and made into car parks. While Bristol is foolishly trying to run its port down as hard as it can, and putting every possible difficulty in the way of traders who would like to use it, Watchet is actually making money by unloading fertilizer ships and sending their cargoes to *Bristol* by lorry! This little port imports packaged timber and loose timber, olive stones and olive pulp to be made into animal foodstuffs, bone meal for the same purpose, tinned tomato and tomato purée, orange, apricot and peach pulp for making into jam (one wonders what sort of jam it makes!), such fresh fruit as does not require refrigeration, and wood pulp for the paper mills. The latter comes from the Baltic, the former all from Portugal or the Mediterranean. Ships of up to 2600 tons can lie against the quay, but the average is from 500 to 1000 tons, and about 150 ships a year come in, bringing about 90,000 tons of cargo. About 15,000 tons go out, mostly waste paper and scrap metal to Spain and Italy and fertilizer for Ireland. This is quite enough shipping to keep Watchet a busy little port. There are about ten full-time dockers, and the rest come off the labour exchange when there is work for them. The only other considerable industry in Watchet is the big paper factory of the Reed and Smith Group, which runs albeit on a reduced scale in this time of recession when many other paper factories have closed down, and a paper bag factory operated in a lovely old mill near the town centre.

Watchet got cut up twice by the Danes, according to the Anglo-Saxon Chronicle, but was supposed to have been founded by them originally, but it certainly existed pre-Danes because St Decuman, one of those innumerable 6th-century Welsh or at least Brythonic saints, came across the Severn Sea floating on a hurdle and carrying a cow for company, had his head cut off some time after he had arrived, and picked it up and carried it to his holy well which is just to the west of the church. The well, alas, is now represented by a prosaic tap which, when I last saw it, needed a new washer and was all pretty messy. Without wishing to relapse into paganism one feels that something more fitting and suitable could be built here than this. The head-carrying story is from a 17th-century manuscript, but there certainly was a St Decuman, for he is known to Welsh literature as well. His church at Watchet is well worth seeing, in its incongruous setting just above the paper mills. I like Tom Allen's anchor gravestone – this is an anchor which, though it is of stone, one feels one could entrust one's ship to.

In the Jurassic rocks at Watchet – the Raetic and Lower Lias – have been found many fossils – even Defoe was impressed by them. There have been found Pterodactyl, Ichthyosaurus, Plesiosaurus (one twelve foot long) and Dapedius, a fish. Two mammoth tusks were dredged out of the harbour in 1861 when it was being deepened. In the cliffs nearby alabaster and gypsum have been extracted. In the Civil War Watchet was the scene of perhaps the only action ever fought between cavalry and naval vessels in which the former won. The Parliamentary troopers of Popham's Troop rode into the shallow water at low tide and captured some stranded Royalist vessels.

Watchet didn't become much of a port until Sir William Wyndham, the local landowner, got acts of parliament to improve it in 1702 and 1714. Defoe, in 1724, was pretty disparaging about it. By the end of the 18th century most of what little trade there was from the port was apparently export of kelp, which was the ashes of seaweed and used in the manufacture of glass, and laver weed, which is an edible seaweed much esteemed by Welshmen. It was sent away pickled in stone jars.

Things revived with a bang, though, in 1859, when the unusual West Somerset Mineral Railway was opened, which connected the port to Gupworthy Mines in the Brendon Hills. This brought iron ore down which was shipped to South Wales. In 1862 the main line railway came, and in the same year a breakwater was built out from the pier. Later another pier was built on the east side. Watchet was becoming a large and prosperous harbour. There were once a hundred and fifty ships owned in this port.

Then in 1898 the first disaster struck. Iron ore started to come more cheaply from Spain (where perhaps the miners were not paid so much as the Gupworthy ones?) and the Gupworthy Mines and mineral railway closed down. Then, on 28th December 1900 a gale struck the place, to such effect that the Breakwater and East Pier were smashed almost completely, four ships in the harbour were completely wrecked, five were gravely damaged, one was sunk, and the remaining three all suffered damage. It must have been a frightful blow to the little port. The people formed an Urban District Council so that they could borrow money and set about rebuilding.

In 1903 a further gale destroyed most of their work and wrecked two ships. But again the work was begun and this time completed, and Watchet Harbour now looks a pretty sturdy place. The last Watchet schooner was trading up to the beginning of the Second World War.

Watchet and Minehead have been hit hard by the stupid closing of the railway in 1971. This has very seriously isolated them, and the local people find it very difficult, if they haven't got cars, to get out or back again. The thousands of people, many who do not own cars, who go to Butlins, have to be collected at great trouble and inconvenience – and even more congestion on the roads – by bus. Fortunately a society has been formed which is fighting hard to be allowed to run the railway as a private concern. If you want good rough cider in Watchet, and a good time, go to The Anchor.

There is an army camp at **Doniford**, by the rather desolate stony and shingly shoreline which we are now embarking on. **St Audries** is by the Quantock State Forest and has a Victorian church, large Victorian Tudor mansion and a girls' school. It is also sprouting 'chalets' and a sort of holiday camp. **East Quantoxhead** has a charmingly situated church built hard up against a vast Jacobean mansion that has, with its pre-Jacobean predecessors, been the home of the Luttrells for seven hundred years and still is. The church has great bench ends. There is a lovely path through a rose garden belonging to the mansion up which one is allowed to walk to the church. The most interesting thing here is perhaps the fine collection of buildings of the Home Farm. The curious round house now used as a garage which is stuck on to the side of the huge barn is the horse mill. Many big barns once had this: in it a horse walked round in a circle and turned a beam which provided power for threshing, winnowing, and grinding machinery within the barn.

There is a lovely footpath to **Kilve** (but you can walk along the top of the low cliffs if you wish). Kilve has a church with a Saxon font. Near the church are the ruins of a 15th-century chantry. The story is that about 1837 this was packed with smuggled brandy and caught fire. The flames were terrific and the parson made heroic efforts (which were successful) to stop them from spreading on the strong gale to the church. When his heroism was being extolled it was pointed out that the *church* was also well stocked with liquor, in which the parson no doubt had a share, and that this it was that he was so concerned about.

There is rolling cornland here, edged with hundred-foot cliffs of

237

Lower Lias, and the beach below is made up of huge pebbles some as big as footballs. It is a lonely deserted beach, for the stones are uncomfortable for the tender footed, and you have a good chance of getting away from it all along this shore. We may find Jurassic fossils here. **Kilton** church has a very interesting barrel organ of very early date: 1780, which the vicar is valiantly trying to restore. It may well be unique.

On the shore near here is practised the only sport I have ever heard of which involves the hunting of fish with dogs (although Defoe did record that the salmon netters of the Dart used a dog to chase salmon into the net). This is the ancient craft of *glatting*, which involves hunting for the conger eels which hide in such rock pools as are normally part of the sea at low tide on spring tides of exceptional lowness when these pools are exposed. Dogs, especially trained for the purpose, are used, first to scent out and then to *haul* out the fierce congers. I have never witnessed this activity, and don't even know whether anybody does it at the present day, but if they don't a Glatting Society ought to be formed forthwith and the sport revived.

About opposite **Stockland Bristol** the rock changes from the Lower Lias beds to Keuper Marl, and the land flattens out into marshes. The Marl is Triassic, hence older than the Jurassic Lias. The coast here is pretty desolate, and it ends before the mouth of the Parrett at a place called **Steart**, which could be beautiful in a lonely bird-haunted way. It is haunted by birds, yes, but they are kept inside a great complex of those factory-farming buildings of the type that the rude call Belsen houses.

And so we come to **Bridgwater** which was once a big port but is now no port at all. In the 1950s it quietly committed suicide as the Port of Bristol is trying so hard to do. **Dunball**, a wharf about three miles downstream started in 1844 by some coal merchants who built a horse tramway to connect with the Bristol–Exeter Railway, still has some traffic but the beautiful dock in Bridgwater itself has been allowed to die. This dock was opened on the 25th of March 1841, and could take – and could still take with a little dredging – ships of 180 foot length and 31 foot beam, and drawing 18 feet at spring tides. It is a beautiful dock, of great interest to dock-lovers, with a most amazing system of sluice gates (or 'paddles' in canal parlance) to allow water to rush out and scour the mud from the Outer Basin.

This dock was once connected with Taunton and Tiverton by canal, and was a transhipment port for river barges that could go as far as Chard and Ilchester and thus, even before the railways, tapped a considerable hinterland.

By 1348 Bridgwater was a port in its own right, being then made independent from Bristol. Two years before Bridgwater had sent one ship to the Siege of Calais. In 1578 the buss *Emanuel* of Bridgwater, went in Martin Frobisher's fleet on his third voyage to Baffin Land. She became parted from the fleet and had many strange adventures of her own, as described by Hakluyt. From a port with predominantly coasting trade Bridgwater became, in the 19th century, a deep sea port. Jarman, in his *History of Bridgwater*, states that in 1889 ships of 300 tons were coming to the port, three or four thousand ships a year bringing from 200,000 to 250,000 tons a year of coal, grain, timber, linseed, valonia, gypsum, esparto grass, hides and potatoes. One firm in the 19th century owned thirty-five ships and barques, all deep sea-going, the largest being the *British Empire* of 1347 tons which was in the India trade, but unfortunately foundered off the Azores in 1860.

The motorists who, in their millions, thunder through Bridgwater on their way from the Midlands to the South-West, see nothing but a rather ugly brick town. If they could find it possible to get out of the rat-race of the murderous A 38 and get out of their cars and walk down to the old deserted docks they would find an old town of great charm. The big merchants' houses along the Quays are very beautiful: the place has a Dutch look about it. The houses don't look quite right though without the tracery of masts and spars and rigging between them and the sky. This place was built up entirely by sea trading – every brick of it. Even the church has a painting in it, a 17th-century Italian 'Descent from the Cross', and this is said to have been presented to the church by a privateer who took it from a captured vessel. It is sad that the town has not kept and improved its river navigation and jealously preserved its connection with the sea. If this were a town in the Common Market countries its docks would be congested with barges and small motor coasters.

Robert Blake the great Parliamentary Admiral or 'General at Sea' was the son of a Bridgwater ship owner. Coleridge wrote much of his poetry at Bridgwater.

The **River Parrett** flows many miles through flat marshes, and has a Bore like its great sister the Severn. It also has an elver fishery. The elver is the immature eel which has swum across the Atlantic from the Sargasso Sea where it was hatched. Its mother before it may have come from the Parrett, into which she had swum as an elver maybe seven years before, and in which she reached maturity,

and fatness, and out of which she swam to journey back to the
Sargasso Sea to lay her eggs and die.

Fishermen creep down to the banks of the Parrett at night (I use
the word *creep* because very often they are trespassing – but they
work when the landowners are in bed), and they catch the elvers
as these tiny thread-like fish wriggle through the water on their
way upstream. The fishing is always done on the ebb, when the
elvers are forced close to the bank to take advantage of the slack
water there. The elverers use large hand nets on sticks – something
like huge butterfly nets – which they hold in the water and allow the
elvers to swim into them. If the elvers are for the 'fresh' trade they
are tipped into buckets and that is that. But nowadays most elvers
are luckier – they go for the 'live' trade, and are carefully tipped on
to nylon trays where they lie and wriggle in layers an inch or two
deep and are taken to the 'elver station' of Mr Hancock, at Combe
Tudleigh Mill, up near Chard. He pays for them and tips them into
big aerated tanks, and from there they are taken to a bigger elver
station on the Severn at Epney and bulked into bigger tanks, and
then most of them are flown across the North Pole to Japan, for the
Japanese have learnt the art of rearing them into eels and fattening
them for sale. If they don't get the ride over the North Pole, however, they are rushed by huge tanker motor lorries over the sea to
such Eastern European countries as Poland and Russia and dumped
into the rivers. Such rivers as the Volga and Danube do not get a
natural supply of elvers and therefore once had no eels. Now elvers
are put into them and important eel fisheries are growing up. The
British, with the Norwegians, are about the only European peoples
who have not discovered that not only can you eat eels, but that if
you smoke them or cook them properly they are the most delicious
fish that swims. Lampreys sometimes swim into Parrett, and salmon
are caught with the 'dip net' – similar to the lave net of Severn.

If you wish to sail into the Parrett you must be careful of Bridgwater Bar, and guide yourself through the deep water by getting the
High Light in line with the Low Light. These two lights are just
north of Burnham-on-Sea.

Burnham-on-Sea was connected by a canal to Glastonbury. The
canal was opened in 1832 but in 1852 it was dried out and a railway
was laid along its bed. The church has a collection of carvings by
Grinling Gibbons of great charm and virtuosity: it is worth going to
this otherwise dreary little late Victorian seaside resort just to see
these. They were commissioned by James II for the chapel of his
Whitehall Palace, which was being designed by Wren. The altar

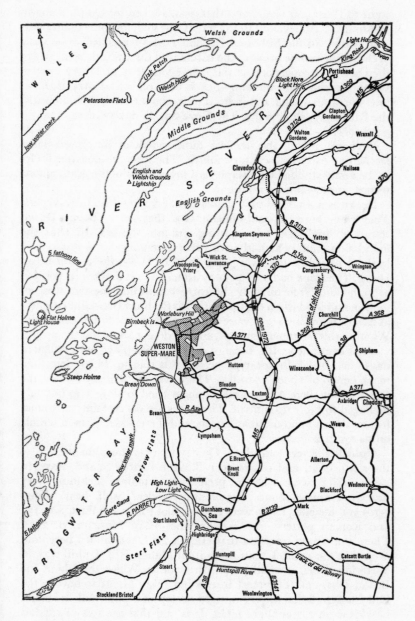

went to Hampton Court and thence was taken by Queen Anne to Westminster Abbey, and from there it was sold, for some unaccountable reason, to the Bishop of Rochester who happened to be vicar of Burnham and he brought the carvings to this unlikely spot, where they are as incongruous as the marvellous font at Prickwillow in Cambridgeshire. Burnham-on-Sea is only on sea at high tide – at low, the sands stretch out in front of it, channelled by the mouth of the Parrett, for three miles. The **Gore Sands** have wrecked many a good ship.

Berrow, among the desolate dunes north of Burnham, has a fascinating early 10th-century church. The strange wooden cylinder in the vestry studded with staples is a predecessor of the gramophone record: it played a barrel organ.

Brean is a kind of sandy desolation of caravans and caravaners. They come here for sand and my God they get it. **Brean Down** stands up high and solid, jutting out into the sea. In 1864 the foundation stone was laid with great ceremony for a grand new harbour of refuge that was going to sprout from the end of Brean Down. The stone had a large buoy attached to it to show its position at high tide. Unfortunately the cable connecting the two was not long enough and when the tide came up the buoy buoyed the stone – and both buoy and stone were floated away never to be seen again. Whether this omen was enough or not I do not know but the project was not continued with. Brean was an obvious place for a refuge in days gone by. A Breton-type beaker was dug up below low tide-mark here – of about 1700 B.C. There was an artillery fort on the Down about 1800. A disgruntled gunner tried to blow it up but only managed to blow up himself. There was almost certainly a Roman fort on the east end of Brean Down, and there was a Roman temple on its south slope.

Uphill is a very old place. Quarrying operations on the hill to the south of it, and others near Bleadon further inland, revealed caves which were rich in prehistoric remains, including very numerous animal bones: mammoth, reindeer, wolf, bear, rhinoceros and hyaena. There were also coins of Julian the First, A.D. 131 and Roman pottery (see Weston-super-Mare Museum, p. 243). There is a strong tradition that Hubba the Dane landed here, and even that the name Uphill came from Hubba Hill. Uphill was, in Victorian times, a small port with trade to Wales and about the Bristol Channel. The most interesting thing about it now is the Old Church, fallen into ruin, right on top of Uphill Hill. It should be visited on a moonlight night. It is said that the sort of vandals that infest large seaside resorts nowadays seem intent on knocking it down.

Weston-super-Mare is the largest seaside resort in the Bristol Channel, and has everything that such places have and also a good Municipal Museum which is well worth a visit. On **Worlebury Hill** was a great Iron Age camp, four lines of ramparts across the limestone spur. It was excavated in 1851 and charred wood and human skeletons were found in it, and a skull pierced by three sword cuts. Many of the skeletons too showed sword wounds. The skulls were Iberian. Wheat and barley was discovered, and several hundred pits – presumably grain storage pits as well as hut foundations. The carboniferous limestone of this hill is full of fossils.

At **Birnbeck Island** a lifeboat was established in 1881. A bridge was built between this island and the mainland and a pier extended into the sea. This was opened in 1867, and steamers used to embark and disembark here. The pier however was washed away. There is another pier right in the bite of Weston Bay, but this can only be approached at high tide. This part of the Bristol Channel has the second highest rise and fall of tide in the world. The little harbour, now called the Marine Lake, once had coal ketches unloading in it. These were coming up to 1933. Weston has all grown up since the beginning of the 19th century: in 1801 there were only 138 people in it. For the rest we will leave Weston-super-Mare in the very capable hands of its publicity department.

At **Woodspring Priory** are the scant remains of a 13th-century priory founded by Tracey, one of the murderers of Thomas à Becket. Up the fascinating little **Yeo River** (what fun to explore it by canoe) lies **Icelton** where a wharf was built to supply coal for the locomotives of the Weston–Portishead Light Railway, now defunct and gone but one can walk its bed. Further up the river are grassy banks on which fattening Herefords graze and which mark the site of a Roman villa. This once had a wharf and a boathouse. It is very strange to stand there now and wonder what on earth the Romans wanted to build a villa for on these desolate, and obviously very easily floodable, marshes. Once trows sailed up this river to **Congresbury**.

Kingston Seymour has a notice in its church recording a disastrous flood on 20th January 1606. The water in the church was five foot high. The marshland country now on these great flats is very beautiful. No agri-businessman has yet got down to ripping out the hedges and willow trees with his bulldozers, there are leafy lanes, old brick farmsteads, and cattle standing deep in grasses, clovers and buttercups. Good old-fashioned pastoral husbandry which is preserving and not destroying the beauty and fertility of the land.

Clevedon has its own little trow harbour, now used by small yachts, just north of the Blackstone Rocks. The winding mouth of the **Land Yeo River** can be entered, and is marked by wands which, on entering, you must keep to port. Up to 1934 a ketch, the *Bessie*, was still unloading gravel here. Clevedon church is up on one of the isolated hills peculiar to this region, and is Norman in origin and beautiful and interesting. Buried here is Arthur Henry Hallam, the friend of Tennyson about whose death the poet wrote 'In Memorandum', and Tennyson spent much time staying in the vicinity with Hallam at Clevedon Court. Coleridge honeymooned at 55 Old Church Road.

Clevedon Pier is currently in eclipse. It is a most elegant structure of iron, a thousand feet long and opened in 1869 with enormous ceremony, but, alas, it was tested 'to destruction' in 1970 and now there is a great gap in it. Many local people feel strongly about repairing it, but it is said that this would cost £250,000. Repaired it should be though, for it is a splendid period piece. The Arts Council may possibly give a grant towards it. There is a notice on the base of the pier saying that the tide here is the second highest in the world (next to the Bay of Funday) and has a rise and fall of 47 feet!

The seascape here is dominated by the **Holmes** – Steep Holme and Flat Holme. On Flat Holme is a lighthouse and several buildings, once a farm. On Steep Holme was a priory, the walls of which were still seven foot high when a battery was built there in 1867. Gildas, a 6th-century Brythonic saint, was supposed to have refuged here until disturbed by pirates when he retired to Avallon (i.e. Glastonbury). Gildas wrote *De Excidio Brittaniae*. Githa, Harlond of England's mother, took refuge here after Hastings.

On Flat Holme there is a well that is said to ebb at high tide and flow at low. You can land here and wander about. You can land on Steep Holme too if nobody is looking, but it is a reserve.

On the rather uncompromising shore to Portishead we pass the National Nautical School, opened in 1906 to replace the training ship *Formidable*, the Black Nore Lighthouse first lit in 1894, the Black Tower of Walton Bay Signal Station.

Portishead I am told is pronounced 'Posset' but I have never heard that pronunciation. The place is dominated by an enormous power station, up to recently supplied by ship from South Wales with coal; chemicals come in, and tankers up to 12,000 tons have managed to get in at the top of the tide – with both lock gates open because the ships have been too long for the lock chamber. The coal-fired power station is in process of being transformed into oil-firing, and so the tonnage into the port is going down: from 850,000 tons in 1966 to 667,000 tons in 1970. Besides fuel, wood pulp for the St Anne's Board Mills comes in from Scandinavia and a bizarre import: liquid phosphorus from Newfoundland for Albright and Wilson's storage depot here. The two ships which bring it have hot water jackets about their tanks to keep the stuff liquid. There are big developments in the air for this port. It may be that before very long large imports will begin of wood pulp for a large new company. The ships bringing it may have to lie out at anchor in Kingroad and discharge into lighters.

Kingroad used to be the anchorage for all ships coming out of Bristol, or bound for that port, or bound to the ports higher up Severn. Here outward-bounders cast off their tugs, or their hobblers, and lay awaiting a fair wind to make sail and set off down Channel. Portishead must have been a roaring place in those days, with sailors, held up by the wind, pulling ashore in droves to get drunk. It is now a strange little place, but not without charm and character: a cross between a very modern port and a rather *passé* seaside resort. In the 1830s it was intended to make it a luxurious seaside resort. The Royal Hotel, on Woodhill Ridge, stems from this period. Once there was a fleet of paddle steamers which plied up and down the Avon carrying pleasure-seekers from Bristol. There was a fort at **Battery Point**, taken by Fairfax in 1644 from the Royalists who held it, and used in both world wars for defence against the enemy.

Portishead is not much of a place for yachts at the moment, but there is talk of building a yacht harbour, and this would be a very good place for one. It must be emphasized though that the Bristol Channel and its approaches, are no place for the inexperienced yachtsman. The tides in the spring, have to be seen to be believed. I have sailed from Minehead to Bristol on one tide – and had an hour to spare – in an open boat, and in doing so have seen the huge navigation buoys out in the channel practically pulled right under the water by the ferocious speed of the tide and have found it touch and go getting into the Avon – it would have been so easy to have been swept right past it. If Portishead opened up its dock area to the public it would be a much nicer and happier place. After all – we are all supposed to be on the same side.

Pill, up the Avon, was the home port of the Bristol Pilots, who sailed little ships which were as famous, in their day, as the Brixham

Trawlers. They were evolved for sailing down the Bristol Channel, often against the predominating south-westerlies, having to use the ebb tide which gave them wind-against-tide conditions which can be ferocious in the Bristol Channel, competing against each other to go further and further out into the Irish Sea to get a pilotage. All incoming ships had to take a pilot from Lundy on. A few of these magnificent little ships still survive, turned into yachts, and are little short of worshipped by their lucky owners. The men of Pill are traditionally called 'Pill Sharks', owing to alleged past allegiance to a gentleman named Captain Morgan, who was a pirate. To this day many Pill men who go to sea (as many still do) have a shark tattooed on their arm to celebrate this fact.

Index

❧

247

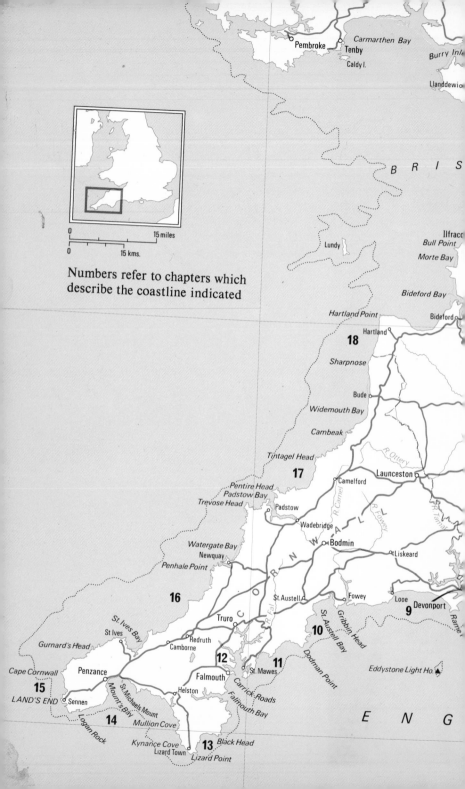

Pembroke Carmarthen Bay
Tenby
Caldy I.
Burry Inle
Llanddewi

B R I S

Ilfraco
Bull Point
Morte Bay

Bideford Bay

Lundy

Hartland Point   Bideford

Hartland
18

Sharpnose

Bude
Widemouth Bay
Cambeak

Tintagel Head
17
Camelford   Launceston

Pentire Head
Padstow Bay
Trevose Head
Padstow
Wadebridge
Bodmin
Liskeard
Watergate Bay
Newquay
Penhale Point
Fowey
Looe Devonport
St.Austell
9
16
10
St. Austell Bay
Truro
Gribbin Head
St.Ives Bay
St Ives
Redruth
Camborne
12
11
Godman Point
Penzance
Falmouth
St.Mawes
Helston
Carrick·Roads
Eddystone Light Ho.
15
St Michaels Mount
Falmouth Bay
LAND'S END Sennen
Mount's Bay
Logan Rock
14 Mullion Cove
Black Head
Kynance Cove
13
Lizard Town
Lizard Point

Gurnard's Head

Cape Cornwall

R. Ottery
R. Camel
R. Fowey
R. Tamar
R. Fal

C O R N W A L L

E N G

0 _____ 15 miles
0 _____ 15 kms.

Numbers refer to chapters which
describe the coastline indicated